2013-2014 AT A GLANCE

Essential Tables for Financial Remedies

FAMILY LAW BAR ASSOCIATION

Copyright © The Family Law Bar Association 2013
All rights reserved

First edition published 1992, reprinted 1992
Subsequent editions 1993 and annually thereafter
Twenty-second edition published 2013

A CIP catalogue record for this book is available from the
British Library

ISBN 978 18595 938 2 0

**Further copies of this publication
and future editions
may be ordered from**

**Class Legal
The Barns
Carr Farm
Cadney
Brigg
DN20 9HP**

**Telephone: 01652 652222
Fax: 01652 651050
DX: 24360 Brigg**

Produced for The FLBA by
Class Legal
The Barns, Carr Farm
Cadney, Brigg DN20 9HP

Cover design by Wendy Bann
Typeset by Stephen Theaker
Printed and bound by
CPI Group (UK) Ltd
Croydon CR0 4YY

Acknowledgements

The Family Law Bar Association thanks those who have agreed to the inclusion of their material in this volume:

        Automobile Association   Fostering Network

        Bank of England   Lloyds Banking Group plc

        Church of England   Independent Schools Council

        Economist Intelligence Unit   Jordans

        Financial Times Business Centre   Office for National Statistics

Individual thanks for their very considerable assistance to David Salter and Richard Jennings (Table 28), Adrian Gallop (Table 15), Laura Poots (Tables 18 to 21) and John Eames and Philippa Johnson (Table 26).

The Family Law Bar Association thanks the Editorial Committee
for the production of this volume:

    Sir Peter Singer   Mr Justice Mostyn
    Lewis Marks QC   Gavin Smith

The Family Law Bar Association publishes At A Glance annually, incorporating fresh and up-dated material. The Editorial Committee would welcome suggestions, whether for the improvement of existing or for the addition of further Tables.

Although care has been taken to ensure the reliability of the contents of this volume neither the members of the Editorial Committee nor The Family Law Bar Association nor any of its officers or members warrant their accuracy.

Sir Peter Singer (PS), Sir Nicholas Mostyn (NM), Lewis Marks QC (LM) and Gavin Smith (GS) have in accordance with the Copyright, Designs and Patents Act 1988 asserted their rights in the Tables specified, which may not be reproduced without their permission: PS/NM 6 and 28; PS/NM/LM 16, 22 and 23; PS/LM 11 and 15; PS 18, 19, 20, 21 and 25; NM 3; NM/GS 27, 31 and Leading Cases; LM 9, 14 and 17; and GS 4, 5, 10 and 32.

Preface

We write at a funerary time. Baroness Thatcher has been laid to rest. Almost exactly contemporaneous with her passing was the tragically melancholy demise on 1 April 2013 (a black even though bank holiday Monday) of public funding for vast swathes of the community as cover was axed and provision scythed by the Legal Aid, Sentencing and Punishment of Offenders Act 2012. A consequence (unintended perhaps, but in fact entirely foreseeable) which threatens swiftly to engulf and maybe even to overwhelm the judicial system is that family courts at all levels will become thronged with a tsunami of LIPs (as they are again to be acronymised, but self-representing nevertheless). The quality of justice will be strained, its administration delayed, its delivery potentially denied. Iron resolve rather than a handbag will be needed to avert implosion.

The next sepulchral guest at the wake will be the passing of the power of the civil courts to grant decrees of divorce and otherwise to adjudicate on family law disputes. By virtue of the Crime and Courts Act 2013 all such powers will be vested in a new Family Court (although the High Court will have power to transfer to itself Family Court proceedings). We have observed before that what goes around comes around. When statutory divorce was invented in 1857 it was to be administered by a brand new Family Court – the Court for Divorce and Matrimonial Causes – but this was abolished in 1875 and its powers transferred to the Probate, Divorce and Admiralty Division of the High Court. Residence and contact orders are further fatalities waiting to happen, having only as comparatively recently as 1989 ousted the now historic formulae of custody and access. The Children and Families Bill with scant ceremony despatches them in favour of the supposedly less disputatious 'child arrangement orders'.

The **Child Support** system may, perhaps, be one body to emerge from what has been its chronic state of morbid torpor. The 2008 reforms have been partially implemented for an experimental path-finding cohort (to use the pre-perestroika jargon of the nomenklatura). It remains to be seen whether these reforms will raise the patient Lazarus-like from the procrustean death-bed to which it has seemed chained, and stretched to the limits of endurance – if not beyond. These labours now devolve on to the no doubt underwhelmed shoulders of the Secretary of State for Work and Pensions – surely a Pandora's Box if not indeed a Trojan Horse the cleansing of whose stables will be epically augean.

On the procedural front the most significant changes are the wholesale overhaul of the rules concerning **expert evidence** contained in the reformulated FPR Part 25 and its sextuple Practice Directions. One wonders how the average LIP will cope with such detailed elaboration, requiring for comprehension that several digits be simultaneously inserted in the volumes of both the CPR and the FPR codes. Similarly, the **Costs Rules** in Part 28 have been reformulated to usher in the new CPR régime presaged by Sir Rupert Jackson's *Review of Civil Litigation Costs*, but will their subtlety and detailed differentiation between applications which attract the 'no order' principle and those which do not perhaps elude the grasp of even the most astute of LIPs (and lawyers)?

The promulgation of the **Legal Services Payment Order** is hardly worthy of the description of sticking plaster when set against these unhappy developments. The new **Matrimonial Causes Act** sections 22ZA and 22ZB bow their début into this edition. Maybe in the coming months guidance on how the new scheme will operate will be formulated whether by Rules and/or PD, or by the courts *ad hoc*.

Preface

From a large crop of important cases by a long chalk the most significant will surely be **Petrodel Resources Limited and others v Prest,** where we await the judgments of the Supreme Court. One can only hope that the money-maker who Toad-like takes to the 'open road and fast car' (as Thorpe LJ put it) in order to deny his (it is usually he cheating her) spouse's just deserts will lose his licence and have his conveyance confiscated. That surely should be the fair fate to befall those who take advantage of the escape route which the Court of Appeal majority in that case opened wide, giving the go-ahead to let them drive a coach and horses through the principles of equal division of available assets developed by the House of Lords. Any such road-hog's barouche should be consigned and confined back to the garage. The willingness of family courts to recognise reality and to peer behind the corporate veil (or rather carapace) in order fairly to assess the pool of divisible resources shocked Patten LJ so that he pronounced 'that must now cease'. May a less dogmatic and more worldly-wise view prevail on the summit.

It remains a universal truth that **Life Cover** comes inevitably to an end when you run out of it. Premiums up to that mortal moment have since December 2012 been 'harmonised'. The ECJ judgment which precipitated this chorus has advanced the march of (wo)mankind along the road to non-discrimination by not as much as a single centimetre. Would they had refrained. But it is only our insurers who sing all the way to the bank. Their lot has improved profitably, whereas the premium-burden for women has increased markedly: on average by 25% to 30%, but for family income policies by more than 40%, and by almost 50% for women smokers. Counter-intuitively male smokers, in particular, have marginally benefitted: although premiums for men have on average increased by about 2% above last year's.

Why, you may ask, do **Principal Points of Interest** year in year out tally the statutory charge at the profiteering annual rate of 8% (equivalent to over 14.5% gross if the government had to pay top-rate **Income Tax** on it, which of course it doesn't)? In reply to a Parliamentary Question in March 2012 the then junior justice minister Jonathan Djanogly suggested that that punitive rate was intended to encourage people owing money to pay promptly (though it bears most unfairly on those who lack the means to do so), as 'money recovered helps to keep legal aid on a sustainable footing, which reduces demand on the taxpayer'. Since then the government has found a more effective savings route by reducing wholescale the availability of public funding: so is it not time to bring down this rate, in force since October 2005 when **Interest Base Rates** stood 4% points higher than they have since March 2009?

At A Glance in its current format is at capacity. Yet some pages perforce expand and burst their bounds: the **Pensions Overview** to accommodate the new National Employment Savings Trust (a NEST, though we hope not one of vipers); and **Social Security Benefits** to encompass the controversial Benefits Cap plus Universal Credit and Personal Independence Payments. The staples, we are warned, cannot contain more pages. But for this year at least the tide has been contained, and this expanded volume presents a new **Procedural Table** to accompany the overview of **The IFLA Arbitration Scheme** and its Rules.

All this and more, dexterously downloadable, printable, saveable, transmissible and continuously updated is compendiously contained in the companion program *@eGlance*. A special gift-wrapped offer for purchasers of this volume is for the asking: worth looking it in the mouth. And at **classlegal.com/ateglance/detail** you can download a free 35 day trial and cast more than the proverbial glance at its benefits.

Essential Tables

Retail Prices Index...1

Interest Base Rates..2

School Fees...3

Child Care Costs..4

Tertiary Education Costs and Funding..5

Child Support...6

House Price Index...7

Mortgage Costs..8

New Car Data..9

Car Running Costs..10

Company Cars...11

Office Salary Survey...12

Financial Times FTSE 100 and All Share Indexes...................................13

Life Cover...14

Life Expectancy..15

Duxbury Calculations...16

Annuities..17

Income Tax...18

Capital Gains Tax..19

Inheritance Tax..20

Taxing Times...21

Gross Salary and Net Income..22

Grossed-up Net Maintenance...23

National Insurance Contributions...24

Principal Points of Interest...25

Social Security Benefits...26

Pension Sharing Procedure..27

Pensions Overview..28

Exchange Rates...29

International Living Costs...30

Financial Remedy Procedure...31

The IFLA Arbitration Scheme..32

Useful Websites..33

Other Financial Remedy Materials...34

Table 1 Retail Prices Index

	1974	1975	1976	1977	1978	1979	1980	1981	1982	1983
Jan	25.35	30.39	37.49	43.70	48.03	52.52	62.18	70.29	78.73	82.61
Feb	25.78	30.90	37.97	44.13	48.31	52.95	63.07	70.93	78.76	82.97
Mar	26.00	31.51	38.17	44.56	48.62	53.38	63.93	71.99	79.44	83.12
Apr	26.89	32.72	38.91	45.70	49.33	54.30	66.11	74.07	81.04	84.28
May	27.28	34.09	39.34	46.06	49.61	54.73	66.72	74.55	81.62	84.64
Jun	27.55	34.75	39.54	46.54	49.99	55.67	67.35	74.98	81.85	84.84
Jul	27.81	35.11	39.62	46.59	50.22	58.07	67.91	75.31	81.88	85.30
Aug	27.83	35.31	40.18	46.82	50.54	58.53	68.06	75.87	81.90	85.68
Sep	28.14	35.61	40.71	47.07	50.75	59.11	68.49	76.30	81.85	86.06
Oct	28.69	36.12	41.44	47.28	50.98	59.72	68.92	76.98	82.26	86.36
Nov	29.20	36.55	42.03	47.50	51.33	60.25	69.48	77.79	82.66	86.67
Dec	29.63	37.01	42.59	47.76	51.76	60.68	69.86	78.28	82.51	86.89

	1984	1985	1986	1987	1988	1989	1990	1991	1992	1993
Jan	86.84	91.20	96.25	100.0	103.3	111.0	119.5	130.2	135.6	137.9
Feb	87.20	91.94	96.60	100.4	103.7	111.8	120.2	130.9	136.3	138.8
Mar	87.48	92.80	96.73	100.6	104.1	112.3	121.4	131.4	136.7	139.3
Apr	88.64	94.78	97.67	101.8	105.8	114.3	125.1	133.1	138.8	140.6
May	88.97	95.21	97.85	101.9	106.2	115.0	126.2	133.5	139.3	141.1
Jun	89.20	95.41	97.79	101.9	106.6	115.4	126.7	134.1	139.3	141.1
Jul	89.10	95.23	97.52	101.8	106.7	115.5	126.8	133.8	138.8	140.7
Aug	89.94	95.49	97.82	102.1	107.9	115.8	128.1	134.1	138.9	141.3
Sep	90.11	95.44	98.30	102.4	108.4	116.6	129.3	134.6	139.4	141.9
Oct	90.67	95.59	98.45	102.9	109.5	117.5	130.3	135.1	139.9	141.8
Nov	90.95	95.92	99.29	103.4	110.0	118.5	130.0	135.6	139.7	141.6
Dec	90.87	96.05	99.62	103.3	110.3	118.8	129.9	135.7	139.2	141.9

	1994	1995	1996	1997	1998	1999	2000	2001	2002	2003
Jan	141.3	146.0	150.2	154.4	159.5	163.4	166.6	171.1	173.3	178.4
Feb	142.1	146.9	150.9	155.0	160.3	163.7	167.5	172.0	173.8	179.3
Mar	142.5	147.5	151.5	155.4	160.8	164.1	168.4	172.2	174.5	179.9
Apr	144.2	149.0	152.6	156.3	162.6	165.2	170.1	173.1	175.7	181.2
May	144.7	149.6	152.9	156.9	163.5	165.6	170.7	174.2	176.2	181.5
Jun	144.7	149.8	153.0	157.5	163.4	165.6	171.1	174.4	176.2	181.3
Jul	144.0	149.1	152.4	157.5	163.0	165.1	170.5	173.3	175.9	181.3
Aug	144.7	149.9	153.1	158.5	163.7	165.5	170.5	174.0	176.4	181.6
Sep	145.0	150.5	153.8	159.3	164.4	166.2	171.7	174.6	177.6	182.5
Oct	145.2	149.8	153.8	159.5	164.5	166.5	171.6	174.3	177.9	182.6
Nov	145.3	149.8	153.9	159.6	164.4	166.7	172.1	173.6	178.2	182.7
Dec	146.0	150.7	154.4	160.0	164.4	167.3	172.2	173.4	178.5	183.5

	2004	2005	2006	2007	2008	2009	2010	2011	2012	2013
Jan	183.1	188.9	193.4	201.6	209.8	210.1	217.9	229.0	238.0	245.8
Feb	183.8	189.6	194.2	203.1	211.4	211.4	219.2	231.3	239.9	247.6
Mar	184.6	190.5	195.0	204.4	212.1	211.3	220.7	232.5	240.8	248.7
Apr	185.7	191.6	196.5	205.4	214.0	211.5	222.8	234.4	242.5	
May	186.5	192.0	197.7	206.2	215.1	212.8	223.6	235.2	242.4	
Jun	186.8	192.2	198.5	207.3	216.8	213.4	224.1	235.2	241.8	
Jul	186.8	192.2	198.5	206.1	216.5	213.4	223.6	234.7	242.1	
Aug	187.4	192.6	199.2	207.3	217.2	214.4	224.5	236.1	243.0	
Sep	188.1	193.1	200.1	208.0	218.4	215.3	225.3	237.9	244.2	
Oct	188.6	193.3	200.4	208.9	217.7	216.0	225.8	238.0	245.6	
Nov	189.0	193.6	201.1	209.7	216.0	216.6	226.8	238.5	245.6	
Dec	189.9	194.1	202.7	210.9	212.9	218.0	228.4	239.4	246.8	

These 'all items index' figures derive from Office for National Statistics (ONS) (© Crown Copyright 2013). Later figures obtainable from www.ons.gov.uk/ons/key-figures/index.html, ONS' recorded message service on ☎ 01633 456961 or its enquiry service on ☎ 01633 456900 or by emailing cpi@ons.gov.uk. More detailed information may be obtained at www.ons.gov.uk/ons/rel/cpi/consumer-price-indices/index.html.

For full RPI analysis, data back to 1950 (and comparable data for Consumer Prices Index) see @eGlance.

How to calculate the effect of inflation from one month to any subsequent month*

The formula is **X x A ÷ B**

Where **X** is the figure to be inflated
A is the RPI for the later month
B is the RPI for the earlier month

*if you don't already have **@eGlance** which with ease does this and so much more

Table 2 Interest Base Rates

Base rate change dates

Date	New rate (%)	Date	New rate (%)	Date	New rate (%)
1982		7 August	10.00	9 June	6.50
12 January	14.00	26 October	9.50	11 July	6.75
25 February	13.50	5 November	9.00	8 August	7.00
12 March	13.00	4 December	8.50	7 November	7.25
8 June	12.50	**1988**		**1998**	
13 July	12.00	2 February	9.00	5 June	7.50
2 August	11.50	17 March	8.50	9 October	7.25
18 August	11.00	11 April	8.00	6 November	6.75
31 August	10.50	18 May	7.50	11 December	6.25
7 October	10.00	3 June	8.00	**1999**	
14 October	9.50	6 June	8.25*	8 January	6.00
4 November	9.00	7 June	8.50	5 February	5.50
26 November	10.125*	22 June	9.00	8 April	5.25
1983		29 June	9.50	10 June	5.00
12 January	11.00	5 July	10.00	8 September	5.25
15 March	10.50	19 July	10.50	4 November	5.50
15 April	10.00	8 August	10.75*	**2000**	
15 June	9.50	9 August	11.00	13 January	5.75
4 October	9.00	25 August	11.50*	10 February	6.00
1984		26 August	12.00	**2001**	
7 March	8.875*	25 November	13.00	8 February	5.75
15 March	8.625*	**1989**		5 April	5.50
10 May	9.125*	24 May	14.00	10 May	5.25
27 June	9.25	5 October	15.00	2 August	5.00
9 July	10.00	**1990**		18 September	4.75
11 July	11.00*	8 October	14.00	4 October	4.50
12 July	12.00	**1991**		8 November	4.00
9 August	11.50	13 February	13.50	**2003**	
10 August	11.00	27 February	13.00	6 February	3.75
20 August	10.50	25 March	12.50	10 July	3.50
7 November	10.00	12 April	12.00	6 November	3.75
20 November	9.875*	24 May	11.50	**2004**	
23 November	9.625*	12 July	11.00	5 February	4.00
1985		4 September	10.50	6 May	4.25
11 January	10.50	**1992**		10 June	4.50
14 January	12.00	5 May	10.00	5 August	4.75
28 January	14.00	16 September	12.00	**2005**	
20 March	13.75*	17 September	10.00	4 August	4.50
21 March	13.50	22 September	9.00	**2006**	
29 March	13.25*	16 October	8.00	3 August	4.75
2 April	13.125*	13 November	7.00	9 November	5.00
12 April	12.875*	**1993**		**2007**	
19 April	12.675*	26 January	6.00	11 January	5.25
12 June	12.50	23 November	5.50	10 May	5.50
7 July	12.25*	**1994**		5 July	5.75
16 July	12.00	8 February	5.25	6 December	5.50
29 July	11.75*	12 September	5.75	**2008**	
30 July	11.50	7 December	6.25	7 February	5.25
1986		**1995**		10 April	5.00
9 January	12.50	2 February	6.75	8 October	4.50
19 March	11.50	13 December	6.50	6 November	3.00
8 April	11.25*	**1996**		4 December	2.00
9 April	11.00	18 January	6.25	**2009**	
24 April	10.50	8 March	6.00	8 January	1.50
27 May	10.00	6 June	5.75	5 February	1.00
14 October	11.00	30 October	6.00	5 March	0.50
1987		**1997**		**2013**	
10 March	10.50	7 May	6.25		
19 March	10.00				
29 April	9.50				
11 May	9.00				

An asterisk denotes that, for that period, there was a spread not exceeding ± 0.5%.

For instantaneous and detailed interest calculations for these (and any other) rates and periods, simple and compound, use @eGlance.

Table 3 School Fees

The table *right* drawn from the 2012 Independent Schools Council census shows termly fees for various types of independent school at the start of that year, together with the percentage increase over the previous year.

The overall average increase for the year to January 2012 was **4.69%**. This compares to **4.82%** inflation over 2011 as measured by the RPI. There was thus no real rate of increase in school fees over that year, for the second year running and for only the second time since 1992.

Annual RPI inflation over the ten years to 2011 averaged **3.28%**, while the average annual rate of increase in school fees over that period has been **5.42%**. A reasonable projected **real rate of increase** in fees is thus **2.1% p.a.**, so that the prediction is that each year they will cost 2.1% more in real terms than the year before.

The table *right* shows the effect of this real rate of increase on a fee-payer with an initial net income of £85,000. The table assumes that this net income increases annually at the average RPI rate increase (3.28%) over the ten years to 2011; and that fees will increase annually at the average rate over that same period (see *above*) of 5.42%.

The full ISC census is at www.isc.co.uk/Resources/Independent Schools Council/Research Archive/Annual Census/2012/ISC_Census_2012_Final.pdf.

Data as at January 2012	Full boarding fee (£)	Day fee (boarding schools) (£)	Day fee (day schools) (£)	Day fee (average) (£)
Sixth-form	9,184	5,622	4,000	4,351
Senior	8,706	5,196	3,863	4,136
Junior	6,517	4,032	3,452	3,513
Nursery	N/A	2,330	2,497	2,476
Overall	8,776	4,848	3,625	3,825
% increase in 12 months	4.7%	2.9%	5.0%	4.7%

Year	Net income (£)	School fees (£)	% of income paid
1	85,000	8,000	9.41%
2	87,786	8,433	9.61%
3	90,664	8,890	9.81%
4	93,636	9,371	10.01%
5	96,705	9,879	10.22%
6	99,875	10,414	10.43%
7	103,149	10,978	10.64%
8	106,530	11,573	10.86%

Table 4 Child Care Costs

Indicative weekly cost of child upbringing: year from 6 April 2013

Age of child (years)	Outside London (£ per week)	London (£ per week)
0-4	99	116
5-10	112	132
11-15	140	164
16+	170	199

The figures derive from minimum weekly foster care allowances recommended by the Fostering Network (FN). FN reflect the extra cost of a fostered child's care by adding 50% to the estimated cost of bringing up a child in its own home, and recommend an uplift (incorporated within the Table *above*) of four extra weeks' allowance for birthday, holidays and a religious festival.

FN's recommended minimum fostering allowances for 2013-14 have increased by 2% over the preceding year.

More information about fostering allowances is available from FN at 87 Blackfriars Road, London SE1 8HA, ☎ 020 7620 6400 or at www.fostering.net/all-about-fostering/foster-carers/finances/allowances.

Table 5 Tertiary Education Costs and Funding

This summary relates to the academic year 2013-14, and to students resident in England who commenced full-time undergraduate courses at UK universities or higher education colleges on or after 1 September 2012. See previous editions for the régime for courses started on or before 1 September 2011. Other régimes apply to part-time courses, and for students resident elsewhere in the United Kingdom.

Tuition fees and loans

The maximum annual tuition fee for 2013-14 is £9,000. Non means-tested tuition fee loans are available from Student Finance England to meet the entire cost. Payment is made direct to the university or college.

Maintenance grants

Means-tested, non-repayable grants are available to assist with maintenance costs. The maximum grant for 2013-14 is £3,354. It is reduced by £1 for every £5.33 by which relevant gross household income exceeds £25,000 but does not exceed £42,611. No grant is payable if gross household income exceeds £42,611.

The rules concerning the assessment of household income are complex. It includes most forms of income received by the student apart from earned income, and parental income where the student is a dependant. Where parents are divorced or separated Student Finance England takes into account the income of the parent (and of any new partner of that parent) on whom the student is financially dependent. Maintenance payments are not treated as income.

Students claiming income-related benefits may be eligible for a special support grant instead of a maintenance grant.

Maintenance loans

The maintenance loan comprises a non means-tested element (65% of the total), and a means-tested element (35%). The latter is reduced by £1 for every £10 of gross household income over £42,875.

The maximum loan amounts for 2013-14 are:
- £4,375 (student living at home)
- £5,500 (student living away from home outside London)
- £7,675 (student living away from home in London).

The loan is reduced by 50 pence for every £1 of maintenance grant to which the student is entitled.

The combined effect for a first-year student living away from home and studying outside London is shown *below*:

Gross household income	Maintenance grant	Maintenance loan	Total
£25,000 or less	£3,354	£3,823	£7,177
£30,000	£2,416	£4,292	£6,708
£35,000	£1,478	£4,761	£6,239
£40,000	£540	£5,230	£5,770
£42,611	£50	£5,475	£5,525
£42,875	£0	£5,500	£5,500
£45,000	£0	£5,288	£5,288
£50,000	£0	£4,788	£4,788
£55,000	£0	£4,288	£4,288
£60,000	£0	£3,788	£3,788
£62,125 or more (£60,785 in final year)	£0	£3,575	£3,575

Repayment of student loans

Student loans become repayable once the student has left his course and is earning more than £21,000 gross per annum. Annual repayment is at the rate of 9% of gross income over £21,000. Interest accrues from the date of drawdown at varying rates depending on income.

Other financial assistance

Other assistance may be available under the National Scholarship Programme (where household income is less than £25,000 per annum) and in the form of bursaries granted by individual institutions.

For more information on loans and grants see www.gov.uk/student-finance; www.studentfinancewales.co.uk; www.studentfinanceni.co.uk (Northern Ireland); and www.saas.gov.uk (Scotland).

Table 6 Child Support

The 2008 Régime

In last year's edition we presaged the Government's intention in 2012 to abolish C-MEC and to introduce the 2008 régime, and speculated whether the embedded woes and tears engendered by the child support scheme would thereby be wiped away. C-MEC was abolished on 30 July 2012 and its functions transferred to the Secretary of State for Work and Pensions. The Department continues however to use the brand-name Child Support Agency (**CSA**) for those using the 1993 and 2003 régimes.

Also in July 2012 the Government published a consultation document *Supporting Separated Families: Securing Children's Futures* that announced the commencement of the **Child Maintenance Service** which would operate the 2008 régime. To use this service a range of fees for assessment, collection and enforcement were to be introduced – demonstrating the old adage that what goes around comes around: fees were a feature of the original scheme in 2003 but were later abolished.

The consultation document (replete with jargon) set out a **delivery timeline** which stated that in 2012 the first elements of the new support services for separated families were to be launched, including the **Innovation Fund, a web app and a quality mark**. The Child Maintenance Service would be 'opened to a **pathfinder group** of new applicants from October 2012.' It states that in 2013 the **second phase** of the statutory Child Maintenance Service, would be launched – but not until the new service has been shown to be working well. This second phase will consist of the **gateway service** to the new statutory scheme; the introduction of charging; and the beginning of the **case closure process**. A review is to be carried out not more than 30 months after the introduction of the second phase. All existing CSA cases will be closed by 2017, except for cases with 'ongoing arrears action only.' Only then will there be a single Child Maintenance Service, operating but one scheme – fully nine years after the 2008 Act. It is accepted that 'for a significant period, until we close all existing cases, we will be managing cases on three different statutory schemes: the 1993, 2003, and 2012 schemes.'

This partial implementation of the 2008 régime was given effect by the Child Support Maintenance Calculation Regulations 2012 (SI 2012 No. 2677); the Child Support Maintenance (Changes to Basic Rate Calculation and Minimum Amount of Liability) Regulations (SI 2012 No. 2678); and the Child Maintenance and Other Payments Act 2008 (Commencement No. 10 and Transitional Provisions) Order 2012 (SI 2012 No. 3042). The Child Maintenance Service began a limited intake of new cases on 10 December 2012.

Arts 3(2) to 3(5) of that (Commencement No. 10 and Transitional Provisions) Order define the specific and very limited cohort of cases which will be guinea pigs for the pathfinder experiment. Only the following scenarios qualify:

(a) The application is made on or after 10 December 2012 and relates to four or more children; and
  i. there is no existing case which has both the same person with care (**PWC**) and non-resident parent (**NRP**); *or*
  ii. there is an existing case which has both the same PWC and NRP *and* the applicant has requested the Secretary of State to cease acting *and* has made a fresh application after 10 December 2012 but before 13 weeks has elapsed following the date of cessation of action by the Secretary of State.
(b) An existing case which has the same NRP (but not the same PWC) as a case falling within (a).
(c) An existing case where the NRP is the partner of a NRP falling within (a), *and* where either of them is in receipt of a benefit giving rise to the flat rate of maintenance (see *below*).

It is difficult to divine what logic led to the selection of this pathfinder cohort. Why four children? Why a benefit-receiving partner of a pathfinder?

By s. 2 of the 2008 Act (in force since 24 July 2008) the main objective of C-MEC (now the Secretary of State) is stated to be 'to maximise the number of those children who live apart from one or both of their parents for whom effective maintenance arrangements are in place.' The subsidiary objectives are (1) 'to encourage and support the making and keeping by parents of appropriate voluntary maintenance arrangements for their children' and (2) 'to support the making of applications for child support maintenance under the Child Support Act 1991 and to secure compliance when appropriate with parental obligations under that Act.' In early 2010 C-MEC had 'established the **Child Maintenance Options** service to provide free, impartial information and support to help people make informed decisions about the type of maintenance arrangement that best suits their circumstances. The service is delivered by phone, via a website (www.cmoptions.org), and for those in most need of more personalised help, through a 'face-to-face service.' The helpline is ☎ 0800 988 0988.

The effect of the repeal of ss. 6 and 46 of the 1991 Act is that the existing s. 6 cases are now to be treated as cases under s. 4. Thus the resident parent can force a termination of an existing assessment or calculation and reach private agreement with the NRP. To this end, from November 2008 existing 'clients' are 'supported to make choices', either to negotiate private arrangements or to continue with their current arrangements. A standard form for private agreement has been promulgated (http://www.cmoptions.org/en/pdfs/Private%20Form.pdf) the final words of which state '*This is not a legal document but signing this agreement is a clear statement of our commitment to our children.*' This is inaccurate and misleading, as in fact the agreement will be legally binding as a maintenance agreement under s. 9(1) and (2) of the 1991 Act, and its existence will entitle the court to make an order in its terms under s. 4(10) which will have the effect of preventing any further child support calculation for 12 months.

From within a mass of detail delivered in undeservedly self-commendatory tones in the final accounts of C-MEC for 2011-12 we note just one claim: '*Value for money improved during the year as the Commission worked to become more efficient in all its work, with overall operating costs reducing by 6%. The cost per £1 of maintenance collected under the statutory schemes fell to around 35 pence, down 10% on last year.*' However, £1,187M was collected or arranged over the year and net operating costs were £484M – so the true cost of collecting £1 of maintenance was 41p. Whether the morph into the Child Maintenance Service will reduce this absurd cost remains to be seen.

Another uncommendable reality is that £3.81B of accumulated debt existed as at September 2012 – up from £3.79B a year earlier. Only a £0.2B increase one might say – but still £20M of anyone's (and particularly PWCs') money!

In the year to March 2012 30 people were sent to prison for not paying child maintenance and 45 driving licences confiscated. Just 555 people were prosecuted for offences under the Child Support Act.

Key features of the 2008 Régime which as at March 2013 are (only if noted to be so) in force, and others which may become so at some later date:

- Redefinition of 'a child' so that the maximum upper age will be 20 rather than 19. *(In force)*
- The abolition of the rule under s. 6 of the 1991 Act that requires benefit claimants to make an application for child support and the consequential abolition of the power to make a Reduced Benefit Direction under s. 46 in relation to parents who fail to cooperate with that requirement. *(In force)*
- A strong emphasis on encouraging parents to make consensual arrangements – see s. 2(2)(a) of the 2008 Act. *(In force)*
- The assessment basis is gross, not net, income. For the

Table 6 Child Support

purposes of calculating gross income the gross income returned to HMRC for the most recent tax year will generally be used, but relievable pension contributions will be deducted. *(In force only for the pathfinder cohort)*
- More complex rates than under the 2000 Régime:
  (a) A nil rate for NRPs who fall into certain categories, such as a student in full-time education or where their income is less than £5 p.w.;
  (b) A £5 p.w. flat rate for gross incomes of less than £100 p.w, or where certain prescribed benefits are received by the NRP or (in some instances) their partner. The increase in the flat rate from £5 to £7 contained in the 2008 Act has not been brought into force;
  (c) A 'reduced rate' now prescribed in the Child Support Maintenance Calculation Regulations 2012 (SI 2012 No. 2677) for gross incomes between £100 and £200 p.w.;
  (d) For gross incomes of £200 to £800 p.w., basic rates of 12% (1 child), 16% (2 children) and 19% (3 or more children) are to be applied; and for gross incomes above £800 p.w. the basic rates are 9% (1 child), 12% (2 children) and 15% (3 or more children);
  (e) Gross income above £3,000 p.w. disregarded.
  ((a) to (e) are in force for the pathfinder cohort)
- A significant increase in the maintenance disregard to the totality of the maintenance paid. *(In force)*
- Reduced liability in cases of shared or split care, comparable to the 2000 Régime. *(In force only for the pathfinder cohort)*
- Where the NRP cares for other children in his new family, reductions of gross weekly income of 11% (1 child in new family), 14% (2 children) and 16% (3 or more children). *(In force only for the pathfinder cohort).*
- The Secretary of State will be empowered to make liability orders. There will be significantly stronger enforcement procedures (including orders for surrender of passports and curfew, which may be made by the Secretary of State). A new offence of failing to notify a change of address (2008 Act, s. 36) is *in force*. S. 24, which supplies an anti-avoidance procedure similar to s37 MCA 1973, *came into force on 6 April 2010.*
- Enhancements to recover the £3.81B of accumulated debt to include the right to sell it to factors.

It is noteworthy that while the minimum weekly payment remains at £5 the absolute maximum has decreased from £500 to £482. In percentage terms a NRP with no other children living in his household with a gross weekly income of £400 who pays for one child will be required to pay 12% in CSM; his counterpart earning £3,000 per week will have to pay only 9.8%.

A Table giving calculations of liability under the 2008 Régime appears below.

The 1991 Régime

Although the then Secretary of State stated in early 2003 that all remaining cases with an **effective date** prior to 3 March 2003 would be brought into the (then) new 2000 scheme 'when we can see how the arrangements are working', no such transfer has been achieved. It is clear that this will not take place before 2014 (at best), the target year for migration of all old cases to the 2008 Régime. Accordingly the Child Support Régime 1991 Table *post*, incorporating 2013-14 data, is retained for use in those active unmigrated cases (151,500 at September 2012) for which assessment under that Régime continues.

Any application for an assessment with an effective date earlier than 3 March 2003 is dealt with under the 1991 Régime, as is any application pending on that date for revision or supersession of, or appeal against, a maintenance assessment then current. By art [8] of the Child Support, Pensions and Social Security Act 2000 (Commencement No. 12) Order 2003 (SI 2003 No. 192) **the effective date** means the date which would be the effective date of a maintenance assessment under the 1991 Régime. Broadly, this is the date 8 weeks after the date on which the maintenance enquiry form is sent to the NRP; but this is subject to qualifications: see Chapter 2 of *Child's Pay: The Complete Guide to the Child Support Acts (Sweet and Maxwell, 2nd edition, 1996)*.

The only exception to the above is in multiple cases where a new application is made against an NRP already subject to an assessment in respect of another child. In such a case the earlier assessment is recalculated under the 2000 Régime, but subject to phasing: discussed fully in *Child's Pay: The Complete Guide to Child Support Law and Practice (Butterworths, 3rd edition, 2002)* at Chapter 21. For the details of these multiple cases reference should be made to the somewhat dense provisions of art [3] of the Order.

The 2000 Régime

The 2000 Régime was introduced on 3 March 2003 for cases with an **effective date** (see *above*) on or after that date. The second Table *post* shows the weekly CSM liability of NRP for cases where the 2000 Régime applies. The basic principle under the 2000 Régime is that NRP pays 15% of his net weekly income (on up to a maximum income of £2,000 p.w.) for one child, 20% for two, and 25% for three or more. Part of that income is disregarded for each other child (up to three) living with NRP.

The Child Support (Maintenance Calculations and Special Cases) Regulations 2000 (SI 2001 No.155) define important aspects. **Net weekly income** is net of tax, and national insurance. Pension contributions are deductible in full. Any bonus, commission or overtime payments is included; as are receipts from a pension scheme, Working Family Tax Credit, Employment Credits and Disabled Person's Tax Credits. Income from savings, investments, benefits and student grants and loans is excluded. Capital allowances are again permissible deductions for the calculation of assessable net income: the decision to the contrary in **Smith v Secretary of State for Work and Pensions** [2006] 1 WLR 2024, [2006] 3 All ER 907, HL, has been reversed by Regulation 4 of the Child Support (Miscellaneous Amendments) Regulations 2007 (SI 2007 No. 1979).

The minimum **flat rate** liability of £5 p.w. arises when net income is less than £100 p.w, and upon those in receipt of certain benefits. But liability is nil if NRP is of a 'prescribed description' (e.g. students, children, prisoners, persons in nursing homes in receipt of benefits) or has a net income of less than £5 p.w. (So NRP with only but ample investment income will be assessed at nil although at risk of a **variation**.)

The **reduced rate band** covers liabilities calculated (not by reference to the percentages, but on a sliding scale) for NRPs whose net income is between £100 and £199.99 p.w.

The **standard rate** (based on the percentages) applies when weekly income lies between £200 and £2,000 p.w.: income above that band is disregarded.

The 2000 Régime Table (*post*) shows these calculations. For weekly incomes between those shown, simple interpolation will give a reasonable approximation of the liability, subject always to rounding to the nearest pound. NRP's liability may be reduced by the rules on **apportionment** and **shared care**.

For **apportionment** the rule is that if NRP is liable for more than one qualifying child, in respect of whom there is more than one **PWC**, then the child support (**CS**) payable is to be divided by the number of qualifying children, and shared rateably among the PWCs according to the number of qualifying children each has (see **Worked examples**).

For **shared care** the rule is that if the care of a qualifying child is shared so that from time to time NRP has care of the child overnight, the CS otherwise due to PWC is decreased by reference to the number of nights in a prescribed 12 month period

Table 6 Child Support

the child in question stays with NRP. The rate of reduction is as follows:

	Fraction to subtract
<52	Nil
52-103	1/7 (14.29%)
104-155	2/7 (28.57%)
156-174	3/7 (42.86%)
175+	1/2 (50%) and deduct further £7 p.w. per child

If PWC cares for more than one qualifying child of NRP, and shares care with NRP, then the applicable decrease is the sum of the appropriate fractions in the Table divided by the number of such qualifying children. If the applicable fraction is one-half in relation to any qualifying child, the total amount payable to the person with care is then to be further decreased by £7 p.w. for each such child. Any such reduction cannot reduce the amount payable below £5 p.w. (although that will be apportioned between different PWCs where appropriate).

The ordinary rules are subject to modification if the case falls within one of the seven prescribed **Special Cases.** Of these the most prominent are:
- where the child's care is in part provided by the local authority, in which event the liability of NRP is reduced as in **shared care**
- where NRP is the subject of a court order for maintenance in respect of other children, in which event CS is reduced by apportionment
- where a child attends boarding school or is a hospital in-patient, when PWC is deemed to be the person providing such care notwithstanding the child's absence.

The liabilities in the Table are subject to **variation** (formerly known as departure) of which there are three classes: (1) Special expenses, (2) Pre-April 1993 property transfers (now obsolete) and (3) Additional cases.
- **Special expenses** are confined to contact costs, the costs of illness or disability of another relevant child, the cost of discharging certain debts incurred when the parties were together as a couple, and the maintenance (as opposed to the educational) element of boarding school fees. Where such expenses arise they are deducted from NRP's net weekly income.
- **Additional cases** are where NRP has assets; NRP's income is not taken into account or has been diverted; and where NRP's lifestyle is inconsistent with stated income.

The **assets** variation category applies where NRP has net assets worth over £65,000 (disregarding any compensation for personal injury, assets used in the course of a trade or business, or real property which is the home of NRP or any child of his). Assets subject to a trust or which are held abroad are included. Where there are such assets an annual income calculated by reference to the Judgment Debt rate is attributed to all the assets (not just to the excess over £65,000) and no allowance is made for income tax. The consequence for an NRP whose marginal tax rate is 45% is that notional investment income of 14.55% p.a. (the current rate, 8%, grossed up) is attributed to all assets. The weekly equivalent of this notional income increases NRP's net weekly income for CS purposes.

The **income not taken into account** variation category applies where NRP's income would ordinarily be disregarded because it includes prescribed benefits or because NRP would otherwise fall outside the Act altogether (for example because he is a student), but where it is established that he has net weekly income in excess of £100. In such a case the whole of such income (not merely the excess over £100) is taken into account if the application for variation is successful.

The **diverted income** variation category applies where the CSA is satisfied that NRP is diverting his income. NRP must have the ability to control his income and the CSA must be satisfied that he has unreasonably reduced his income by diverting it to other destinations in order to reduce his liability to pay maintenance. The purpose of any diversion of income must be shown to be avoidance of CS. In such a case the whole of the diverted income is taken into account for the purposes of the calculation.

The **lifestyle inconsistent with income** variation category applies where the CSA is satisfied that the income which has been, or would be, taken into account for the purposes of CS is substantially lower than the level of income required to support the overall life-style of NRP. Where this is proved, the additional income taken into account is the difference between the income which the CSA is satisfied NRP requires to support his overall life-style and the income already taken into account for the purposes of the calculation. In **WM v C-MEC** [2011] UKUT 226 (AAC) at [22] Upper Tribunal Judge Turnbull stated 'one can see arguments both ways on whether, as a matter of policy, there should be an exception in the case where a non-resident [parent] is able to afford a higher lifestyle by evading tax': the point remains undecided.

Before a **variation** can be directed the CSA must be additionally satisfied that it is **just and equitable** to do so. See **RC v C-MEC** [2009] UKUT 62 (AAC), where the Senior President (Carnwath LJ) and Judge Jacobs give an exposition of the principles referable to this requirement.

In **GW v RW** [2003] 2 FLR 108 at [74] it was suggested that when the circumstances are such that a court makes a child maintenance order the appropriate starting point should almost invariably be the figure thrown up by the new child support rules. An interesting question now that the 2008 régime has been partially implemented is: which rules? An authoritative decision must be awaited.

The rules for special cases and variation for the 2008 régime are very similar and are set out in the Child Support Maintenance Calculation Regulations (SI 2012 No. 2677).

In **R (Kehoe) v Secretary of State for Work and Pensions** [2006] 1 AC 42, [2005] 3 WLR 252, the House of Lords decided that a PWC has no right to play any part in the enforcement processes of the CSA, and that they do not engage her rights under Art 6(1) of the European Convention on Human Rights. Her only remedy, per Lord Walker of Gestingthorpe, would be to take judicial review proceedings if the CSA's refusal to enforce a claim arose from an error of law (such as misunderstanding the extent of its statutory powers).

In **Gray v Secretary of State for Work and Pensions & Anor** [2012] EWCA Civ 1412 the Court of Appeal decided that the Secretary of State is not bound to accept that the liable parent's gross income is as stated in the information provided by him to HMRC; he is entitled to make his own findings of fact as to the parent's actual income. In his judgment at [22] Ward LJ observed that 'nothing to do with child support is ever simple and straightforward' and at [23] 'the sad experience of this Act is that algebra may be a source of happiness for mathematicians but it is not much of a panacea for angry parents.'

Caveat: *Notwithstanding the asserted transparency and simplicity of the 2000 and 2008 Régimes, calculations may still be highly complex, both legally and algebraically. This short guide is intended as a basic survey only, and should not be regarded as comprehensive. Reference should be made to the Child Support Act 1991 as amended and to the numerous applicable Regulations, compendiously discussed in* Child's Pay *(3rd edition, 2002, op. cit.).*

@eGlance *offers Child Support calculators for all three Régimes.*

Child Support Régime 1991

2013-14 maintenance requirements and maximum assessments, and Child Support rates

Number of children aged				Total no. of children	Relevant MR	Maximum assessment		
under 11	11 - 13	14 - 15	16 - 18			Total	Per child	Income threshold
1	-	-	-	1	134.42	258.95	258.95	112,074
2	-	-	-	2	186.64	435.70	217.85	164,626
3	-	-	-	3	238.86	612.45	204.15	200,423
4	-	-	-	4	291.08	789.20	197.30	261,442
5	-	-	-	5	343.30	965.95	193.19	322,461
1	1	-	-	2	186.64	435.70	217.85	164,626
2	1	-	-	3	238.86	612.45	204.15	200,423
3	1	-	-	4	291.08	789.20	197.30	261,442
1	2	-	-	3	238.86	612.45	204.15	200,423
1	1	1	-	3	238.86	612.45	204.15	200,423
1	1	2	-	4	291.08	789.20	197.30	261,442
1	1	1	1	4	291.08	789.20	197.30	261,442
2	1	1	-	4	291.08	789.20	197.30	261,442
2	2	1	-	5	343.30	965.95	193.19	322,461
2	1	2	-	5	343.30	965.95	193.19	322,461
2	0	1	1	4	291.08	789.20	197.30	261,442
3	1	1	-	5	343.30	965.95	193.19	322,461
-	1	-	-	1	116.50	241.03	241.03	107,008
-	2	-	-	2	168.72	417.78	208.89	160,995
-	1	-	1	2	168.72	417.78	208.89	160,995
-	1	1	-	2	168.72	417.78	208.89	160,995
-	1	1	1	3	220.94	594.53	198.18	196,793
-	-	1	-	1	98.57	223.10	223.10	102,339
-	-	1	1	2	150.79	399.85	199.93	157,365
-	-	-	1	1	62.72	187.25	187.25	95,705

See text on previous pages for the extent of the continuing applicability of this 1991 Régime Table.

For a range of specimen family profiles the Table illustrates:
- the maintenance requirement
- the maximum possible assessment
- each child's share of the maximum
- the approximate threshold of the non-resident parent's gross income at which that maximum could arise.

Assumptions in calculating the income threshold are:
- the parent with care has no assessable income
- the non-resident parent is single, has housing costs of £150 p.w., pays 3% contributory pension, and is contracted out of NIC.

General rates		
Personal allowances		
Adult		71.70
Child aged	Under 11	65.62
	11 - 15	65.62
	16 - 18	65.62
Premiums		
Family		17.40
Disabled child		57.89
Carer		33.30
Disability	Single	31.00
Severe disability	Single	59.50
Child Benefit		
Only/elder/eldest child (not lone parent)		20.30
Each subsequent child		13.40

Rates used only to calculate Protected Income			
Personal allowance			
Adult	Couple		112.55
Premiums			
Pensioner	Couple		109.50
Disability		Couple	44.20
Severe disability		Couple	
		- one qualifies	59.50
		- both qualify	119.00

Child Support Régime 2000

Weekly maintenance calculations

Qualifying children	1	2	3+	1	2	3+	1	2	3+	1	2	3+	
Other children living with paying parent	None			One other			Two other			Three (or more) other			
<100	5	5	5	5	5	5	5	5	5	5	5	5	Min.
100	5	5	5	5	5	5	5	5	5	5	5	5	
105	6	7	7	6	6	7	6	6	7	6	6	7	
110	8	9	10	7	8	9	7	8	9	7	8	8	
115	9	10	12	8	9	11	8	9	10	8	9	10	
120	10	12	14	9	11	13	9	10	12	9	10	12	
125	11	14	16	10	12	14	10	12	14	9	11	13	
130	13	16	19	11	14	16	11	13	16	10	13	15	
135	14	17	21	12	15	18	12	14	17	11	14	16	Reduced rate band
140	15	19	23	13	17	20	13	16	19	12	15	18	
145	16	21	25	14	18	22	14	17	21	13	16	20	
150	18	23	28	15	20	24	15	19	23	14	18	21	
155	19	24	30	16	21	26	15	20	24	15	19	23	
160	20	26	32	17	22	28	16	21	26	16	20	25	
165	21	28	34	18	24	29	17	23	28	16	21	26	
170	23	30	37	19	25	31	18	24	30	17	23	28	
175	24	31	39	20	27	33	19	25	31	18	24	29	
180	25	33	41	21	28	35	20	27	33	19	25	31	
185	26	35	43	22	30	37	21	28	35	20	26	33	
190	28	37	46	23	31	39	22	29	37	21	28	34	
195	29	38	48	24	33	41	23	31	38	22	29	36	
199.99	30	40	50	25	34	42	24	32	40	22	30	37	
200	30	40	50	26	34	43	24	32	40	23	30	38	
210	32	42	53	27	36	45	25	34	42	24	32	39	
225	34	45	56	29	38	48	27	36	45	25	34	42	
250	38	50	63	32	43	53	30	40	50	28	38	47	
300	45	60	75	38	51	64	36	48	60	34	45	56	
350	53	70	88	45	60	74	42	56	70	39	53	66	
400	60	80	100	51	68	85	48	64	80	45	60	75	
450	68	90	113	57	77	96	54	72	90	51	68	84	
500	75	100	125	64	85	106	60	80	100	56	75	94	
550	83	110	138	70	94	117	66	88	110	62	83	103	
600	90	120	150	77	102	128	72	96	120	68	90	113	
650	98	130	163	83	111	138	78	104	130	73	98	122	Standard rate band
700	105	140	175	89	119	149	84	112	140	79	105	131	
750	113	150	188	96	128	159	90	120	150	84	113	141	
800	120	160	200	102	136	170	96	128	160	90	120	150	
900	135	180	225	115	153	191	108	144	180	101	135	169	
1,000	150	200	250	128	170	213	120	160	200	113	150	188	
1,100	165	220	275	140	187	234	132	176	220	124	165	206	
1,200	180	240	300	153	204	255	144	192	240	135	180	225	
1,300	195	260	325	166	221	276	156	208	260	146	195	244	
1,400	210	280	350	179	238	298	168	224	280	158	210	263	
1,500	225	300	375	191	255	319	180	240	300	169	225	281	
1,600	240	320	400	204	272	340	192	256	320	180	240	300	
1,700	255	340	425	217	289	361	204	272	340	191	255	319	
1,800	270	360	450	230	306	383	216	288	360	203	270	338	
1,900	285	380	475	242	323	404	228	304	380	214	285	356	
>2,000	300	400	500	255	340	425	240	320	400	225	300	375	Max.

Net weekly income of paying parent

AT A GLANCE

Child Support Régime 2000 Examples

Apportionment: F has 4 children. Two live with M1, 1 lives with M2 and 1 lives with F. There are thus 3 qualifying children. F's net weekly income is £350.

The calculation is £74 p.w. (see Table). $2/3$ is payable to M1 (£49.33 p.w.) and $1/3$ to M2 (£24.67 p.w.).

Shared care (1): F has 3 children. 1 lives with him, 2 live with M, but they spend every other weekend (Friday p.m. to Sunday p.m.) with him, and two weeks in the Summer holidays. F's net weekly income is £1000.

The basic calculation would be £170 p.w. (see Table). However, this is reduced by $1/7$ as the qualifying children spend about 64 nights p.a. with him, reducing the calculation to £145.71 (rounded to £146).

Shared care (2): as *left*, save that one qualifying child spends every Friday p.m. to Monday a.m. with him during term-time and three-quarters of the school holidays (say 9 weeks) – for a total of 177 nights, although the other child is still spending time with F in accordance with the régime *left* (i.e. 64 nights p.a.).

The calculation is: a basic calculation of £170 p.w.
- subject to a reduction of $1/2$ for one child and a reduction of $1/7$ for the other
- which (added together and divided by two) gives a total reduction of $9/28$ (32.14%)
- which equals £115.36, less £7 for the '50% child', rounded down to a net total of £108 p.w.

Child Support Régime 2008

Weekly maintenance calculations

Qualifying children	1	2	3+	1	2	3+	1	2	3+	1	2	3+	
Other children living with paying parent	None			One other			Two other			Three (or more) other			
<100	5	5	5	5	5	5	5	5	5	5	5	5	Min.
100	5	5	5	5	5	5	5	5	5	5	5	5	Reduced rate band
120	9	10	12	8	10	11	8	10	11	8	9	10	
140	13	16	18	12	14	17	11	14	16	11	14	16	
160	16	21	25	15	19	22	14	19	22	14	18	21	
180	20	27	31	18	24	28	17	23	27	17	23	27	
199.99	24	32	38	21	28	34	21	27	33	20	27	32	
200	24	32	38	21	28	34	21	28	33	20	27	32	Gross weekly income of paying parent / Standard rate band
210	25	34	40	22	30	36	22	29	34	21	28	34	
225	27	36	43	24	32	38	23	31	37	23	30	36	
300	36	48	57	32	43	51	31	41	49	30	40	48	
350	42	56	67	37	50	59	36	48	57	35	47	56	
400	48	64	76	43	57	68	41	55	65	40	54	64	
450	54	72	86	48	64	76	46	62	74	45	60	72	
500	60	80	95	53	71	85	52	69	82	50	67	80	
550	66	88	105	59	78	93	57	76	90	55	74	88	
600	72	96	114	64	85	101	62	83	98	60	81	96	
650	78	104	124	69	93	110	67	89	106	66	87	104	
700	84	112	133	75	100	118	72	96	114	71	94	112	
750	90	120	143	80	107	127	77	103	123	76	101	120	
800	96	128	152	85	114	135	83	110	131	81	108	128	
850	101	134	160	91	121	144	88	117	139	86	114	136	
900	105	140	167	96	128	152	93	124	147	91	121	144	
950	110	146	175	100	133	159	98	130	155	96	128	152	
1,000	114	152	182	104	139	166	101	135	161	100	133	158	
1,100	123	164	197	112	149	179	109	146	174	107	143	171	
1,200	132	176	212	120	160	192	117	156	187	115	153	183	
1,300	141	188	227	128	171	206	125	166	200	122	163	196	
1,400	150	200	242	136	182	219	132	176	213	130	173	208	
1,500	159	212	257	144	192	232	140	187	226	137	183	221	
1,600	168	224	272	152	203	246	148	197	238	145	193	234	
1,700	177	236	287	160	214	259	156	207	251	153	203	246	
1,800	186	248	302	168	224	272	163	218	264	160	213	259	
1,900	195	260	317	176	235	286	171	228	277	168	224	271	
2,000	204	272	332	184	246	299	179	238	290	175	234	284	
2,100	213	284	347	192	256	312	187	249	303	183	244	297	
2,200	222	296	362	200	267	326	194	259	316	190	254	309	
2,300	231	308	377	208	278	339	202	269	329	198	264	322	
2,400	240	320	392	216	288	352	210	280	342	205	274	334	
2,500	249	332	407	224	299	366	218	290	355	213	284	347	
2,600	258	344	422	232	310	379	225	300	367	221	294	360	
2,700	267	356	437	240	320	392	233	311	380	228	304	372	
2,800	276	368	452	248	331	406	241	321	393	236	314	385	
2,900	285	380	467	256	342	419	248	331	406	243	324	397	
2,999	294	392	482	264	352	432	256	341	419	251	334	410	
>3,000	294	392	482	264	352	433	256	342	419	251	334	410	Max.

Table 7 House Price Index

Standardised indices showing change in property prices over 10 years since 2003

UK indices (by property type)

	All houses			Existing houses		
Year	Index	%	Av'ge price	Index	%	Av'ge price
03	429.1	22.4	132,589	440.9	22.5	133,808
04	507.6	18.3	156,831	521.0	18.2	158,111
05	536.6	5.7	165,807	549.6	5.5	166,810
06	581.3	8.3	179,601	596.6	8.6	181,081
07	635.9	9.4	196,478	650.4	9.0	197,384
08	585.9	(7.9)	181,032	592.5	(8.9)	179,826
09	524.6	(10.5)	162,085	535.6	(9.6)	162,541
10	539.6	2.9	166,739	550.1	2.7	166,958
11	525.4	(2.6)	162,322	535.6	(2.6)	162,550
12	522.1	(0.6)	161,308	530.5	(0.9)	161,009

Regional indices (all houses)

	North		Yorks/Humb.		N. West		E. Midlands		W. Midlands		E. Anglia	
Year	Index	%	Index	%	Index	%	Index	%	Index	%	Index	%
03	370.6	36.5	395.6	32.9	366.3	25.1	457.5	26.5	460.7	26.7	465.0	20.5
04	490.3	32.3	495.0	25.1	472.8	29.1	541.4	18.3	540.5	17.3	522.3	12.3
05	533.3	8.8	549.3	11.0	523.7	10.8	564.9	4.3	565.4	4.6	536.4	2.6
06	567.3	6.4	602.4	9.7	565.1	7.9	599.4	6.1	602.8	6.6	581.1	8.4
07	601.8	6.1	640.5	6.3	596.8	5.6	632.4	5.5	640.4	6.2	637.3	9.7
08	547.2	(9.1)	580.0	(9.4)	558.3	(6.5)	582.0	(8.0)	591.9	(7.6)	600.8	(5.7)
09	500.2	(8.6)	526.3	(9.3)	492.8	(11.7)	518.2	(11.0)	534.1	(9.8)	520.2	(13.4)
10	511.5	2.3	538.2	2.3	486.7	(1.3)	541.7	4.5	549.5	2.9	540.9	4.0
11	483.1	(5.6)	513.2	(4.6)	485.0	(0.4)	517.9	(4.4)	530.9	(3.4)	544.1	0.6
12	478.1	(1.0)	509.1	(0.8)	468.6	(3.4)	523.1	1.0	528.8	(0.4)	540.7	(0.6)

	S. West		S. East		Gr. London		Wales		Scotland		N. Ireland	
Year	Index	%	Index	%	Index	%	Index	%	Index	%	Index	%
03	477.7	18.4	483.8	17.0	563.3	12.8	397.2	32.5	274.5	15.1	340.3	10.7
04	545.4	14.2	528.8	9.3	608.5	8.0	516.3	30.0	330.6	20.4	397.9	16.9
05	552.6	1.3	537.0	1.5	621.4	2.1	553.7	7.3	375.7	13.6	486.0	22.1
06	587.5	6.3	571.2	6.4	680.9	9.6	589.7	6.5	421.7	12.2	644.4	32.6
07	641.9	9.3	636.9	11.5	777.6	14.2	640.7	8.7	488.2	15.8	844.5	31.1
08	583.2	(9.1)	588.6	(7.6)	705.3	(9.3)	579.4	(9.6)	478.2	(2.1)	679.2	(19.6)
09	540.0	(7.4)	532.1	(9.6)	622.0	(11.8)	512.0	(11.6)	426.6	(10.8)	563.7	(17.0)
10	568.5	5.3	561.4	5.5	659.9	6.1	530.3	3.6	421.4	(1.2)	506.2	(10.2)
11	547.3	(3.7)	553.1	(1.5)	659.6	0.0	521.5	(1.7)	406.8	(3.5)	444.1	(12.3)
12	553.1	1.1	558.8	1.0	674.4	2.2	505.6	(3.0)	384.3	(5.5)	405.4	(8.7)

Index 1983 = 100

The percentage figure is the change from the preceding year (with falls bracketed).

Data from the Halifax House Price Index (www.lloydsbankinggroup.com/housepricecalculator.asp).

The @eGlance House Price Index module contains data for a greater range of indices (including the Savills Prime Central London Residential Capital Value Index) **than it is possible to include in this publication, and affords an opportunity to approximate changes in value for given properties over any given period of time.**

AT A GLANCE

Table 8 Mortgage Costs

The annual cost of a repayment mortgage over various terms

Initial borrowing	Annual cost (monthly instalment x 12) over 25 year term, at interest rates of:										
	1.5%	2.0%	2.5%	3.0%	3.5%	4.0%	4.5%	5.0%	5.5%	6.0%	6.5%
30,000	1,440	1,526	1,615	1,707	1,802	1,900	2,001	2,105	2,211	2,319	2,431
40,000	1,920	2,034	2,153	2,276	2,403	2,534	2,668	2,806	2,948	3,093	3,241
50,000	2,400	2,543	2,692	2,845	3,004	3,167	3,335	3,508	3,684	3,866	4,051
60,000	2,880	3,052	3,230	3,414	3,604	3,800	4,002	4,209	4,421	4,639	4,861
70,000	3,360	3,560	3,768	3,983	4,205	4,434	4,669	4,911	5,158	5,412	5,672
80,000	3,839	4,069	4,307	4,552	4,806	5,067	5,336	5,612	5,895	6,185	6,482
90,000	4,319	4,578	4,845	5,121	5,407	5,701	6,003	6,314	6,632	6,958	7,292
100,000	4,799	5,086	5,383	5,691	6,007	6,334	6,670	7,015	7,369	7,732	8,103
150,000	7,199	7,629	8,075	8,536	9,011	9,501	10,005	10,523	11,054	11,597	12,154
200,000	9,598	10,173	10,767	11,381	12,015	12,668	13,340	14,030	14,738	15,463	16,205
250,000	11,998	12,716	13,458	14,226	15,019	15,835	16,675	17,538	18,423	19,329	20,256
300,000	14,398	15,259	16,150	17,072	18,022	19,002	20,010	21,045	22,107	23,195	24,307

Initial borrowing	Annual cost (monthly instalment x 12) over 20 year term, at interest rates of:										
	1.5%	2.0%	2.5%	3.0%	3.5%	4.0%	4.5%	5.0%	5.5%	6.0%	6.5%
30,000	1,737	1,821	1,908	1,997	2,088	2,181	2,277	2,376	2,476	2,579	2,684
40,000	2,316	2,428	2,544	2,662	2,784	2,909	3,037	3,168	3,302	3,439	3,579
50,000	2,895	3,035	3,179	3,328	3,480	3,636	3,796	3,960	4,127	4,299	4,473
60,000	3,474	3,642	3,815	3,993	4,176	4,363	4,555	4,752	4,953	5,158	5,368
70,000	4,053	4,249	4,451	4,659	4,872	5,090	5,314	5,544	5,778	6,018	6,263
80,000	4,632	4,857	5,087	5,324	5,568	5,817	6,073	6,336	6,604	6,878	7,158
90,000	5,211	5,464	5,723	5,990	6,264	6,545	6,833	7,128	7,429	7,737	8,052
100,000	5,791	6,071	6,359	6,655	6,960	7,272	7,592	7,920	8,255	8,597	8,947
150,000	8,686	9,106	9,538	9,983	10,439	10,908	11,388	11,879	12,382	12,896	13,420
200,000	11,581	12,141	12,718	13,310	13,919	14,544	15,184	15,839	16,509	17,194	17,894
250,000	14,476	15,177	15,897	16,638	17,399	18,179	18,979	19,799	20,637	21,493	22,367
300,000	17,372	18,212	19,077	19,965	20,879	21,815	22,775	23,758	24,764	25,791	26,841

Initial borrowing	Annual cost (monthly instalment x 12) over 15 year term, at interest rates of:										
	1.5%	2.0%	2.5%	3.0%	3.5%	4.0%	4.5%	5.0%	5.5%	6.0%	6.5%
30,000	2,235	2,317	2,400	2,486	2,574	2,663	2,754	2,847	2,942	3,038	3,136
40,000	2,980	3,089	3,201	3,315	3,431	3,551	3,672	3,796	3,922	4,050	4,181
50,000	3,724	3,861	4,001	4,143	4,289	4,438	4,590	4,745	4,902	5,063	5,227
60,000	4,469	4,633	4,801	4,972	5,147	5,326	5,508	5,694	5,883	6,076	6,272
70,000	5,214	5,406	5,601	5,801	6,005	6,213	6,426	6,643	6,864	7,088	7,317
80,000	5,959	6,178	6,401	6,630	6,863	7,101	7,344	7,592	7,844	8,101	8,363
90,000	6,704	6,950	7,201	7,458	7,721	7,989	8,262	8,541	8,825	9,114	9,408
100,000	7,449	7,722	8,001	8,287	8,579	8,876	9,180	9,489	9,805	10,126	10,453
150,000	11,173	11,583	12,002	12,430	12,868	13,314	13,770	14,234	14,708	15,189	15,680
200,000	14,898	15,444	16,003	16,574	17,157	17,753	18,360	18,979	19,610	20,253	20,907
250,000	18,622	19,305	20,004	20,717	21,447	22,191	22,950	23,724	24,513	25,316	26,133
300,000	22,347	23,166	24,004	24,861	25,736	26,629	27,540	28,469	29,415	30,379	31,360

These tables show the annual cost of various levels of borrowing over various terms, at the rates of interest shown. As tax relief on mortgage interest was abolished in 2000 instalments are paid from taxed income.
Use your @eGlance *for infinitely bespoke quotes.*

Table 9 New Car Data

Approximate April 2013 'on the road' list and best prices and company car tax rates

Category	Model	Basic Model			Mid-range Model			Luxury Model			Performance Model		
		list	tax	best	list	tax	best	list	tax	best	list	tax	best
Superminis	Fiat 500	1.2 Pop S/S 3dr			1.2 Lounge S/S 3dr			1.4 T-Jet Abarth 3dr			1.4 T-Jet Abarth Esseesse 3dr		
		9,960	13%	9,590	11,360	13%	10,935	14,167	22%	14,467	17,212	22%	17,212
	Ford Fiesta	1.25 60 Studio 3dr			1.6 TDCi 75 Style 3dr			1.6 TDCi 95 Titanium Econetic 3dr			1.6T 180 Ecoboost ST2 3dr		
		9,795	15%	9,305	13,395	13%	12,058	16,945	13%	15,452	17,995	18%	17,995
	Mercedes-Benz A1	A180 BlueEFFICIENCY 5dr			A180 CDI BlueEFF SE 5dr			A200 CDI BlueEFF Sport 5dr			A250 AMG Sport 5dr		
		18,970	16%	18,208	21,225	13%	20,370	23,295	17%	22,353	28,800	20%	27,635
	Mini Cooper	1.6 3dr			1.6D Sport Pack 3dr			1.6T S JCW Chili/Media 3dr			2.0D SD 3dr		
		14,900	16%	14,161	19,075	13%	18,121	25,335	21%	24,068	18,870	16%	17,927
	Renault Clio	1.2 75 Expr. 3dr			1.2 75 Expr.+ 3dr			1.5 dCi 90 Expr.+ 5dr					
		10,595	16%	10,181	11,995	16%	11,523	14,095	13%	13,536			
	Skoda Fabia	1.2 12v 60 S 5dr			1.2 TSI 105 Elegance 5dr			1.4 TSI 180 vRS 5dr			1.6 TDI CR 90 S 5dr		
		9,835	16%	8,322	13,785	15%	11,627	17,145	20%	14,461	12,510	15%	10,560
	Vauxhall Corsa	1.0 12v wcoFLEX Expr. 3dr			1.3 CDTi 75 ecoFLEX S 5dr			1.7 CTDi 130 ecoFLEX SRi 5dr			1.6 VXR 3dr		
		9,495	15%	9,495	14,000	16%	12,476	18,080	17%	16,087	18,910	25%	17,422
	Volkswagen Polo	1.2 60 S 3dr			1.4 85 Match 5dr			1.6 TDI 90 SEL 3dr			1.4 TSI 180 GTI 3dr		
		10,490	16%	10,054	13,705	18%	12,847	16,120	16%	15,095	19,430	18%	18,194
Family Cars / Hatchbacks	Audi A3	1.4 TFSI 122 SE 3dr			1.6 TDI 105 SE 3dr			2.0 TDI 150 S line 3dr					
		19,205	15%	18,251	20,155	13%	19,152	24,880	15%	23,634			
	BMW 1 Series	116i ES 3dr			118i SE 3dr			120d M Sport 3dr			125I M Sport 5dr		
		19,180	17%	17,992	21,670	18%	20,320	26,135	18%	24,233	26,280	21%	24,380
	Ford Focus	1.6 85 Studio 5dr			1.6 105 Zetec 5dr			1.6 TDCi 115 Titanium X 5dr			2.0 TDCi 163 Titanium X 5dr		
		13,995	16%	13,185	17,300	15%	15,182	22,145	15%	19,630	23,645	18%	21,010
	Honda Civic	1.4 i-VITEC SE 5dr			1.8 i-VETEC EX 5dr			2.2 i-DTEC ES 5dr					
		16,955	16%	15,682	21,960	19%	20,306	21,495	16%	19,867			
	Vauxhall Astra	1.4i VVT 87 Expr. 5dr			1.7 CDTi 110 eFLEX ES 5dr			2.0 CDTi 165 Elite auto 5dr			2.0 CDTi 195 BiTurbo S/S 5dr		
		12,995	16%	12,995	19,380	13%	18,012	25,175	24%	22,088	25,110	20%	22,144
	Volkswagen Golf	1.2 TSI 85 S 3dr			1.4 TSI 122 S 3dr			2.0 TDI 150 SE 5dr			2.0 TDI 150 GT 5dr		
		16,285	13%	15,210	18,710	15%	17,469	22,015	15%	20,547	23,465	15%	21,898
Estate Cars	Audi A4 Avant	1.8 TFSI 120 SE 5dr			1.8 TFSI 170 S line 5dr			2.0 TDI 177 Black Edition 5dr			3.0 TDI quattro 245 Black Edit 5dr		
		24,980	21%	22,850	29,165	19%	26,664	32,730	19%	29,902	39,795	24%	36,360
	Ford Focus Estate	1.6 105 Edge 5dr			1.6T 150 Ebst. Titanium 5dr			2.0 TDCi 163 Titanium X 5dr					
		17,400	18%	15,274	21,150	18%	18,724	24,745	18%	22,022			
	Mercedes-Benz C-Class Estate	C180 BlueEff. Exec. SE 5dr			C220 CDI BlueEFF. SE 5dr			C250 CGI BlueEff. Sport 5dr			C350 CDI BlueEff. Sport Plus 5dr		
		27,470	18%	24,403	29,860	18%	26,645	33,020	20%	29,627	37,930	26%	34,251
	Skoda Octavia Estate	1.4 16v 80 S 5dr			1.8 TSI 160 Elegance 5dr			2.0 TDI CR 140 L&K 5dr					
		14,425	20%	12,113	19,345	22%	16,211	23,860	19%	19,937			
	Volvo V70	2.0 D3 SE S/S 5dr			2.4 D5 SE S/S 5dr			3.0 T6 AWD SE Lux Auto 5dr					
		30,120	17%	26,363	33,020	19%	28,894	41,185	35%	36,123			
People Carriers / MPVs	Citroën C4 Picasso	1.6 VTi 120 Edition 5dr			1.6 HDi 110 Edition 5dr			1.6 HDi 110 Platinum 5dr					
		17,950	22%	14,324	19,550	20%	15,863	20,750	21%	17,019			
	Ford Galaxy	1.6 160 Ecoboost Zetec S/S 5dr			2.0 TDCi 163 Titanium 5dr			2.2 TDCi 200 Titanium X 5dr					
		24,955	24%	23,209	28,450	22%	26,446	32,155	29%	29,901			
	Renault Grand Scenic	1.6 VVT 110 Dyn. TomTom 5dr			1.2 TCe115 DynTmTm. S/S 5dr			1.6 dCi 130 Dyn. TmTm. S/S 5dr					
		19,735	26%	16,888	20,830	19%	17,785	22,725	16%	19,375			
	Toyota Verso	1.6 V-matic T2 5st 5dr			2.0 D-4D Active 7st 5dr			2.0 D-4D Excel 7st 5dr					
		17,495	22%	17,130	19,495	19%	19,083	23,445	19%	22,946			
	Vauxhall Zafira	1.4T 140 Exclusiv 5dr			2.0 CDTi 130 Exclusiv 5dr			2.0 CDTi 165 Elite auto 5dr					
		22,760	21%	19,370	24,070	21%	20,550	28,820	25%	24,586			
	Volkswagen Touran	1.2 TSI Bluemotion Tech S 5dr			2.0 TDI 140 SE 5dr			2.0 TDI 170 Sport DSG 5dr					
		19,650	18%	16,945	24,090	22%	21,103	27,330	24%	24,140			
4 Wheel Drive / SUVs	Land Rover Discovery	3.0 SDV6 255 GS 5dr			3.0 SDV6 255 XS 5dr			3.0 SDV6 255 HSE 5dr					
		38,825	35%	36,502	45,510	35%	42,440	52,450	35%	49,293			
	Range Rover	3.0 TDV6 Vogue 5dr			4.4 SDV8 Vogue SE 5dr			5.0 V8 Supercharged 5dr					
		71,295	33%	71,295	84,695	35%	84,695	98,395	35%	98,395			
	Toyota Land Cruiser	3.0 D-4D 188 LC3 3dr			3.0 D-4D 190 LC4 5dr			3.0 D-4D 190 LC5 5dr					
		32,745	35%	30,595	47,445	35%	44,288	52,895	35%	49,364			
	Toyota Rav4 Crossover	2.2 D-4D 150 XT-R 2WD 5dr			2.2 D-CAT XT-R 4WD 5dr			2.2 D-CAT 150 SR 4WD 5dr					
		24,340	25%	22,336	26,040	25%	23,890	28,350	31%	26,027			
Executive / Luxury Cars	Audi A6 Saloon	2.0 TDI 177 SE 4dr			3.0 TDI 204 SE 4dr			3.0 TDI 245 Quattro S line 4dr			4.0 TFSI 420 S6 4dr		
		30,810	19%	27,487	35,030	21%	31,256	42,130	25%	37,579	56,365	35%	52,871
	BMW 5 Series Saloon	520i SE 4dr			530i M Sport 4dr			550i M Sport 4dr			4.4 V8 M5 4dr		
		31,595	22%	28,684	39,105	27%	35,495	56,315	35%	51,117	73,350	35%	70,121
	Jaguar XJ Series Saloon	3.0D V6 Luxury 4dr			3.0D V6 Portfolio 4dr			3.0 V6 S/C Portfolio LWB 4dr					
		56,260	25%	50,008	67,260	25%	59,770	75,815	35%	67,410			
	Mercedes-Benz S-Class Saloon	S350 BlueEFFICIENCY 4dr			S500L BlueEFFICIENCY 4dr			S600L 4dr			S65L AMG 4dr		
		63,090	26%	53,440	83,360	34%	72,536	115,555	35%	102,865	165,060	35%	149,461
Hybrids / Electrics	Honda Insight	1.3 IMA HE 5dr			1.3 IMA HS 5dr			1.3 IMA HX 5dr					
		19,535	11%	18,383	20,335	12%	19,134	22,535	12%	21199			
	Nissan Leaf (EV)				80kw 5 door								
					25,990	0%	25,990						
	Renault Fluence (EV)	Z.E. Expression+ 4dr			Z.E. Dynamique 4dr								
		17,495	0%	17,495	18,395	0%	18,395						
	Toyota Prius	1.8 VVT-i T3 5dr			1.8 VVT-i T4 5dr			1.8 VVT-i T Spirit 5dr			1.8 plug-in (EV)		
		21,845	10%	20,246	23,595	10%	21,864	25,145	10%	23,296	33,245	5%	30,860

Table 10 Car Running Costs

Total car running and maintenance costs according to cost of new car (petrol) as at April 2013

Cost per mile (pence)

Annual mileage	Cost of new car (£s)				
	up to 13,000	13,001 to 18,000	18,001 to 25,000	25,001 to 32,000	over 32,000
5,000	64.11	85.69	104.82	144.18	276.42
10,000	43.95	56.12	66.61	87.88	159.09
15,000	37.39	46.53	54.22	69.63	121.07
20,000	34.24	41.94	48.28	60.89	102.87
25,000	32.15	38.86	44.31	55.03	90.65
30,000	30.71	36.74	41.57	50.99	82.23

Standing charges: cost per year (£)

	Cost of new car (£s)				
	up to 13,000	13,001 to 18,000	18,001 to 25,000	25,001 to 32,000	over 32,000
VED (Road Tax)	125	175	200	260	455
Insurance	667	806	1,078	1,617	3,395
Depreciation	1,223	2,006	2,597	3,857	8,159
Breakdown cover	50	50	50	50	50
Total	2,065	3,037	3,925	5,784	12,059

Standing charges: cost per mile (pence)

Annual mileage	Cost of new car (£s)				
	up to 13,000	13,001 to 18,000	18,001 to 25,000	25,001 to 32,000	over 32,000
5,000	40.81	59.94	77.46	114.14	237.92
10,000	20.65	30.37	39.25	57.84	120.59
15,000	14.09	20.78	26.86	39.59	82.57
20,000	10.94	16.19	20.92	30.85	64.37
25,000	8.85	13.11	16.95	24.99	52.15
30,000	7.41	10.99	14.21	20.95	43.73

Running costs: cost per mile (pence)

	Cost of new car (£s)				
	up to 13,000	13,001 to 18,000	18,001 to 25,000	25,001 to 32,000	over 32,000
Petrol	12.67	14.19	15.77	17.32	21.80
Tyres	1.28	1.83	2.16	2.90	3.75
Service and parts	7.35	7.73	7.43	7.82	10.95
Parking and tolls	2.00	2.00	2.00	2.00	2.00
Total	23.30	25.75	27.36	30.04	38.50
For each 1p change in the cost of petrol from 138 pence per litre, add/subtract	0.10	0.11	0.13	0.14	0.17

These figures are compiled from information published by the AA in April 2013 and include VAT.
The **Cost per mile** is calculated from the **Standing charges** and **Running costs**.

The following assumptions are applied:
Road tax (Vehicle Excise Duty) is shown as the average for each price group. Insurance is the average cost of a fully comprehensive policy (60% NCD, man aged 35 living on the outskirts of London).
Depreciation is averaged over four years from purchase and is adjusted for different annual mileages.
Breakdown cover is based on the cost of basic roadside assistance.
Petrol is unleaded costing 138 pence per litre. Typical fuel consumption figures are used for each car group listed.
It is assumed that the car will use six tyres in a four year period. Online prices are used.
Service and parts are based on average dealer labour rates and normal replacement parts/materials for each price group. Parking and tolls are based on national averages for urban drivers.

The equivalent data for diesel cars are available in @eGlance.

Table 11 Company Cars

HMRC Car Benefit Charges 2013-14

Percentage of the list price to be taxed					
CO_2 g/km	Taxable %		CO_2 g/km	Taxable %	
	Petrol	Diesel		Petrol	Diesel
Up to 75	5	8	130 to 134	18	21
76 to 94	10	13	For every additional 5g/km band from '135 to 139' up to '195 to 199' add 1%, then:		
95 to 99	11	14			
100 to 104	12	15			
105 to 109	13	16			
110 to 114	14	17	200 to 204	32	35
115 to 119	15	18	205 to 209	33	35
120 to 124	16	19	210 to 214	34	35
125 to 129	17	20	215 and over	35	35

The taxable benefit of a company car is based solely on the carbon dioxide each vehicle model produces, measured in grams per kilometre (the CO_2 g/km rating). Tax is levied on Car Benefit calculated by reference to the appropriate percentage (*above*) of the manufacturer's list price for the vehicle (whatever the actual price paid), plus the list price of options/extras. There is no maximum chargeable limit on the list price, but a capital contribution made to the purchase by an employee reduces the list price commensurately.

For 2013-14 the percentage benefit chargeable for vehicles producing up to 75 g/km is 5% for petrol, 8% for diesel engines (as diesel powered cars attract a 3% surcharge). The maximum percentage is 35% (215 g/km and above for petrol vehicles; 200 g/km and above for diesel). Second and subsequent cars are taxed in an identical manner.

Cars which cannot produce CO_2 engine emissions under any circumstances attract a 0% rate.

For cars registered on or after 1 March 2001 the CO_2 g/km rating is shown on the DVLA Registration Form V5.

Table 9, *ante*, shows taxable benefit percentages for a range of new cars. For both old and new cars find indicative ratings at carfueldata.direct.gov.uk/search-new-or-used-cars.aspx.

HMRC Fuel Benefit Charge 2013-14

The taxable benefit where an employer supplies fuel for private use (or allows reimbursement for fuel for private journeys) is based on the CO_2 g/km rating of the car used. To calculate the Fuel Benefit Charge the appropriate percentage (see Table *above*) is multiplied by a set figure (£20,200 for 2013-14). The minimum chargeable benefit for 2013-14 is £1,010 (5%), the maximum is £7,070 (35%). So where a petrol vehicle's CO_2 g/km rating is 117 and thus 15% applies, the taxable fuel benefit is £3,030 (15% x 20,200).

No charge arises if fuel is provided only for business or if the employee must pay for private fuel use.

HMRC Approved Mileage Allowance Payments (AMAPs) 2013-14

Vehicle	Pence per mile
Cars and vans	
up to 10,000 miles	45
above 10,000 miles	25
plus per passenger*	5
Motorcycles	24
Cycles	20

Mileage payments to employees using their own transport for business purposes attract no tax if within these authorised rates.

*When paid to driver for each fellow employee carried as passenger on shared business trip.

Table 12 Office Salary Survey

Regional salaries (rounded £000s) in December 2012 for a range of secretarial and office employment

	London	South East	South West	East Anglia	South Midlands	Midlands
Office manager	23-33	22-30	19-26	20-30	24-34	18-27
PA	22-34	33-30	20-28	19-29	22-36	18-27
Legal secretary	21-28	19-24	17-21	16-21	18-25	15-21
Administrator	16-23	15-20	14-18	14-20	15-25	14-20
Receptionist	16-21	15-19	13-16	13-18	14-20	13-17
Customer service manager	23-33	23-32	23-33	23-33	24-39	21-31
Customer service operative	16-20	15-19	14-18	13-18	15-22	13-18
Tele-sales manager	21-29	23-31	21-27	22-27	22-34	20-27
Tele-sales executive	15-20	15-19	15-20	13-18	15-23	13-18
Sales manager	35-45	35-45	32-40	30-40	30-40	25-30
Sales executive	30-40	30-40	19-25	25-35	25-35	18-30
Marketing executive	22-40	22-40	22-30	26-33	17-35	21-34
Graphic designer	22-45	22-45	18-30	17-37	14-28	17-37
Bookkeeper	25-36	18-25	17-21	18-27	19-28	19-26

	Yorkshire and Humber	North East	North West	Scotland	Wales	Northern Ireland
Office manager	18-35	19-30	22-31	20-40	18-24	20-26
PA	17-30	18-27	18-28	17-38	18-25	18-25
Legal secretary	14-26	15-18	16-20	18-26	15-18	15-17
Administrator	13-22	13-17	13-18	16-22	14-17	12-18
Receptionist	13-22	12-17	13-17	13-19	13-16	12-16
Customer service manager	18-40	19-30	22-36	20-35	20-25	20-26
Customer service operative	13-22	13-18	14-18	12-21	13-17	12-16
Tele-sales manager	18-40	18-29	25-41	20-36	20-25	20-25
Tele-sales executive	13-22	14-19	15-20	14-25	15-18	13-19
Sales manager	30-40	25-42	20-35	20-40	32-37	20-35
Sales executive	25-35	16-27	18-26	18-32	18-25	18-25
Marketing executive	18-30	17-27	18-25	20-32	20-28	20-27
Graphic designer	18-36	16-29	20-30	18-31	18-30	16-25
Bookkeeper	16-22	18-22	16-20	17-26	17-23	17-23

Notes

From data collected during **December 2012**, the Table shows salaries paid and offered to office, secretarial and sales staff by private and public sector employers and demonstrates the pay differentials across the country. The figures quoted are annual basic salary only and do not reflect any additional allowances or benefits.

These Salary Surveys (with commentary on trends, skills shortages and benefits) are published each year by Reed Specialist (☎ 0845 241 9249 or press.office@reedglobal.com).

Table 13 Financial Times Indexes

Level of the FTSE 100 Index at month-end

Year	Jan	Feb	Mar	Apr	May	Jun	Jul	Aug	Sep	Oct	Nov	Dec
96	3,759.28	3,727.57	3,699.66	3,817.93	3,747.78	3,711.02	3,703.20	3,867.58	3,953.67	3,979.10	4,058.04	4,118.51
97	4,275.79	4,308.32	4,312.90	4,435.97	4,621.27	4,604.63	4,907.47	4,817.47	5,244.18	4,842.33	4,831.77	5,135.54
98	5,458.46	5,767.31	5,932.22	5,928.35	5,870.72	5,832.55	5,837.05	5,249.38	5,064.36	5,438.37	5,743.89	5,882.58
99	5,896.00	6,175.10	6,295.30	6,552.18	6,226.22	6,318.53	6,231.93	6,246.44	6,029.84	6,255.72	6,597.17	6,930.20
00	6,268.54	6,232.56	6,540.22	6,327.43	6,359.35	6,312.71	6,365.26	6,672.66	6,294.24	6,438.42	6,142.19	6,222.46
01	6,297.53	5,917.87	5,633.70	5,966.95	5,796.15	5,642.50	5,529.05	5,344.97	4,903.39	5,039.71	5,203.55	5,217.35
02	5,164.78	5,100.96	5,271.76	5,165.58	5,085.07	4,656.36	4,246.21	4,227.28	3,721.75	4,039.66	4,169.41	3,950.36
03	3,567.41	3,655.58	3,613.28	3,925.97	4,048.14	4,031.17	4,157.02	4,161.06	4,091.31	4,287.59	4,342.60	4,476.87
04	4,390.68	4,492.21	4,385.67	4,489.70	4,430.70	4,464.10	4,413.10	4,459.30	4,570.80	4,624.20	4,703.20	4,814.30
05	4,852.30	4,968.50	4,894.40	4,801.70	4,964.00	5,113.20	5,282.30	5,296.90	5,477.70	5,317.30	5,423.20	5,722.60
06	5,760.30	5,791.50	5,964.60	6,023.10	5,723.80	5,833.40	5,928.30	5,906.10	5,960.80	6,129.20	6,048.80	6,152.40
07	6,203.10	6,171.50	6,308.00	6,449.20	6,621.40	6,607.90	6,360.10	6,303.30	6,466.80	6,721.60	6,432.50	6,456.90
08	5,879.80	5,884.30	5,702.10	6,087.30	6,053.50	5,625.90	5,411.90	5,636.60	4,902.50	4,337.30	4,288.00	4,434.20
09	4,149.60	3,830.10	3,926.10	4,243.70	4,417.90	4,249.20	4,608.40	4,908.90	5,133.90	5,044.50	5,190.70	5,412.90
10	5,188.50	5,354.50	5,679.60	5,533.30	5,188.40	4,916.90	5,258.00	5,225.20	5,548.60	5,675.20	5,528.30	5,899.90
11	5,862.90	5,994.00	5,908.80	6,069.90	5,990.00	5,945.70	5,815.20	5,394.50	5,128.50	5,544.20	5,505.40	5,572.30
12	5,681.60	5,871.50	5,768.50	5,737.80	5,320.90	5,571.10	5,635.30	5,711.50	5,742.10	5,782.70	5,866.80	5,897.80
13	6,276.90	6,360.80	6,411.70	6,430.10								

Calculated on a daily basis, this Index represents the value of the 100 most highly capitalised blue chip companies in the UK.

Level of the All Share Index at month-end

Year	Jan	Feb	Mar	Apr	May	Jun	Jul	Aug	Sep	Oct	Nov	Dec
96	1,841.96	1,840.77	1,843.44	1,914.61	1,885.78	1,856.33	1,835.44	1,915.98	1,945.00	1,956.90	1,985.17	2,013.66
97	2,087.61	2,107.86	2,099.70	2,135.31	2,200.91	2,184.52	2,295.18	2,276.72	2,455.02	2,293.87	2,288.64	2,411.00
98	2,536.68	2,683.40	2,781.66	2,788.99	2,802.18	2,743.46	2,734.72	2,440.89	2,344.82	2,504.85	2,626.86	2,673.92
99	2,695.99	2,825.39	2,894.79	3,028.40	2,889.65	2,949.17	2,925.14	2,939.11	2,826.11	2,904.38	3,086.90	3,242.06
00	2,975.87	2,989.93	3,110.56	3,001.92	3,017.23	3,029.74	3,062.41	3,207.99	3,029.36	3,078.22	2,945.06	2,983.81
01	3,030.05	2,868.00	2,711.40	2,869.04	2,811.22	2,728.12	2,663.92	2,590.17	2,340.48	2,413.50	2,514.07	2,523.88
02	2,496.02	2,466.98	2,557.40	2,512.04	2,475.57	2,263.11	2,050.81	2,046.21	1,801.48	1,938.71	2,002.97	1,893.73
03	1,722.28	1,759.08	1,735.72	1,891.50	1,968.83	1,971.26	2,045.82	2,064.74	2,027.72	2,125.37	2,146.72	2,207.38
04	2,187.10	2,243.41	2,196.97	2,237.30	2,201.80	2,228.70	2,192.22	2,214.19	2,271.67	2,297.66	2,345.21	2,410.75
05	2,441.22	2,495.46	2,457.73	2,397.05	2,483.35	2,560.17	2,644.75	2,659.21	2,745.79	2,664.40	2,741.05	2,847.02
06	2,928.56	2,956.12	3,047.96	3,074.26	2,916.85	2,967.58	3,004.28	3,007.51	3,050.44	3,140.47	3,119.85	3,178.59
07	3,211.84	3,198.28	3,283.21	3,355.60	3,438.70	3,404.14	3,289.12	3,260.48	3,316.89	3,454.12	3,280.87	3,286.67
08	3,000.10	3,013.02	2,927.05	3,095.68	3,082.26	2,855.69	2,749.21	2,868.69	2,483.67	2,183.69	2,133.99	2,209.29
09	2,078.92	1,929.75	1,984.17	2,173.06	2,252.64	2,172.08	2,353.47	2,520.66	2,634.79	2,584.59	2,648.43	2,760.80
10	2,660.49	2,736.80	2,910.19	2,863.35	2,673.17	2,543.47	2,715.36	2,696.72	2,867.58	2,936.15	2,861.61	3,062.85
11	3,044.27	3,106.58	3,067.73	3,155.03	3,121.07	3,096.72	3,026.02	2,800.51	2,654.38	2,860.86	2,835.84	2,857.88
12	2,932.91	3,043.91	3,002.78	2,984.67	2,760.62	2,891.45	2,927.27	2,972.63	2,998.86	3,024.40	3,065.30	3,093.41
13	3,287.38	3,349.39	3,380.64	3,390.18								

Calculated on a daily basis, this Index represents the aggregation of the FTSE 100, the FTSE 250 and the FTSE SmallCap indexes.

Equivalent data for other Indexes (Dax, Dow, Hang Seng and Nasdaq) can be found in @eGlance.

Table 13 Financial Times Indexes

Level of FTSE 100 Index at year-end

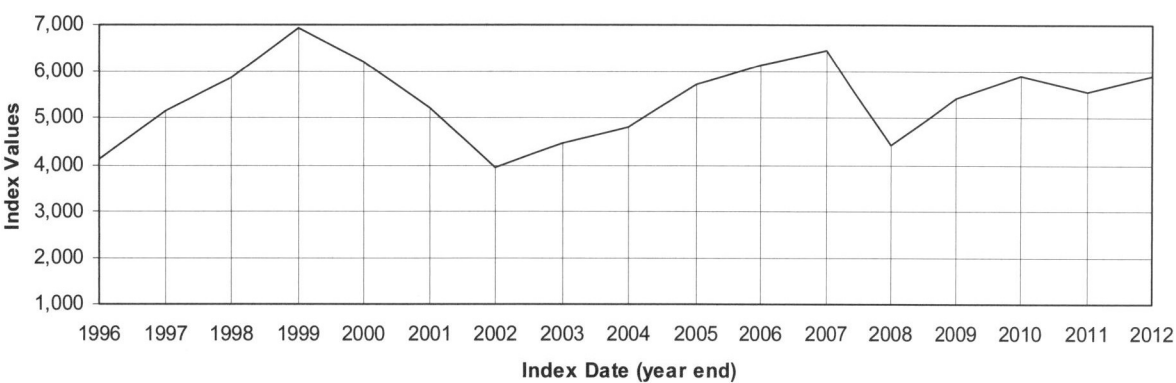

Level of FTSE 100 Index at month-end for 2012

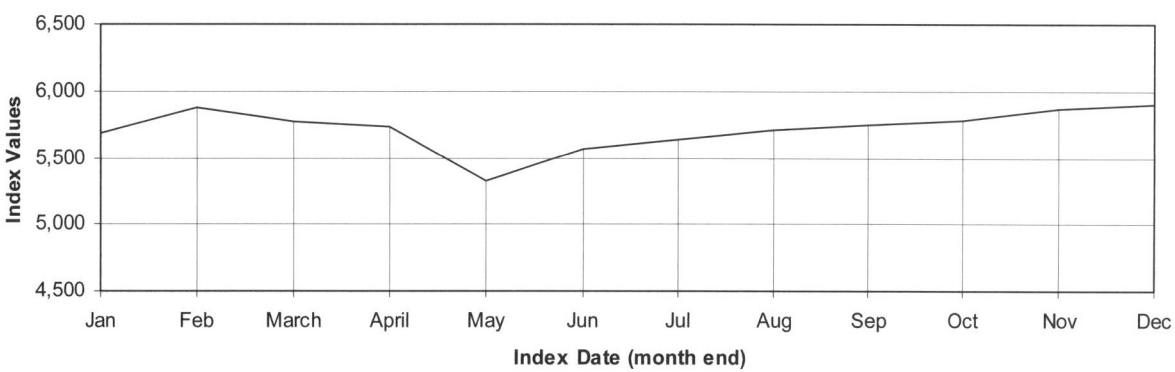

Level of All Share Index at year-end

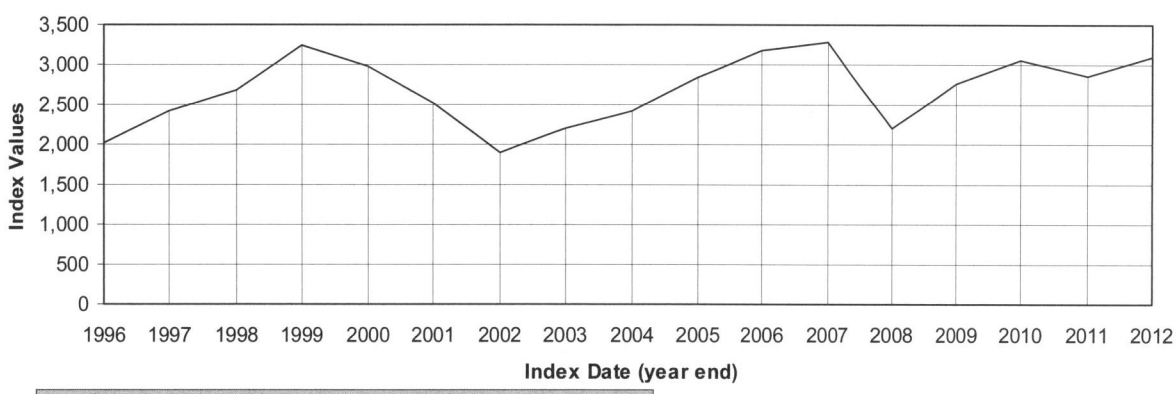

Level of All Share Index at month-end for 2012

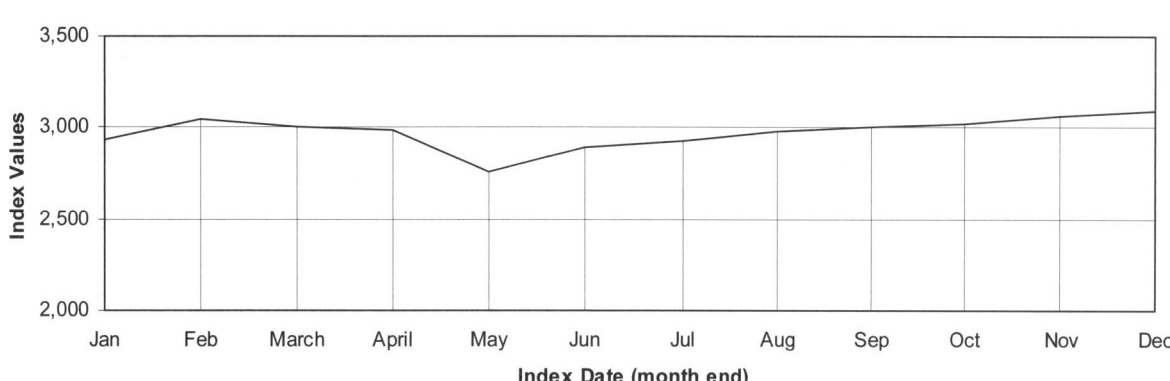

Table 14 Life Cover

Level Term: per £100,000 of sum assured

Age	Policy length (years)									
	10		15		20		25		30	
	NS	S	NS	S	NS	S	NS	S	NS	S
25	5.45	7.13	5.70	7.18	5.70	7.24	5.90	7.65	6.07	8.33
30	6.15	7.57	6.15	8.04	6.15	8.64	6.56	9.48	7.16	10.52
35	6.96	9.78	7.16	10.36	7.57	11.59	8.30	13.01	9.18	15.31
40	8.63	13.41	9.25	15.52	10.04	17.64	11.21	20.49	12.74	23.77
45	11.72	21.37	13.08	24.64	14.74	28.84	16.68	32.81	20.23	40.48
50	16.98	34.30	19.39	41.14	22.25	47.51	26.82	57.86	33.85	67.83

Family Income Benefit: £25,000 income per annum for the balance of the chosen term

Age	Policy length (years)									
	10		15		20		25		30	
	NS	S	NS	S	NS	S	NS	S	NS	S
25	7.82	10.59	9.96	13.60	11.87	16.68	14.01	20.09	16.02	24.55
30	8.04	11.68	10.49	15.16	12.94	19.55	15.71	25.29	19.27	32.25
35	9.12	14.47	12.04	19.74	15.36	26.32	21.12	37.19	24.70	46.69
40	11.32	19.43	15.85	29.59	21.53	43.38	28.34	60.43	37.26	77.74
45	15.57	29.96	23.97	48.94	33.21	71.05	46.02	103.76	60.80	133.77
50	23.27	49.66	37.89	83.81	54.68	123.70	77.54	179.13	108.64	233.08

Mortgage Protection: per initial sum assured of £100,000, reducing in line with a repayment mortgage

Age	Policy length (years)									
	10		15		20		25		30	
	NS	S	NS	S	NS	S	NS	S	NS	S
25	5.08	6.17	5.08	6.17	5.28	6.18	5.39	6.78	5.70	7.19
30	5.59	6.86	5.59	6.90	5.80	7.15	5.92	7.75	6.03	8.58
35	5.92	8.14	6.00	8.38	6.11	9.04	6.59	10.42	7.06	11.43
40	6.59	10.18	7.03	11.78	7.54	13.66	8.39	15.82	9.34	17.61
45	8.19	14.38	9.25	18.12	10.71	20.71	12.10	24.30	13.99	30.17
50	11.79	25.25	14.02	30.15	15.97	35.36	19.28	43.51	22.64	54.37

Policy features

All premiums are monthly, payable throughout the term. All the above quotations are based on guaranteed premium rates for the term of the plan. None of these types of policy achieves a capital or surrender value.

A **level term policy** pays out the sum assured should the life assured die or suffer from a terminal illness during the term of the plan.

A **family income benefit policy** pays out a tax free income for the remaining term of the plan from the death or prior terminal illness of the policy holder.

A **mortgage protection policy** is designed so that the sum assured decreases in line with a repayment mortgage: on death the payment is the amount of the loan then outstanding (assuming all payments have been made in accordance with the mortgage terms).

These rates were representative in March 2013.

Harmonisation of rates for men and women was imposed pursuant to an ECJ ruling in March 2011. This took effect on 21 December 2012, and has primarily improved the lot of insurers. Some men, particularly smokers, have marginally benefitted, although on average men's premiums have increased by about 2% above those published last year. Women's have increased markedly: on average by 25% to 30%, but for family income policies by over 40%, and by almost 50% for women smokers.

Table 15 Life Expectancy

Remaining life expectancy in years according to age and sex (for use in the year 2013)

Age	Men ONS10M	Men PMA92	Women ONS10F	Women PFA92	Age	Men ONS10M	Men PMA92	Women ONS10F	Women PFA92
20	68.3	66.3	71.9	69.3	55	30.7	30.1	33.8	33.1
21	67.1	65.3	70.8	68.3	56	29.7	29.1	32.8	32.1
22	66.0	64.3	69.7	67.3	57	28.7	28.1	31.8	31.1
23	64.9	63.3	68.6	66.3	58	27.7	27.0	30.8	30.1
24	63.8	62.3	67.5	65.2	59	26.8	26.0	29.8	29.1
25	62.7	61.2	66.3	64.2	60	25.9	25.0	28.8	28.1
26	61.6	60.2	65.2	63.2	61	25.0	24.0	27.9	27.1
27	60.4	59.2	64.1	62.2	62	24.1	23.0	26.9	26.1
28	59.3	58.2	63.0	61.1	63	23.2	22.1	26.0	25.1
29	58.2	57.1	61.9	60.1	64	22.3	21.1	25.0	24.1
30	57.1	56.1	60.8	59.1	65	21.4	20.2	24.1	23.2
31	56.0	55.1	59.7	58.0	66	20.6	19.2	23.1	22.2
32	54.9	54.0	58.6	57.0	67	19.7	18.3	22.2	21.3
33	53.9	53.0	57.5	56.0	68	18.8	17.4	21.3	20.4
34	52.8	52.0	56.4	54.9	69	18.0	16.6	20.4	19.5
35	51.7	50.9	55.3	53.9	70	17.2	15.7	19.5	18.6
36	50.6	49.9	54.2	52.9	71	16.4	14.9	18.6	17.8
37	49.6	48.9	53.1	51.8	72	15.6	14.1	17.7	16.9
38	48.5	47.8	52.0	50.8	73	14.8	13.3	16.9	16.1
39	47.4	46.8	50.9	49.8	74	14.1	12.6	16.0	15.3
40	46.3	45.7	49.8	48.7	75	13.3	11.8	15.2	14.6
41	45.3	44.7	48.7	47.7	76	12.6	11.2	14.4	13.8
42	44.2	43.7	47.6	46.6	77	11.9	10.5	13.6	13.1
43	43.1	42.6	46.5	45.6	78	11.2	9.9	12.8	12.4
44	42.1	41.6	45.4	44.5	79	10.5	9.3	12.0	11.7
45	41.0	40.5	44.3	43.5	80	9.8	8.7	11.2	11.1
46	40.0	39.5	43.3	42.5	81	9.2	8.2	10.4	10.5
47	38.9	38.4	42.2	41.4	82	8.5	7.6	9.7	9.9
48	37.9	37.4	41.1	40.4	83	7.9	7.2	9.0	9.3
49	36.8	36.3	40.1	39.3	84	7.4	6.7	8.3	8.8
50	35.8	35.3	39.0	38.3	85	6.9	6.3	7.7	8.3
51	34.7	34.3	38.0	37.3	86	6.4	5.9	7.1	7.8
52	33.7	33.2	36.9	36.2	87	6.0	5.5	6.6	7.4
53	32.7	32.2	35.9	35.2	88	5.6	5.2	6.1	6.9
54	31.7	31.1	34.8	34.2	89	5.2	4.8	5.6	6.5

This Table contains data from two of the numerous life expectancy tables for men and women in the UK.

PA92 (PMA92 for males and PFA92 for females) shows data for members of insured pension schemes, and underlies the **Duxbury Calculations** in this edition.

ONS10 (ONS10M for males and ONS10F for females) provides data from the latest published UK national population projections.

These figures are 'cohort life expectancies' and incorporate future mortality changes projected beyond 2013, as the experience is that people live progressively longer.

Until the 2007-2008 edition *At A Glance* carried detailed expositions of the characteristics of various life expectancy tables. That material is reproduced in the Life Expectancy module of *@eGlance* where additional life expectancy tables (PA80 and ELT16) are available; or search for 'cohort life expectancy' at www.ons.gov.uk.

Table 16 Duxbury Calculations

Capitalising (to nearest £1,000) female and male lifetime net income needs

Age	£10,000		£15,000		£20,000		£25,000		£30,000		£40,000		£50,000		£60,000	
	F	M	F	M	F	M	F	M	F	M	F	M	F	M	F	M
40	191	189	303	298	417	409	537	525	664	647	924	900	1,187	1,154	1,460	1,41
41	189	186	300	294	413	404	531	518	656	639	914	889	1,174	1,141	1,444	1,39
42	186	183	296	290	408	399	525	512	649	631	904	878	1,161	1,127	1,427	1,38
43	182	180	292	286	403	394	518	505	641	622	893	867	1,148	1,113	1,410	1,36
44	179	177	287	282	398	388	512	498	633	614	882	855	1,134	1,098	1,392	1,34
45	176	173	283	277	392	382	505	491	624	605	871	843	1,120	1,083	1,374	1,32
46	170	167	276	270	384	374	496	481	613	593	857	828	1,104	1,065	1,354	1,30
47	165	162	269	263	375	364	484	468	598	577	836	805	1,076	1,035	1,318	1,26
48	161	158	264	258	369	358	476	460	588	567	823	791	1,060	1,018	1,299	1,24
49	157	154	259	252	362	351	468	452	579	557	810	777	1,044	1,001	1,279	1,22
50	153	150	254	247	356	344	460	443	569	546	797	763	1,027	983	1,259	1,20
51	149	146	248	241	349	337	452	435	559	536	783	748	1,010	964	1,238	1,18
52	145	141	243	235	342	329	444	425	549	525	769	733	992	945	1,216	1,15
53	140	136	237	229	335	321	435	416	538	513	755	718	974	925	1,194	1,13
54	135	131	230	222	327	313	426	406	527	502	740	702	955	905	1,172	1,11
55	130	126	224	215	319	305	416	396	516	490	724	685	936	885	1,149	1,08
56	125	121	218	208	311	297	407	386	504	477	709	669	916	863	1,125	1,05
57	120	116	211	201	303	288	397	375	492	465	693	651	896	841	1,100	1,03
58	115	110	204	194	294	278	386	364	480	452	676	634	875	819	1,075	1,00
59	109	104	196	186	285	269	376	353	467	438	659	615	853	796	1,049	97
60	94	94	179	174	268	255	357	337	447	420	634	593	824	768	1,015	94
61	82	87	166	165	253	244	341	325	430	406	612	573	797	744	984	9
62	70	81	152	156	237	234	324	312	410	391	588	553	769	719	951	8
63	68	74	148	147	231	222	315	299	400	376	573	533	749	693	926	8
64	67	66	145	138	225	211	307	285	389	360	557	511	728	666	900	8
65	65	59	141	128	219	198	298	270	378	342	541	489	706	638	873	7
66	63	57	137	124	212	191	289	260	366	329	524	470	684	614	845	7
67	61	55	132	119	205	184	279	250	354	316	506	451	661	589	817	7
68	59	53	128	114	198	176	270	239	342	303	489	432	638	563	788	6
69	59	53	128	114	198	176	270	239	342	303	489	432	638	563	788	6
70	57	50	124	109	191	168	260	229	329	289	470	412	614	537	758	6
71	55	48	119	104	184	160	250	218	316	275	451	392	589	510	727	6
72	53	46	114	99	176	152	239	206	303	261	432	371	563	483	696	5
73	50	43	109	93	168	144	229	194	289	246	412	349	537	454	663	5
74	48	43	104	93	160	144	218	194	275	246	392	349	510	454	630	5
75	48	40	104	88	160	135	218	182	275	230	392	327	510	425	630	5
76	46	38	99	82	152	126	206	170	261	214	371	304	482	395	595	4
77	43	38	93	82	144	126	194	170	246	214	349	304	454	395	560	4
78	40	35	88	75	135	116	182	157	230	198	327	280	425	364	524	4
79	40	32	88	69	135	106	182	143	230	181	327	256	425	332	524	4
80	38	32	38	69	126	106	170	143	214	181	304	256	395	332	487	4

Table 16 Duxbury Calculations

£75,000		£100,000		£125,000		£150,000		£175,000		£200,000		£250,000		£300,000		Age
F	M	F	M	F	M	F	M	F	M	F	M	F	M	F	M	
907	1,844	2,673	2,580	3,447	3,325	4,261	4,100	5,061	4,875	5,859	5,640	7,461	7,182	9,064	8,725	40
884	1,820	2,641	2,546	3,405	3,280	4,207	4,042	4,999	4,808	5,787	5,563	7,368	7,083	8,951	8,605	41
861	1,795	2,608	2,511	3,362	3,235	4,151	3,983	4,935	4,740	5,712	5,484	7,273	6,983	8,836	8,483	42
837	1,770	2,574	2,475	3,319	3,189	4,094	3,922	4,869	4,670	5,637	5,404	7,176	6,880	8,719	8,358	43
813	1,744	2,540	2,439	3,275	3,142	4,036	3,861	4,802	4,599	5,559	5,322	7,077	6,775	8,600	8,231	44
788	1,717	2,505	2,401	3,229	3,094	3,976	3,799	4,734	4,525	5,480	5,238	6,976	6,668	8,477	8,102	45
760	1,688	2,467	2,361	3,181	3,042	3,914	3,734	4,661	4,448	5,398	5,151	6,871	6,557	8,351	7,967	46
710	1,635	2,395	2,284	3,087	2,943	3,792	3,607	4,519	4,296	5,234	4,977	6,661	6,335	8,096	7,696	47
683	1,606	2,357	2,244	3,038	2,890	3,729	3,542	4,444	4,216	5,148	4,886	6,552	6,219	7,963	7,555	48
655	1,577	2,318	2,202	2,988	2,836	3,665	3,475	4,367	4,134	5,061	4,793	6,441	6,101	7,828	7,411	49
627	1,547	2,278	2,160	2,936	2,782	3,600	3,407	4,289	4,051	4,972	4,698	6,328	5,981	7,690	7,265	50
598	1,517	2,237	2,116	2,883	2,726	3,535	3,339	4,209	3,966	4,881	4,601	6,212	5,858	7,549	7,115	51
569	1,486	2,195	2,072	2,829	2,668	3,468	3,269	4,127	3,879	4,788	4,501	6,094	5,733	7,405	6,962	52
539	1,454	2,153	2,027	2,774	2,610	3,400	3,197	4,043	3,791	4,692	4,400	5,973	5,605	7,258	6,806	53
508	1,422	2,109	1,980	2,718	2,550	3,331	3,124	3,958	3,703	4,595	4,296	5,850	5,474	7,108	6,648	54
477	1,389	2,064	1,933	2,661	2,489	3,261	3,049	3,871	3,612	4,496	4,190	5,725	5,342	6,955	6,486	55
445	1,356	2,019	1,885	2,602	2,427	3,189	2,973	3,784	3,521	4,394	4,082	5,597	5,206	6,799	6,322	56
413	1,322	1,973	1,835	2,543	2,364	3,116	2,895	3,695	3,428	4,290	3,971	5,467	5,068	6,641	6,154	57
380	1,287	1,925	1,785	2,482	2,299	3,041	2,815	3,604	3,334	4,184	3,859	5,334	4,927	6,479	5,982	58
347	1,251	1,877	1,734	2,419	2,233	2,965	2,734	3,513	3,238	4,075	3,746	5,198	4,783	6,314	5,808	59
305	1,211	1,822	1,678	2,350	2,162	2,881	2,648	3,414	3,137	3,961	3,628	5,054	4,633	6,141	5,627	60
265	1,174	1,768	1,625	2,282	2,093	2,798	2,564	3,317	3,037	3,847	3,511	4,910	4,483	5,967	5,446	61
225	1,136	1,712	1,570	2,211	2,022	2,714	2,477	3,218	2,934	3,730	3,393	4,763	4,329	5,789	5,261	62
192	1,097	1,663	1,514	2,146	1,950	2,633	2,389	3,122	2,830	3,616	3,272	4,618	4,173	5,613	5,073	63
158	1,056	1,612	1,457	2,080	1,877	2,551	2,300	3,025	2,723	3,501	3,149	4,471	4,013	5,435	4,880	64
124	1,014	1,560	1,398	2,012	1,801	2,468	2,207	2,925	2,615	3,384	3,024	4,321	3,850	5,252	4,684	65
088	976	1,507	1,342	1,943	1,728	2,382	2,116	2,824	2,507	3,266	2,899	4,167	3,687	5,067	4,487	66
052	936	1,453	1,285	1,873	1,653	2,295	2,024	2,720	2,397	3,146	2,771	4,010	3,523	4,877	4,286	67
014	895	1,398	1,228	1,801	1,576	2,207	1,930	2,615	2,285	3,024	2,641	3,850	3,356	4,684	4,080	68
014	895	1,398	1,228	1,801	1,576	2,207	1,930	2,615	2,285	3,024	2,641	3,850	3,356	4,684	4,080	69
976	853	1,342	1,171	1,728	1,498	2,116	1,834	2,507	2,170	2,899	2,508	3,687	3,186	4,487	3,871	70
936	810	1,285	1,111	1,653	1,419	2,024	1,736	2,397	2,054	2,771	2,373	3,523	3,014	4,286	3,659	71
895	766	1,228	1,050	1,576	1,338	1,930	1,636	2,285	1,935	2,641	2,235	3,356	2,838	4,080	3,443	72
853	720	1,171	988	1,498	1,256	1,834	1,534	2,170	1,814	2,508	2,095	3,186	2,659	3,871	3,225	73
810	720	1,111	988	1,419	1,256	1,736	1,534	2,054	1,814	2,373	2,095	3,014	2,659	3,659	3,225	74
810	673	1,111	923	1,419	1,174	1,736	1,430	2,054	1,690	2,373	1,952	3,014	2,476	3,659	3,004	75
766	625	1,050	857	1,338	1,089	1,636	1,324	1,935	1,565	2,235	1,806	2,838	2,291	3,443	2,777	76
720	625	988	857	1,256	1,089	1,534	1,324	1,814	1,565	2,095	1,806	2,659	2,291	3,225	2,777	77
673	576	923	789	1,174	1,003	1,430	1,217	1,690	1,436	1,952	1,658	2,476	2,102	3,004	2,547	78
673	525	923	719	1,174	914	1,430	1,109	1,690	1,306	1,952	1,506	2,476	1,909	3,004	2,313	79
625	525	857	719	1,089	914	1,324	1,109	1,565	1,306	1,806	1,506	2,291	1,909	2,777	2,313	80

Table 16 Duxbury Calculations

Duxbury calculators are based on an iterative computation, seeking the amount which if invested to achieve capital growth and income yield (both at assumed rates and after income tax on the yield and CGT on the realised gains) could theoretically be drawn down in equal inflation-proofed instalments over a period (usually, but not always, the estimated actuarial life expectancy of the recipient) but would be completely exhausted at the end of the period. It is not, and never has been, an attempt to identify the sum necessary to guarantee a particular level of expenditure, but should rather be viewed as a guide to the net present value of a right to receive periodical payments at the target annual rate for the remainder of the payee's life.

The underlying 'assumptions' are (1) a uniform income yield; (2) a uniform rate of capital growth; (3) a uniform rate of inflation; (4) a consistent régime of taxation - with bands/allowances increasing in line with inflation; (5) a constant level of drawdown in real terms; (6) a consistent rate of 'churn' (the realisation of capital gains other than to fund expenditure); and that the recipient will (7) survive for precisely the expected average of her (or occasionally his) contemporaries; and (8) be or become entitled to a 'full' state pension; which will (9) increase in line with prices; while (10) the age at which a state pension is payable will not alter in the meantime.[1] All of the assumptions are necessary simplifications which will not materialise: as Ward LJ said in **B v B** [1990] 1 FLR 20 *'the only certainty is that it will not happen as we have predicted'*. At best the assumptions are 'guesstimates', or approximations of what may be an average of events to happen over a future of something between about 15 and 50 years. The assumptions include three key financial predictions – an average income yield of 3% p.a., average capital growth of 3.75% p.a. and average inflation of 3% p.a.[2]

In turbulent economic times predicting what might be the investment yields and capital returns available over such a long future period is particularly challenging. While there is scope for debate about the appropriate assumptions to use, it is clear that predictions about what may happen over the next 15 to 50 years cannot be overly reliant upon what has happened in the last 15 to 50 months, let alone the last 15 to 50 weeks. The past is an imperfect guide, indeed a very imperfect guide, but it is the least/most (un)reliable guide devised so far, and history tells us that average real returns of 3.75% p.a. are – over the long term – achievable even with a cautious investment strategy. Although interest rates remain obstinately low, the FTSE 100 is up 13% in the year to 2 April 2013, while the FTSE Mid-250 is up 23% in the same period.

Before the October 2000 decision of the House of Lords in **White v White** [2000] 3 WLR 1571 Duxbury calculations were commonly the determinant of awards in ancillary relief cases. Since the development first of 'the yardstick' (in **White**) and subsequently of 'the sharing principle' (in **Miller; McFarlane**), their most common use has been either (i) as a guide to the appropriate sum for which an existing periodical payments order might be capitalised (**Pearce** [2004] 2 FLR 236) or (ii) as a cross-check on whether the application of the sharing principle is likely to meet the needs of the recipient. In both instances, but particularly the former, the assumptions must be such as strive to achieve fairness between the parties. A financial remedy award is a 'nil gain sum' – so any benefit to one party is necessarily a detriment to the other. The capitalisation of a periodical payments award should therefore aim to achieve as fair a balance as possible between ensuring that the payer does not pay too much and that the payee receives enough but no less. Standardisation inevitably leads to anomalies and occasionally unfair results in individual cases. A payee who receives capitalised periodical payments calculated on Duxbury assumptions is a net winner if she soon remarries (or cohabits in circumstances which would have led to a reduction in her periodical payments) or, more paradoxically, if she dies young. On the other hand she will be a net loser if she lives singly for longer than her average contemporary. The likelihood of re-marriage by the payee, or a payer's inability to continue to make periodical payments long into his old age, are factors which would tend to favour the former over the latter. For a fuller discussion of these topics see '***An Alternative view of Duxbury***' [2010] Fam Law 614 and, for the intellectually curious, the judgment of Baroness Hale in **Simon v Helmot** [2012] UKPC 5 especially at [70] to [72].

Notwithstanding the implementation into UK insurance law of the March 2011 decision of the European Court of Justice prohibiting the inclusion of differential gender-based risks on the calculation of insurance premia and annuity rates (see Tables 14 and 17 respectively) the editors continue to publish distinct Duxbury calculations for male and female recipients. Reasons for persisting in this discrimination include that (i) Duxbury is but a 'guide' to assist the Court to determine the fair outcome of a discretionary exercise, (ii) unification of rates would result in women receiving markedly lower and, perhaps, men more generous awards which would be difficult to justify objectively, and (iii) the ECJ decision is not directly applicable to the task in hand. It may be that it will be successfully argued (presumably by a husband – whether claimant or respondent), that differential rates are inapposite, but until then *At A Glance* will continue to publish comparative figures.

The Table shows figures for recipients in the age range 40 to 80 but the usefulness of Duxbury calculations for recipients with a life expectancy of less than about 15 years (women over about 74 and men over about 71) must be doubtful. The likelihood is that recipients of that age will fall foul of the so-called 'Duxbury paradox' - that the longer the marriage the smaller the lump sum requirement. The proportionate margin of error in relation to life expectancy (in particular) is also extremely high, with some recipients living more than twice longer than expected: not a fate which can afflict recipients at the outset aged 40, 50 or even 60 years. And the shorter the expectancy the less likely it is that the average returns will return to those historically achievable over longer terms.

More refined calculations are available within ***@eGlance*** and yet more bespoke via ***Capitalise***.

---

1. No account is yet taken of the proposed adjustments to state pension ages, the effect of which would be, if implemented, to add very slightly to the sums identified for young recipients.
2. The quantitative easing introduced in 2009-10 and intended to last for only two years has been extended into this, the fifth year, by a temporary reduction in the assumed yield in year one to 1.5% before returning to the normative level of 3% p.a.

Table 17 Annuities

Gross annuity payable annually in advance for life per £100,000 of purchase money

Since the implementation of the EU Gender Directive, effective 21 December 2012, annuity providers are obliged to provide the same rates to women as to men.

It had been anticipated that the consequence would be annuity rates for both men and women somewhat closer to the (more generous) rates previously available to men than to the rates previously available to women.

In fact rates (in March 2013) are markedly lower for both men (broadly 10% to 15%) and for women (broadly 5% to 14%) compared to the rates available in April 2012 shown in the previous edition.

If one ignores both taxation and inflation, the survival age necessary to recoup even the original purchase cost of an annuity is in the range from 77 (for an annuity purchased at age 50) to about 90 (for an annuity purchased at age 75) for both level and +3% p.a. annuities.

To recoup an RPI linked annuity at current rates of inflation the annuitant must survive significantly longer. Inflation would need to average about 4.5% p.a. to bring survival ages for recoupment in line with other annuity types.

The Table shows examples available in March 2013: rates from different providers vary significantly and the figures shown are the average of the best three rates from various providers available to all applicants on the sample date.

Age at purchase	Level		+3% p.a.		RPI
	Gross	T	Gross	T	Gross
50	**4,027**	56%	**2,462**	61%	**1,937**
51	4,070	55%	2,509	59%	1,986
52	4,119	54%	2,562	56%	2,042
53	4,173	53%	2,620	54%	2,104
54	4,233	52%	2,684	52%	2,172
55	**4,298**	51%	**2,755**	50%	**2,247**
56	4,377	50%	2,824	47%	2,311
57	4,465	49%	2,902	45%	2,383
58	4,564	47%	2,989	43%	2,463
59	4,672	46%	3,084	41%	2,551
60	**4,790**	45%	**3,188**	39%	**2,647**
61	4,886	44%	3,275	37%	2,747
62	4,994	43%	3,373	35%	2,860
63	5,113	41%	3,482	33%	2,985
64	5,245	40%	3,602	31%	3,122
65	**5,389**	39%	**3,733**	29%	**3,272**
66	5,508	37%	3,855	27%	3,391
67	5,641	36%	3,993	25%	3,525
68	5,789	34%	4,147	24%	3,673
69	5,951	33%	4,316	22%	3,837
70	**6,129**	31%	**4,500**	20%	**4,015**
71	6,298	30%	4,663	18%	4,186
72	6,488	28%	4,847	17%	4,377
73	6,699	27%	5,052	15%	4,591
74	6,932	25%	5,277	13%	4,825
75	**7,185**	23%	**5,522**	12%	**5,081**

The rates shown are not guaranteed but do reflect a minimum payment period of 5 years; percentage increases are compound.

Quoted rates are highly sensitive to market fluctuations, and in particular to interest rate changes.

Those shown were for annuitants with supposedly average life expectancy. Adverse medical history, including smoking, obesity and existing medical conditions may enhance the sum payable.

Gross rates are shown for compulsory purchase annuities (i.e. purchased with a pension fund) while those for money purchase annuities tend to be marginally lower.

Pension annuities are fully taxable as income subject to the payee's taxation situation: see Table 18.

For non-pension annuities part is treated as return of capital, and only the remainder (**T%**, approximately) is taxable as income. The fluctuating rate of change in RPI annuities renders it unreliable to identify average taxable, and tax free, elements of non-pension RPI linked annuities.

Example

Age	Escalation Rate p.a.	Purchase Price	Annuity Gross p.a.	Taxable	
				Pension	Non-pension
68	3%	£200,000	£8,294	100% = **£8,294**	24% = **£1,990**
55	Level	£500,000	£21,490	100% = **£21,490**	51% = **£10,960**

Table 18 Income Tax

In simplified terms, 2013-14 income (net of the reliefs and allowances shown *opposite*) is treated as follows:

Income other than from savings and dividends is taken as the first tranche of income.

Savings income is taxed as the next tranche of income.
- A special savings rate of 10% can apply where an individual has savings income, but has less than £2,790 of taxable non-savings income. To the extent of the shortfall in taxable income below £2,790, savings income is then charged at 10%. This special savings rate only applies if the individual's taxable non-savings income does not exceed £2,790: otherwise income is taxed at basic and/or higher rate.

Dividend income is treated separately, being normally taken as the top tranche of income.
- UK dividends are receivable net of a 10% **tax credit** (equivalent to $1/9$ of the net dividend) so that the recipient's income for tax purposes is the dividend received plus the tax credit (*gross dividend*). For basic rate taxpayers, no further tax on dividends is payable.
- But tax credits are not repayable even if the taxpayer's gross income is below his allowances.
- Gross dividends falling within the higher rate (40%) band are further taxed at the dividend upper rate of 32.5%. Thus a further 22.5% of the gross dividend is payable (900 net = 1000 gross x 32.5% less 100 re 10% tax credit already deducted = 225 balance payable: equivalent to a further 25% of the net dividend received).
- For additional rate (45%) taxpayers whose income exceeds £150,000, gross dividends within that band are further taxed at the 37.5% dividend additional rate. Thus a further 27.5% of the gross dividend is payable (900 net = 1000 gross x 37.5% less 100 re 10% tax credit already deducted = 275 balance payable).
- Special rules, beyond the scope of this Table, apply to dividends from overseas companies.

Examples
- X has taxable earnings of £15,000 taxed under PAYE; gross interest of £200 from which tax of £40 has been deducted; and cash dividends received of £90 (gross equivalent £100). His total taxable income is less than £32,010 so he has no further tax to pay.
- Y has taxable earnings of £15,000 taxed under PAYE; and receives gross interest of £37,010 from which tax (at 20%) of £7,402 has been deducted. His total taxable income (the amount exceeding his personal allowance) is £52,010 of which £20,000 (£52,010 – £32,010) is chargeable at the 40% higher rate (£8,000). Tax at 20% has already been deducted from this income so Y has another £4,000 to pay.
- Z has taxable earnings of £15,000 taxed under PAYE; receives gross interest of £16,000 from which tax (at 20%) of £3,200 has been deducted; and £15,309 cash dividends (gross equivalent £17,010). Earnings and interest have used £31,000 of his basic rate band leaving £1,010 of dividend income within this band. The £16,000 balance of gross dividend income is chargeable at 32.5% (£5,200). Tax at 10% is deemed to have been deducted from that dividend income, so a further £3,600 is payable (£5,200 – £1,600).

Note: these examples assume the PAYE deduction is correct and that tax has been withheld from all interest received. In practice, there may be further tax to pay on earnings or interest, or a refund of tax may be due.

For all individuals irrespective of age whose income exceeds £100,000 the personal allowance is reduced by £1 for every £2 of income over £100,000, and extinguished if it exceeds £118,880.

For individuals born before 6 April 1948 whose income exceeds the **income limit** of £26,100 their personal age allowance reduces by half the excess until it reaches the basic personal allowance of £9,440 (and then further as above by 50% of income over £100,000).

If a tax calculation is needed where one of a **couple** (married or civil partners) **of whom either was born before 6 April 1935** has income over that **income limit** see www.hmrc.gov.uk/incometax/married-allow.htm.

Restricted tax relief is available to the payer of **maintenance** who or whose former spouse was born before 6 April 1935, limited to a tax reduction of 10% of up to a maximum of £3,040** of qualifying payments falling due. No tax is payable on maintenance received.

Income within discretionary and accumulation trusts: The first £1,000 of income is taxed at basic rate. The excess is taxed at 45% on non-dividend income and at 37.5% on grossed-up dividends. Beneficiaries who are not additional rate taxpayers may be entitled to a refund of part of the tax paid by the trustees when the income is distributed, but such intricacies are beyond the scope of this Table.

Working Tax and **Child Tax Credits** and (for those over 60) **Pension Credit** are available to certain lower income families and lone parents, reducing as income rises: see Table 26, *post*, and **@eGlance** for calculators.

Table 18 Income Tax

	Tax year						
	13-14	12-13	11-12	10-11	09-10	08-09	07-08
Income Tax Rates							
20% on first taxable	32,010	34,370	35,000	37,400	37,400	34,800	—
10% on first taxable	—	—	—	—	—	—	2,230
22% on next	—	—	—	—	—	—	32,370
40% on excess over	—	—	—	—	37,400	34,800	34,600
40% higher rate on next	117,990	115,630	115,000	112,600	—	—	—
and 45% additional rate over	150,000	—	—	—	—	—	—
and 50% additional rate over	—	150,000	150,000	150,000	—	—	—
Income Tax Reliefs							
Personal allowance	9,440*	8,105*	7,475*	6,475*	6,475	6,035	5,225
Age allowances							
For ages 65 to 74							
Personal allowance	—	10,500*	9,940*	9,490*	9,490	9,030	7,550
Married couple's allowance**	—	—	—	—	—	6,535**	6,285**
For age 75 and over							
Personal allowance	—	10,660*	10,090*	9,640*	9,640	9,180	7,690
Married couple's allowance**	—	7,705**	7,295**	6,965**	6,965**	6,625**	6,365**
Born after 5 April 1938 but before 6 April 1948*	10,500*	—	—	—	—	—	—
Born before 6 April 1938	10,660*	—	—	—	—	—	—
Born before 6 April 1935: Married couple's allowance**	7,915	—	—	—	—	—	—
Income limit	26,100	25,400	24,000	22,900	22,900	21,800	20,900

* These personal allowances are reduced (potentially to zero) by £1 for every £2 of income over £100,000.
**For allowances thus marked the tax saving is restricted to 10%.

Table 19 Capital Gains Tax

Capital Gains Tax for disposals (actual or notional) during 2013-14

*The information in this Table applies to gains arising in 2013-14. Earlier editions of **At A Glance** should be consulted for gains arising in prior years.*

Basis and rate of tax

Gains (the excess of disposal proceeds over **base cost**, which includes acquisition and disposal costs and enhancement expenditure) which surpass any available **annual exempt allowance** (AEA) are taxable.

For 2013-14:

- The rate is **18%** where total taxable gains **and** income in aggregate do not exceed the upper limit of the income tax basic rate band (£32,010 for 2013-14). Gains (or any parts of gains) above that limit attract a rate of **28%**.
- In calculating total taxable gains and income for this purpose all allowable deductions (including losses, and the income tax personal allowance) and the AEA (see *below*) are taken into account.
- Individual taxpayers when calculating CGT can apply losses and the AEA to reduce their chargeable gain in the way most advantageous to them. So the AEA and losses may be applied to gains which would otherwise attract tax at 28% (unless ***entrepreneurs' relief*** is available: see *below*).
- For trustees and personal representatives of deceased persons, the rate is increased to 28% regardless of the total income and gains arising to them, except where Entrepreneurs' Relief applies.

The annual exempt allowance (AEA). For 2013-14 the first £10,900 of gains made by individuals are exempt from tax. For estates the same exemption applies in the tax year of death and for the next two years. The exemption for trustees is normally half that applicable to individuals.

The base cost of any asset acquired before 31 March 1982 is its market value on that date.

Capital losses are set against current year gains or, so far as losses exceed gains, future gains.

Fungible assets (intangible assets of the same type, such as shares of the same class in a company) acquired in separate transactions at varying base costs, are pooled and treated as a single asset. Where part-disposal of the holding is made, the base cost of the part sold is the average of the aggregate base cost of all acquisitions.

Disposal of the matrimonial home

Any gain on the disposal of the former matrimonial home (if the spouses' principal private residence) will usually be fully relieved from tax, although relief may be restricted or unavailable in some cases such as where:

- the couple has more than one main residence
- the property disposed of was not elected as their principal private residence throughout their period of ownership
- the property has been let
- they have not lived in it throughout the period of their ownership.

Entrepreneurs' Relief

Broadly, individuals and trustees who dispose of all or part of a business or asset used in a business may qualify for relief which has the effect of reducing the tax rate to 10% on gains up to a *lifetime* limit of £10M per individual. The same relief applies also to disposals of shares where the owner holds at least 5% of the ordinary shares in a trading company and is a director or employee.

The rules are complex and specialist advice must be sought where Entrepreneurs' Relief may apply.

Capital gains by companies

These are calculated after applying indexation relief throughout the ownership period. The gains less allowable capital losses are added to the profit for corporation tax and taxed at the company's corporation tax rate. There is no annual exemption. A capital loss that cannot be offset against gains is carried forward for future accounting periods.

Company taxation generally is a complex area outside the scope of this Table.

The information in this Table is necessarily summarised in condensed form: specialist taxation advice should always be sought in all but the most straightforward situations.

Calculators for CGT liabilities arising (actually or notionally) during 2013-14 are to be found in @eGlance

Table 20 Inheritance Tax

Inheritance Tax rates for chargeable transfers during the year commencing 6 April 2013

	First £325,000	Excess over £325,000
Lifetime transfers (other than PETs)	Nil	20%
On death	Nil	40%

Transfer of nil rate band may be available on the death of a surviving spouse after 9 October 2007. This applies whenever the first spouse died. Where one spouse or civil partner dies with a chargeable estate of less than the nil rate band (*above*), the unused *proportion* is transferred to the surviving spouse's estate on the second death. The unused proportion is applied to the nil rate band in force in the year of the second death and is transferred to the surviving spouse. The unused proportion (in addition to the survivor's own nil rate band) will bear no tax.

The chargeable estate of the first to die may be less than the nil rate band where they leave their estate to the surviving spouse or civil partner as such legacy is exempt – either entirely, or subject to legacies and/or lifetime gifts (*below*) within the nil rate band.

Lower rate: A reduced rate of 36% applies on death where 10% or more of the value of the estate (above the nil rate band) is donated to charity. The legislation is complex: expert advice should be sought if this situation appears relevant.

For individuals, **unlimited exemption** applies to gifts in life or on death to –
- a UK domiciled spouse or civil partner (or, if elects to be treated as UK domicilied, to either)
- UK registered charities
- qualifying political parties

and to regular lifetime gifts out of income.

There are also **exemptions** for –
- lifetime gifts of £3,000 per fiscal year in total (plus any unused balance from the previous year)
- small gifts of up to £250 per fiscal year per donee
- lifetime gifts in consideration of marriage or registration of a civil partnership up to:
  - £5,000 by each parent of either party
  - £2,500 by a grandparent or other direct linear ancestor of either party
  - £2,500 from one party to the other
  - £1,000 by any other donee.

The paragraphs *below* apply to transactions after 22 March 2006 only. For previous periods, refer to earlier editions.

Lifetime gifts to individuals constitute potentially exempt transfers (PETs). PETs are not subject to inheritance tax at the date of gift, but if the donor dies within seven years thereafter are taxable at death rates. The rate progressively reduces by 20% upon the donor surviving to the third and each subsequent anniversary of the gift, and thus after seven years the liability is extinguished. Successive lifetime chargeable transfers within seven years are cumulated, as are PETs which have become chargeable transfers on death.

Lifetime gifts not ranking as PETs (such as gifts to most trusts) are initially taxable at the lifetime rates pertaining at the date of the gift. This liability is revised to death rates if the donor dies within seven years, with the rates being progressively reduced as above.

For **trusts**, except for certain trusts for minors and where there was an existing life tenant at 21 March 2006, a charge to tax potentially arises:
- where assets cease to be held on trust
- every ten years from the date on which the trust was set up, with a maximum charge at the ten year anniversary date of 6%.

The effect of these rules is ameliorated for certain trusts for minors and disabled beneficiaries, but the rules and calculations are complex and beyond this note's scope. Specialist advice should be sought in this area.

Caveat: By way of example only, the taxation principles outlined deal **only** with UK domiciled individuals; and other forms of relief apply to certain transfers of business and agricultural property and of shares in specific types of company.

Thus professional advice should invariably be sought as this is only a simplified and condensed summary.

Table 21 Taxing Times

Income tax and capital gains tax

Under the self-assessment régime tax is to be paid on and returns filed by the following dates:

Due date	Requirement	Assessment year
31 July 2013	Second payment on account	2012-13
31 October 2013	Last filing date for paper return	2012-13
31 January 2014	Balance of income tax	2012-13
	Capital gains tax	2012-13
	Last filing date for online return	2012-13
	First payment on account	2013-14
31 July 2014	Second payment on account	2013-14
31 January 2015	Balance of income tax	2013-14
	Capital gains tax	2013-14
	First payment on account	2014-15

Each payment on account is 50% of the preceding year's total net income tax bill, unless the taxpayer applies and HMRC agree that the payment be reduced. If the reduced amount proves insufficient to cover one half of the year's liability, interest will be charged on the balance of the original on account amount from each due date until the balance is paid. Penalties (see *below*) may also arise.

The onus is on the taxpayer to pay the correct tax due, whether or not he has an up-to-date statement and payslip from HMRC and irrespective of the amount of tax shown on the payslip (if he has one).

Interest

Interest is chargeable on tax, national insurance contributions and penalties paid late (i.e. after the date on which they were due to be paid). At the time of writing the rate is 3% per annum.

Penalties: Late and Incorrect Returns

Penalties (cumulative) for *failure to file a tax return on time* without reasonable excuse:
- up to 3 months late: £100
- up to 6 months late: a daily penalty of £10 for 90 days
- up to 12 months late: higher of £300 or 5% of tax established as due on the return when filed (even if already paid on account)
- over 12 months late: a further penalty of the higher of £300 or 5% of tax due (established as above) or up to 100% if information which would enable HMRC to assess the tax due is deliberately withheld.

Further penalties are payable *in the event of an incorrect return*. A tariff applies: between nil and 30% of extra tax due if the error was as a result of a lack of reasonable care; between 20% and 70% if deliberate; or between 30% and 100% if deliberate and concealed.

Penalties will be towards the lower end of the tariff ranges shown if the taxpayer admits the mistake to HMRC unprompted, and also if assistance is given in determining the extra tax due.

Penalties: Late Payment

Penalties (cumulative) for *late payment of tax due* without reasonable excuse:
- after 30 days: 5% of tax due
- after 6 months: additional 5% of tax due
- after 12 months: additional 5% of tax due.

No penalties will be levied where a taxpayer has agreed with HMRC that payment may be deferred for a period.

Major changes were made to the penalty régime to take effect for 2010-11 returns. For prior periods reference should be made to previous editions.

Interest on tax overpaid

'Repayment supplement' is payable on tax repayments, including:
- repayments of interim payments and other tax paid directly, from the date paid until the repayment date
- repayments of tax deducted at source, from 31 January following the year of assessment until the repayment date.

At the time of writing the rate is 0.5% per annum.

Table 21 Taxing Times

Inheritance tax

On chargeable lifetime transfers

Between 2 October and 5 April	Six months after the end of the month in which the chargeable transfer is made
Between 6 April and 1 October	On 30 April in the following year.

On death

Six months after the end of the month in which death occurred (save where payment by instalments is available, see *below*).

Where the IHT account is delivered before six months after the end of the month in which the death occurs, tax must be paid on delivery of the account.

Tax arising in cases where lifetime transfers become chargeable on the death	Six months after the end of the month in which the death occurred (save where payment by instalments is available, see *below*).

Tax arising on the transfer on death of *inter alia* land and buildings, certain shares and businesses may be paid by ten equal yearly instalments.

Interest

Interest is chargeable with effect from the due date on late paid inheritance tax.

At the time of writing the rate is 3% per annum.

Penalties

HMRC are empowered to charge penalties:

- for failure to submit timely inheritance tax accounts without reasonable excuse
- for inaccurate accounts.

Legislation provides for penalties for late payment but no announcement has yet been made of anticipated commencement dates.

Corporation tax

Under self-assessment a company's corporation tax is due nine months after the end of the accounting period. Large companies (broadly companies whose profit exceeds £1.5M) are required to pay corporation tax in quarterly instalments commencing six months and 13 days from the start of the accounting period. Such arrangements are beyond the scope of this Table.

Interest

Corporation tax paid late is subject to an interest charge, at the time of writing at the rate of 3% per annum.

Overpayments of corporation tax

These attract interest ('repayment supplement') of 0.5% per annum at the time of writing.

Value added tax

Return and payment within 1 month of quarter end (plus 7 days if paid online); or 2 months after annual accounting date (plus interim payments meanwhile).

Stamp duty land tax

Payable 30 days from completion.

Sanctions arise on default.

Table 22 Gross Salary and Net Income

Net income derived from gross annual salary for 2013-14

A	B	C	D
Gross salary (£ per annum)	Net income (£ per annum)	Gross salary (£ per annum)	Net income (£ per annum)
Up to 7,760	Same as gross	20,000	16,110
8,000	7,969	25,000	19,460
9,000	8,849	27,500	21,135
10,000	9,617	30,000	22,810
11,000	10,297	32,500	24,485
12,000	10,977	35,000	26,160
13,000	11,657	37,500	27,835
14,000	12,337	40,000	29,510
15,000	13,017	45,000	32,725
16,000	13,697	50,000	35,535
17,000	14,377	55,000	38,345
18,000	15,057	60,000	41,155
19,000	15,737	65,000	43,965
20,000	16,417	70,000	46,775
21,000	17,097	80,000	52,395
22,000	17,777	90,000	58,015
23,000	18,457	100,000	63,635
24,000	19,137	125,000	73,909
25,000	19,817	150,000	87,959
26,000	20,497	175,000	101,022
27,000	21,177	200,000	113,859
28,000	21,857	250,000	139,534
29,000	22,537	300,000	165,209
30,000	23,217	350,000	190,884
35,000	26,617	400,000	216,559
40,000	30,017	500,000	267,909

The assumptions

Columns **A** & **B**: not contracted out of State Second Pension (S2P) for Class 1 NIC.
Columns **C** & **D**: 3% contributory pension; contracted out of S2P for Class 1 NIC.

In each case 2013-14 tax rates are applied.

Table 23 Grossed-up Net Maintenance

The gross-income equivalent of maintenance, and some comparable salaries: 2013-14 tax rates

Maint. (£)	Gross (£)	Comparable gross salaries
£10,000	£10,881	
£11,336	£12,875	National Minimum Wage (adults) £12,875 (i.e. £6.19 p.h. x 40 hrs x 52 weeks)
£12,000	£13,866	Army (new entrant) £14,349
£14,000	£16,851	Healthcare Assistant £17,087, Army Private (B) £17,767
£16,000	£19,836	Nurse (newly qualified) £21,549, Teacher (newly qualified, B) £21,588
£18,000	£22,821	Junior Hospital Doctor (B) £22,636
£20,000	£25,806	Nurse Grade F £26,869, Army Private (T) £29,357
£22,500	£29,537	NHS Registrar (B) £29,705, Nurse (A) £31,446, Bishop (B) £32,060, Sister Grade G (T) £32,883
£25,000	£33,269	Sergeant (B) £33,229, Dean (T) £33,830
£27,500	£37,000	Teacher (Advanced Skills, B) £37,461, Head Teacher (B) £37,461, Sergeant (T) £37,462
£30,000	£40,731	Captain (B) £38,463, Bishop (T) £41,220
£32,500	£44,599	Captain (T) £45,741, NHS Registrar (T) £46,708, Major (B) £48,450
£35,000	£49,047	
£37,500	£53,496	
£40,000	£57,944	Major (T) £58,026, Bishop of London £58,740, Civil Service Band 1 (B) £61,500
£42,500	£62,393	Teacher (Advanced Skills, T) £64,036, Archbishop of York £64,090, MP £66,396
£45,000	£66,841	Lieutenant Colonel (B) £67,999
£47,500	£71,289	NHS Consultant (B) £74,504, Archbishop of Canterbury £74,780
£50,000	£75,738	Lieutenant Colonel (T) £78,737
£52,500	£80,186	Colonel (B) £82,381, Civil Service Band 2 (B) £84,000
£55,000	£84,635	
£57,500	£89,083	Colonel (T) £90,560
£60,000	£93,531	Junior Government Minister £95,170
£62,500	£97,980	Brigadier (B) £98,172, Brigadier (T) £102,145
£65,000	£102,428	Civil Service Band 3 (B) £103,000, District Judge (PRFD) £103,950, GP (A) £104,100
£67,500	£108,871	Minister of State £105,091, Major General (B) £109,770, Head Teacher (T) £112,181
£70,000	£115,665	Civil Service Band 1 (T) £118,978, NHS Consultant (A) £119,800, Major General (T) £120,943
£72,500	£122,458	
£75,000	£126,941	Lieutenant General (B) £127,734, Circuit Judge £129,579
£77,500	£131,389	
£80,000	£135,837	NHS Consultant (T) £135,930, Senior Circuit Judge £139,933
£82,500	£140,286	Permanent Secretary (B) £141,137, Cabinet Minister £143,285
£85,000	£144,734	
£87,500	£149,183	
£90,000	£153,631	Lieutenant General (T) £154,855
£92,500	£158,404	
£95,000	£163,273	Civil Service Band 2 (T) £164,124, General (B) £167,681
£97,500	£168,142	
£100,000	£173,010	High Court Judge £174,481
£105,000	£182,747	General (T) £187,869
£110,000	£192,484	Prime Minister £196,193, Lord Justice of Appeal £198,674
£115,000	£202,221	Supreme Court Justice & Family Division President £208,926
£120,000	£211,958	Civil Service Band 3 (T) £210,181, Master of the Rolls £216,307
£130,000	£231,433	Chief of Defence Staff (B) £241,576, Lord Chief Justice £242,243
£140,000	£250,907	Chief of Defence Staff (T) £256,362
£150,000	£270,381	Permanent Secretary (T) £277,212
£175,000	£319,067	

Assumptions for the grossed-up equivalent: 3% contributory pension; contracted out of S2P for Class 1 NIC.

Most salaries effective April 2013.

All categories are subject to varying terms and conditions, and some benefit from expenses.

(A), (B) and (T) indicate average, bottom and top of range or seniority for post or rank.

Table 24 National Insurance Contributions

Class 1 Earnings Limits and Threshold, and Class 2, Class 3 and Class 4 Limits and Contributions

		2013-14	*2012-13*
Class 1	Lower earnings limit	£109 p.w.	*£107 p.w.*
	Earnings threshold	£149 p.w.	*£146 p.w.*
	Upper earnings limit	£797 p.w.	*£817 p.w.*
Class 2	Flat rate contribution	£2.70 p.w.	*£2.65 p.w.*
	Small earnings exception limit	£5,725 p.a.	*£5,595 p.a.*
Class 3	Flat rate voluntary contribution	£13.55 p.w.	*£13.25 p.w.*
Class 4	Lower profits limit	£7,755 p.a.	*£7,605 p.a.*
	Upper profits limit	£41,450 p.a.	*£42,475 p.a.*
	Contribution rate	9%	*9%*
	plus on profits over upper profits limit	2%	*2%*

Standard Rates of Class 1 Contributions for 2013-14

Primary contribution (employee)		Secondary contribution (employer)	
Not contracted-out rate	**Contracted-out rate**	**Not contracted-out rate**	**Contracted-out rate (salary related schemes)**
Nil on the first £149 p.w. THEN 12% on earnings up to £797 p.w. PLUS 2% thereafter	Nil on the first £149 p.w. THEN 10.6% on earnings up to £797 p.w. PLUS 2% thereafter	Nil on the first £148 p.w. THEN 13.8% on earnings from £148.01 p.w. without upper limit	Nil on the first £148 p.w. THEN 10.4% on earnings from £148.01 p.w. without upper limit

No Class 1 contributions are payable by or for those whose earnings do not exceed £149 p.w.

The Reduced Rate for married women and widow optants is 5.85% of earnings above £149 p.w. and up to £797 p.w., plus 2% on earnings which exceed that amount.

Contracting-out on a money purchase basis was abolished from 6 April 2012.

Table 25 Principal Points of Interest

Statutory Charge Interest Rates

For the period	Rate (%)
Until 31 March 2002	8.00
From 1 April 2002 to 30 September 2005	5.00
From 1 October 2005	8.00

The legal aid statutory charge is now governed by Legal Aid, Sentencing and Punishment of Offenders Act 2012, s. 25. Interest is payable where the charge is postponed and the applicable rate is set by Civil Legal Aid (Statutory Charge) Regulations 2013 (SI No.2013/503), reg. 25.

Judgment Debt Interest Rates since November 1982

For judgments entered since	Rate (%)
10 November 1982	12.00
16 April 1985	15.00
1 April 1993	8.00

These interest rates apply to High Court judgments generally, and since 1 July 1991 to county court judgment debts of not less than £5,000, and are set pursuant to s. 17, Judgments Act 1838.

Stamp duty on residential land (Stamp Duty Land Tax) and shares

Stocks and shares	Where acquisition cost exceeds £1,000	0.5% rounded up to nearest £5
Residential land (rate since 22 March 2012 but see *below*)	Up to £125,000	Nil
	£125,001 to £250,000	1.0%
	£250,001 to £500,000	3.0%
	£500,001 to £1,000,000	4.0%
	£1,000,001 to £2,000,000	5.0%
	Over £2,000,000...	7.0%
	(but if by a corporate body)	15.0%

Council Tax Bands

Council Tax band	Valuation bands (England)	Valuation bands (Wales)
A	Up to £40,000	Up to £44,000
B	£40,001 to £52,000	£44,001 to £65,000
C	£52,001 to £68,000	£65,001 to £91,000
D	£68,001 to £88,000	£91,001 to £123,000
E	£88,001 to £120,000	£123,001 to £162,000
F	£120,001 to £160,000	£162,001 to £223,000
G	£160,001 to £320,000	£223,001 to £324,000
H	Over £320,000	£324,001 to £424,000
I		Over £424,000

Council Tax valuation bands for properties in England (valued as at 1 April 1991) and Wales (as at 1 April 2005). For more about Council Tax visit www.voa.gov.uk.

Table 26 Social Security Benefits

Universal Credit (UC)

A new benefit to replace Income-based Jobseeker's Allowance, Income-related Employment and Support Allowance, Income Support, some aspects of the Social Fund, Child Tax Credit, Working Tax Credit and Housing Benefit. Available to new claimants from April/July 2013 within certain areas of the North-West of England, and from October 2013 nationally. From April 2014 all new claims, including by people in work, to be for UC. Existing claimants for other benefits expected to transfer to UC by 2017, with cash protection on transfer, subject to Benefit Cap (BC) rules, unless circumstances changed.

Normally for those over 18 and under Pension Credit (PC) age, present and habitually resident in UK, with right of residence. Not normally available to those in education. If claimant one of a couple, then must make joint claim; if one fails to meet relevant conditions, he or she ignored for purposes of calculating UC maximum amount, but his/her savings/capital/income and earnings taken into account. If only one over PC age, both to claim UC unless already in receipt of PC. If only one in full-time education, both must claim UC. Available to people in work and on a low income as well as those who are out of work. Different tests applied depending on individual capability and circumstances. Able to do volunteer work for up to half the relevant target for working hours. Applications online or by telephone; online account through which claims managed.

One monthly payment, paid in arrears, into bank account, to include a basic allowance plus up to five additional elements: child element/disabled child additions; childcare element; carer element; limited capability for work element; housing element. Additional amount for disabled child or qualifying young person (QYP): paid at lower rate for DLA mobility or care at less than highest rate of care component; paid at higher rate for highest rate of care component of DLA or registered blind. Childcare costs elements available up to 70% of relevant costs, up to maximum of £532.29 for one child, £912.50 for two or more children; no set number of working hours but if part of couple both must be in work unless one unable to look after child; not available for care provided by close relative wholly or mainly in claimant's home. Housing costs element available for rent or mortgage (owner-occupiers must wait 3 months before paid; not entitled to housing element if in paid work; no deductions from owner occupier benefits for non-dependants). For tenants (private and social housing), rules similar to those for Housing Benefit; tenants' benefit subject to deductions if non-dependants live with them. Subject to BC.

UC withdrawn at a constant rate of 65p for each £1 of net earnings (additional 20p withdrawal if claiming Council Tax Support). Savings/capital limit £16,000 (for both single and joint claimants). Income over £6,000 subject to tariff income of £4.35 per £250 or part thereof. Capital under £6,000 disregarded. Permitted one earnings disregard.

	Per month
Basic Allowance	
Single claimant under 25	246.81
Single claimant over 25	311.55
Joint claimants both under 25	387.42
Joint claimants one or both over 25	489.06
Child Element	
First child or QYP	272.08
Second and each subsequent child (or QYP)	226.67
Additional amount for disabled child or QYP	
Lower rate	123.62
Higher rate	352.92
Capability for work elements	
Limited capability for work	123.62
Limited capability for work and work-related activity	303.66
Carer element	144.70
Earnings disregards (only one to be claimed)	
Single with rental costs (no child or QYP)	110.83
Single with rental costs (child or QYP)	263.25
Single with rental costs (limited capability)	192.16
Single no rental costs (no child or QYP)	110.83
Single no rental costs (child or QYP)	734.33
Single no rental costs (limited capability)	646.58
Couple with rental costs (no child or QYP)	110.83
Couple with rental costs (child or QYP)	221.66
Couple with rental costs (limited capability)	192.16
Couple no rental costs (no child or QYP)	110.83
Couple no rental costs (child or QYP)	535.75
Couple no rental costs (limited capability)	646.58

Benefits Cap (BC)

Housing Benefit adjusted downwards so as to apply a cap on total benefits available to working-age people: applies to Bereavement Allowance, Carer's Allowance, Child Benefit, Child Tax Credit, Employment and Support Allowance (other than support group), Guardian's Allowance, Housing Benefit, Incapacity Benefit, Income Support, Jobseeker's Allowance, Maternity Allowance, Severe Disablement Allowance, and Widowed Parent's Allowance. Introduced in London Boroughs of Bromley, Croydon, Enfield and Haringey on 15 April 2013; to other council areas between 15 July and 30 September 2013.

Total amount paid from benefits claimed limited to £500 p.w. (£2,166 p.m.) for lone parents or part of a couple, or £350 p.w. (£1,516 p.m.) for single claimants. If no housing benefit received, BC will not apply until claimant transferred to UC.

BC does not apply to households qualifying for Working Tax Credits (earning more than £430 p.m.), or receiving Disability Living Allowance or Personal Independence Payment, or Attendance Allowance, or Industrial Injuries Benefits and equivalent payments, or support group component of Employment and Support Allowance. BC does not apply to first 39 weeks after claimant stops work, provided claimant (and/or partner) worked for previous year with combined gross earnings of £430 p.m. Carers not exempt from BC unless the person they care for is their partner, or a dependent child for whom they receive Child Benefit).

The following benefits are **not** subject to BC: Armed Forces Independence Payment, Bereavement Payment and Bereavement Support Payment, Cold Weather Payment, Council Tax Support, Discretionary Housing Payments, Free School Meals, Funeral Payments, Community Care Grants and Crisis Loans, Statutory Adoption Pay, Statutory Maternity Pay, Statutory Paternity Pay, Statutory Sick Pay, Sure Start Maternity Grants, In-work Credit, Return-to-Work Credit.

Table 26 Social Security Benefits

Income replacement

1. Retirement

Retirement Pension		2013-14
Claimant	Category A	110.15
	Category B	66.00

Either spouse/civil partner may qualify in their own right (Category A) or as a spouse or civil partner (Category B).

Special rules apply for parents, carers, divorced people, widows and widowers. Women's State Pension age gradually increasing to 65 by November 2018. For both men and women State Pension age gradually increasing to 67 by 2026.

Highly variable rates according to contribution history.

Contributory and taxable.

For information for Form E submit Form BR20 (for valuation of additional state pension); or Form BR19 (for benefit forecast): downloadable at www.direct.gov.uk, or complete an online form at www.gov.uk/state-pension-statement.

2. Ill Health

i. Statutory Sick Pay	2013-14
Standard rate	86.70

Paid by employer for up to 168 days (28 six-day weeks), to employees earning not less than £109 gross p.w. Taxable. Not replaced by UC.

ii. Employment and Support Allowance (ESA)	2013-14
Maximum Basic Rate	
Single claimant	71.70
Couple (means-tested)	112.55
Work-related activity component	
for those meeting limited capability for work test)	28.45
Support component	
(for those assessed as more severely disabled)	34.80
Premiums (Means-tested)	
Enhanced disability - single	15.15
Enhanced disability - couple	21.75
Severe disability - single/couple (lower rate)	59.50
Severe disability - couple (higher rate)	119.00
Carer premium	33.30

Includes both contributory and 'income-related' (means-tested) benefit, based on either limited capability for work (placed in 'work-related activity group', must attend and take part in work-related activity) or limited capability for work-related activity (not expected to work, placed in 'support group'). New rules in relation to limited capability for work and limited capability for work-related activity from 28 January 2013. Surviving Incapacity Benefit claimants to be moved to ESA by 6 April 2014.

Benefit paid at basic rate during 13-week assessment phase. Lower rates for under 25s during assessment period; contributory youth ESA abolished. Contributory ESA: time-limited to one year for those in work-related activity group; also no age or spouse's additions, and no housing costs allowances. Income-related ESA (IRESA): assessment, housing costs and capital rules modelled on IS. Child maintenance and up to £20 earnings p.w. disregarded (or 16 hours p.w. earning up to £99.50 p.w. for 52 weeks). Passport to other benefits including HB.

Contributory ESA taxable and not replaced by UC (although same system): IRESA not taxable; being replaced by UC from October 2013. BC applies except where support component awarded.

iii. Carer's Allowance	2013-14
Claimant	59.75
Adult dependant - extra	35.15

Paid to people over 16 who spend at least 35 hours p.w. caring for recipient of higher or middle rates of Care Component of DLA, PIP daily living component, Attendance Allowance or Constant Attendance Allowance at or above the normal rate with related pension. Claimant can earn no more than £100 p.w. net and must not be in full-time education; however, entitled to offset against earnings up to half any sums paid to someone else (not close relative) to care for either recipient of allowances or carer's children under 16.

Non-contributory; not means-tested. Taxable. Not replaced by UC. BC applies.

3. Unemployment – Jobseeker's Allowance (JSA)

i. Contribution-based JSA		2013-14
Claimant	18-24	56.80
	25 and over	71.70

ii. Income-based JSA (IBJSA)		2013-14
Claimant	16-24	56.80
	25 and over	71.70
Couple	Both over 18	112.55
Dependent children (existing claimants only – others see Child Tax Credit) till day before 20th birthday		65.62
Premiums: as for IS		

Claimants must be under State Pension age, available for and actively seeking work, and have a current Jobseeker's Agreement. Main rates only given. **Contribution-based JSA** is age-related flat-rate payment (reduced by amount of any part-time earnings); without dependant allowances: paid for up to 26 weeks and not included in UC (although administered by same system). **Income-based JSA** paid with, or from expiry of, contribution-based JSA, with IS-style rules for income, capital, premiums and mortgage interest. Child maintenance disregarded. Not usually available for those under 18 or those working 16+ hours p.w. Men eligible for Pension Credit Guarantee Credit (PC - GC) but not yet 65 may claim PC - GC instead. Basic payment taxable; premiums not. BC applies. IBJSA being replaced by UC from October 2013.

Table 26 Social Security Benefits

4. Maternity/paternity/adoption

i. Statutory Maternity Pay[1] (SMP) 2013-14
Average earnings threshold 109.00
Higher rate (first 6 weeks) 90% of average weekly wage
Lower rate (for up to next 33 weeks) 136.78

Paid by employer for a maximum of 39 weeks. Taxable. Not replaced by UC.

ii. Statutory Paternity Pay[1] (SPP) 2013-14
Average earnings threshold 109.00
Rate 136.78

Payable for up to 2 weeks. Additional SPP at same rate if upon mother's return to work, baby 20 weeks old and she would otherwise still be entitled to SMP, SAP or MA. Not payable beyond mother's 39-week maternity period.

Extended SSP and/or SPP available in some cases until baby's first birthday.

Taxable. Not replaced by UC.

iii. Maternity Allowance (MA) 2013-14
Average earnings threshold 30.00
Standard rate 136.78[2]

Paid to claimants not entitled to SMP but employed or self-employed for at least 26 weeks in 66 weeks before due date, and average pay over £30 p.w. Maximum 39 weeks (during which may work up to 10 days).
Non-taxable. BC applies. Not replaced by UC.

iv. Statutory Adoption Pay[1] (SAP) 2013-14
Average earnings threshold 109.00
Standard rate 136.78

Paid by employer for a maximum of 39 weeks. Taxable. Not replaced by UC.

1 Qualifying conditions based on length of service and average earnings
2 Or (if less) 90% of the parent's weekly average gross earnings

v. Surestart Maternity Grant 2013-14
Standard one-off payment 500.00

Subject to complex conditions. Available only for first child. Being replaced by UC from October 2013.

5. Bereavement

Bereavement Benefit 2013-14
i Bereavement Payment (lump sum) 2,000.00
ii. Bereavement allowance (age-related) 32.49 to 108.30

Available to bereaved spouses/civil partners over 45 but under State Pension age who do not remarry or cohabit and who are not bringing up children. Standard rate £108.30 for those 55 and over. Payable for up to 52 weeks from date of bereavement.

iii. Widowed Parent's Allowance 108.30

Available to bereaved spouses/civil partners under State Pension age and in receipt of child benefit who do not remarry or cohabit.

Widowed Parent's Allowance and Bereavement Allowance cannot be claimed together.

All benefits are contributory (late spouse/civil partner must have satisfied NIC conditions) and (save lump sum) taxable. BC applies (save for lump sum). Not replaced by UC.

Special needs

1. Disability Living Allowance (DLA)

		2013-14
Care Component	Highest	79.15
	Middle	53.00
	Lowest	21.00
Mobility Component	Higher	55.25
	Lower	21.00

The claimant must qualify before reaching 65. Available to under 16s too. Replaced since 8 April 2013 for new claimants 16 to 64 by new Personal Independence Payment (PIP), to be followed later by transfer of existing claimants.

2. Personal Independence Payment (PIP)

Replaced DLA from 8 April 2013 in pilot areas (North-West and parts of North-East). From June 2013 new claims will be to PIP in all remaining areas. From October 2013 extended to some existing DLA recipients.

Available to those aged 16 to 64 who satisfy daily living and/or mobility activities test for 3 months prior to claiming (qualifying period starts when eligible needs arise) and who are likely to continue to satisfy this test for at least 9 months after claim.

Made up of two elements: daily living component paid at either standard rate (limited ability to carry out daily living activities) or enhanced rate (severely limited ability to carry out daily living activities), and mobility component paid at either standard rate (limited mobility) or enhanced rate (severely limited mobility). Claimant suffering from progressive disease where death can be expected within 6 months automatically receives daily living component enhanced rate, and can apply for mobility component. If in a care home, may be entitled to mobility component.

		2013-14
Daily living component	Standard rate	£53.00
	Enhanced rate	£79.15
Mobility component	Standard rate	£21.00
	Enhanced rate	£55.25

3. Attendance Allowance

	2013-14
Higher rate	79.15
Lower rate	53.00

Paid for care needs of those over 65. Not replaced by UC or PIP.

Both DLA and AA are based on need, but without restrictions on how they are used. Both non-contributory, non-means tested, non-taxable and ignored as income for means-tested benefits.

Table 26 Social Security Benefits

Children

1. Child Benefit (CB)

	2013-14
Only/elder/eldest child	20.30
Each subsequent child	13.40

Child must be under 16, or under 20 and in full-time secondary education, or registered for work or work-based training when under 18. From 8 January 2013 onwards tapered income tax charge applies if either parent receives CB and earns more than £50,000; tax charge rate is 1% of CB per £100 of annual income; full CB recovered from those earning £60,000 p.a.

Administered by HMRC. Non-contributory and otherwise non-taxable. BC applies. Not replaced by UC.

2. Guardian's allowance

	2013-14
Guardian's allowance	15.90

Payable with child benefit to those raising the children of deceased (or sometimes imprisoned) parents. Administered by HMRC. Non-contributory, non-taxable. BC applies. Not replaced by UC.

Income Support (IS) 2013-14

For those not expected to look for work, under pension age, on low income (e.g. lone parents of young children, carers, and some students); may not work less than 16 hrs p.w. Not for the unemployed (see JSA) or claimants who are sick/disabled (see ESA: transfer of existing claimants to be complete by March 2014) or most childless people under 18. Children remain dependent while CB is payable, but replacement of allowances by CTC continues. New conditions restrict entitlement for lone parents as youngest child reaches threshold age, currently 5+ (claims thereafter will be for JSA or ESA).

Main rates below. BC applies. Being replaced by UC from October 2013.

A need level is established from allowances and premiums *right*, plus (after 13 week waiting period) mortgage interest at Bank of England's published monthly average mortgage rate (currently 3.63%) on loans of up to £200,000 (restrictions on increases during claim and reduction for resident non-dependants; current maximum interest payment £139 p.w.). IS then paid to supplement other income to the need level. Detailed rules on application of premiums and disregarded income. Payments from former partner may disqualify, including lump sum payment of any amount (treated as income) but all child maintenance disregarded. No disregard for childcare costs.

Capital up to £6,000 disregarded (£10,000 for those in residential/nursing homes; £3,000 for child). Capital between £6,000 and £16,000 deemed to produce tariff income of £1 for each £250 (or part) over £6,000. No entitlement to IS if capital exceeds £16,000, disregarding value of home. Notional capital rules penalise deliberate deprivation of capital.

Non-contributory. Rarely taxable.

Personal allowances	p.w.	p.a.
Single person		
16-24	56.80	2,953.60
25 or over	71.70	3,728.40
Lone parent		
Under 18	56.80	2,953.60
Over 18	71.70	3,728.40
Couple		
Both over 18	112.55	5,852.60
Dependent children (existing untransferred claimants only – others see CTC) till day before 20th birthday/end of secondary education (if earlier)	65.62	3,412.24

Main premiums		
Carer	33.30	1,731.60
Enhanced disability		
Single	15.15	787.80
Disabled child	23.45	1,219.40
Couple	21.75	1,131.00
Severe disability		
Single (or one of couple)	59.50	3,094.00
Couple (both qualifying)	119.00	6,188.00

Existing claimants only (others see CTC):		
Family/lone parent family	17.40	904.80
Disabled child	57.89	3,010.28
Enhanced disability (child)	23.45	1,219.40

Pension Credit (PC) 2013-14

PC comprises 2 elements: Guarantee Credit (GC) for those of qualifying age whose income is below 'standard minimum guarantee'; and Savings Credit for those 65 and over with modest savings or income. Either or both are claimable.

Age at which GC available is rising gradually in line with increases in State Pension age; this is key date for other benefits and retirement age-related provisions: for current law see Pensions Act 1995 and the Pensions Act 2011.

Means-tested, some income disregarded. £10,000 capital disregarded; thereafter tariff income is £1 for every £500 (or part). No upper capital limit.

Administered by Department for Work and Pensions. Not a tax credit. State pension not affected. Child maintenance disregarded; other maintenance disregarded only for savings credit. No provision for childcare costs. Housing costs as for IS until October 2014, after which housing credit will be added to PC.

Non-contributory. Not taxable. Not replaced by UC.

Standard Minimum Guarantee		p.w.
Single		145.40
Couple		222.05
Additional amount for severe disability		
Single		59.50
Couple (both qualify)		119.00
Additional amount for carers		33.30
Savings Credit		
Threshold	Single	115.80
	Couple	183.90
Maximum	Single	18.06
	Couple	22.89

Table 26 Social Security Benefits

Working Tax Credit (WTC) 2013-14

		p.a.
First Income threshold		6,420.00
Withdrawal rate	41%	
Basic element		1,920.00
Additional couple's/lone parent element		1,970.00
30 hour element		790.00
Disabled worker element		2,855.00
Severe disability element		1,220.00
Childcare element		**p.w.**
Maximum eligible cost		300.00
Maximum eligible cost for one child		175.00
(70% of eligible costs are covered)		

Based on gross annual income: in-work support for families with child/children where lone parent (or equivalent) 16+ works at least 16 hours p.w., or couple's combined work hours total 24 hours p.w. and one parent works at least 16 hours p.w. Extra payment for working at least 30 hours p.w. Also in-work support for some households without child, including those 25+ working at least 30 hours p.w. and those 60+ or with disability working at least 16 hours p.w. Up to first threshold, claimants receive maximum. Credit then tapers by 41p per £1 of income as income rises. Above first threshold, claimant loses main element of WTC first, then childcare element, then child element of any CTC.

Elements cumulative. Complex assessment rules. Maintenance ignored. Assessment on annual income, joint incomes for couples (disregarding £300 of some unearned income).

Awards provisional until end of year notice identifies under/overpayments. Disregard of £2,500 before in-year falls in income affect entitlement; disregard of £5,000 before in-year rises in income affect entitlement.

HMRC administered. Being replaced by UC from October 2013.

Child Tax Credit (CTC) 2013-14

		p.a.
First Income threshold (if only entitled to CTC)		15,910.00
Withdrawal rate	41%	
Family element		545.00
Child element (per child)		2,720.00
Disabled child additional element		3,015.00
Severely disabled child additional element		1,220.00

Based on gross annual income, support for families with child/children. First the per child element then the family element taper by 41p per £1 of income once income above £15,910 (WTC abated first).

One family element per family. Child elements cumulative, including any disabled child or severely disabled child additional elements. Paid to nominated main carer.

Replaces most benefit additions for children. BC applies. Being replaced by UC from October 2013.

Housing Benefit (HB) 2013-14

HB for 'eligible' housing costs (not mortgages).

For private rentals all eligible housing costs based on **Local Housing Allowance (LHA)**. LHA is flat rate based on household size/composition (bedrooms). Maximum housing allowance four bedroom rate (£400), with individual caps dependent on number of bedrooms. Most under 35s restricted to bed-sit/shared accommodation rate. For social housing, from April 2013 LHA size criteria also applied to working age claimants, except no four bedroom limit, private rent shared accommodation rate will not apply, and no limits for those reasonably occupying exempt accommodation. One 'empty' bedroom means loss of 14% of maximum eligible rent; two empty bedrooms means loss of 25% of maximum eligible rent. Size criteria will not apply if claimant or partner over state pension credit age; all other social housing tenants retain eligible housing costs based on contractual rent.

Award for HB depends on: money coming in; amount of savings; personal circumstances (children, disability, others in household); eligible rent. BC applies; for those over Cap, HB reduced first. Being replaced by UC from October 2013.

Child benefit disregarded. Childcare costs paid by single parents and working/disabled couples may be disregarded, up to £175 p.w. for one child and £300 p.w. for more than one child.

If income greater than claimant's applicable amount, tapered reduction applies; HB reduced by 65% of excess income.

Usual upper savings limit £16,000; if on Guarantee PC no upper limit (but tariff income). Capital up to £6,000 is disregarded. (£10,000 if above qualifying age for PC). For claimants under women's pension age: each £250 (or part) over £6,000 is deemed to produce tariff income of £1 p.w. For claimants over women's pension age rate is £1 per £500 (or part). Different capital limits for those in residential homes and for children.

Administered by LAs. Non-contributory and non-taxable.

		p.w.
Claimant	18-24	56.80
	25 or over	71.70
Lone parent	Under 18	56.80
	18 or over	71.70
Couple	Both under 18	85.80
	One or both over 18	112.55
Dependent children to day before 20th birthday		65.62
Pensioner		
Single women's pension age to 64		145.40
Couple one or both women's pension age to 64		222.05
Single 65 and over		163.50
Couple one or both 65 and over		244.95
Premiums as for IS, except		
Family/lone parent family premium		17.40
Protected lone parent family premium		22.20
ESA components		
Work-related activity		28.45
Support		34.80

Council Tax Support (CTS) 2013-14

On 1 April 2013 Council Tax Benefit was abolished in England and Wales; replaced by a locally-administered CTS (funds available reduced by 10%). Each LA is responsible for devising its own scheme. Schemes vary from LA to LA so that contribution required from poorest householders ranges from 0% to 33%. No claimant who was receiving maximum CTB to pay more than 85% of annual total.

Table 27 Pension Sharing Procedure

Procedure on an application made on or after 6 April 2011 for a pension sharing order

	Step	Timing	FPR/Reg/ WRP Act 1999
1	**Applicant** (party without pension) makes the application for pension sharing order (PSO) in **Form A / D50F**	On or at any time after filing of application for a matrimonial or civil partnership order (Form A) or at any time after permission granted to apply for a PSO after overseas divorce / dissolution (Form D50F)	9.4 and PD 5A Table 2
2	Applicant serves the person responsible for each pension arrangement ('**PRPA**') with a copy of Form A / D50F	Upon making the application	9.31
3	Unless **Respondent** (party with pension) has or has requested a relevant valuation[1] of his pension rights or benefits (ie the CETV or CEB) (and whether or not a PSO has been applied for), he requests PRPA to provide it	Within 7 days of receiving notice of First Appointment	9.30(1), (2) and (4)
4	PRPA provides the information at step 3	If notified that requested for purpose of proceedings, within 6 weeks of request or as directed	reg. 2(5), 2000 Regs
5	Respondent serves the information at step 4 together with name and address of PRPA	Within 7 days of receipt	9.30(3)
6	If **Court** so directs at the First Appointment, Respondent to file and serve a Pension Inquiry Form (**Form P**), completed in full or part as the Court may direct[2]	As directed	9.15(7)(c); regs. 2, 3 and 4, 2000 Regs
7	PRPA provides as directed the information required by Form P	Within 21 days of receipt or as otherwise directed	reg. 4(1), 2000 Regs
8	The PSO must include a statement that the order provides for pension sharing in accordance with its annex(es)	When drafting or making the PSO	9.35(a)
9	The PSO must be accompanied by an annex for each pension arrangement in the prescribed form (**Form P1**)[3]	When drafting or making the PSO	9.35(b)
10	Where the PSO is made by consent but no service has been effected under step 2, Respondent must request from PRPA the information in Section C of Form P (unless already provided) and on receipt serve copy on Applicant	On making of order	9.32
11	The PSO and annex(es) are sent to PRPA by one of the parties or by Court, as directed, together with copies of the divorce decrees/ dissolution orders	Within 7 days of the later of the making of the PSO or decree absolute / final order of dissolution	9.36(2), (4) and (5)
12	PSO takes effect	On the later of decree absolute or 7 days from expiry of time for appeal against PSO	MCA s 24B(2); reg 9, D(P)R 2000[4]
13	PRPA implements the PSO	Within EITHER 4 months of date PSO takes effect OR after which PRPA receives the order and annex(es), copies of the divorce decrees / dissolution orders, the information specified in the applicable paragraphs of the annex(es) and payment of its charges (whichever the later) OR as directed by Court[5]	WRPA 1999, s 34(1); reg. 5, 2000 Regs WRPA 1999, ss 34(4) and 41(2)(a)

[1] See reg. 2(2), Pensions on Divorce etc (Provision of Information) Regulations 2000 ('2000 Regs').
[2] Form P should always be used for significant pensions where an order may be made: *Martin-Dye* [2006] 2 FLR 901.
[3] The pension share must be expressed as a percentage of CE: *H v H* [2010] 2 FLR 173.
[4] I.e. reg. 9 of the Divorce etc (Pensions) Regulations 2000.
[5] Pursuant to Pension Sharing (Implementation and Discharge of Liability) Regulations 2000 or Pensions on Divorce etc (Charging) Regulations 2000.

Note: additional/other steps must be taken in the case of PPF involvement (rule 9.37), and on applications for pension compensation sharing orders (FPR Part 9, Chapter 9), for all of which, and for Forms P and P1, see *@eGlance*.

Table 28 Pensions Overview

Pensions are a complex area. This text highlights only the key features of pensions in the family proceedings context. It is not (nor is it intended to be) a sufficient basis upon which to advise clients. Specialist advice from an independent financial adviser and/or an actuary will in most cases be essential.

The current pensions 'simplification' rules for registered pension schemes came into force on 6 April 2006 (**A-Day**) and are found in the Finance Act 2004, Part 4. Significant subsequent changes have been made, notably by the Finance Act 2011.

LIFETIME ALLOWANCE

The *lifetime allowance* (**LTA**) is the overall limit on the total amount of tax-relieved pension savings that an individual can have over his/her lifetime.

2010-11	£1.8M
2011-12	£1.8M
2012-13 and 2013-2014	£1.5M
2014-15	£1.25M

- Up to 25% of the value of pension funds may be paid as a tax-free lump sum (a *pension commencement lump sum*) up to a limit of 25% of the LTA;
- Individuals with existing pension funds with a value higher than £1.5M on A-Day were able to apply for *primary protection*, and anyone could apply for *enhanced protection* provided they ceased accruing further pension benefits. It is no longer possible to apply for such protection. These protections were preserved following the changes introduced on 6 April 2011;
- A further form of protection was introduced by the Finance Act 2011 known as *fixed protection* which provides the individual with a personalised lifetime allowance of £1.8M, but only if accrual of benefits in all registered pension schemes ceased before 6 April 2012. Applications for such protection had to be made to HMRC by 5 April 2012;
- The LTA is not reduced by virtue of a pension debit resulting from a pension sharing order, thus permitting pension rebuilding. [The position is more complex where the party suffering the pension debit has elected for primary or enhanced protection];
- Yet another form of protection is to be introduced from 6 April 2014 known as **fixed 2014 protection**, which will provide individuals with a lifetime allowance of £1.5M, but no further provision may be made after this date. Individuals who have applied for the previous forms of protection will be unaffected;
- A pension credit counts towards the recipient's LTA;
- Tax relief on any pension savings above the LTA is recovered by the application of the *lifetime allowance tax charge* to the excess at a rate of 25% if the excess is taken as a pension or 55% if taken as a lump sum.

ANTI-FORESTALLING RÉGIME

- Finance Act 2009, Sched 35 introduced measures to prevent those likely to be affected by the restrictions on tax relief and pension contributions effective from 6 April 2011 front-loading their pension contributions/accruals before that date;
- From 22 April 2009 until 5 April 2011, a *special annual allowance* and an associated *special annual allowance tax charge* applied to high earners in certain circumstances;
- The rules introduced by the Finance Act 2009 were repealed by the Finance Act 2011;
- The former impact of the anti-forestalling régime is mitigated by the carry forward of unused AA introduced by the Finance Act 2011 (see **Annual Allowance**);
- **The anti-forestalling régime is a complex area requiring specialist advice.**

ANNUAL ALLOWANCE

The *annual allowance* (**AA**) is the limit on the total amount of an individual's tax-relieved annual pension savings.

2010-11	£255,000
2011-12 and 2013-14	£50,000
2014-15	£40,000

- Relief is at an individual's marginal rate of tax up to 100% of an individual's UK taxable income (subject to the AA) or £3,600 (whichever is the greater);
- Carry forward of unused AA from up to 3 previous years is available to off-set against excess pension savings. Carry forward is available against a restricted AA of £50,000 for tax years 2008-09, 2009-10 and 2010-11;
- From 6 April 2011, the AA limit applies in the year benefits come into payment;
- The annual allowance is measured by reference to an annual *pension input period* (**PIP**) determined by the pension scheme and is not necessarily aligned to the tax year;
- Transitional rules apply from 14 October 2010 where an individual has pension savings relating to a PIP that started before 14 October 2010 and which ended in 2011-12;
- Neither a pension credit nor a pension debit resulting from a pension sharing order counts towards an individual's AA.

BENEFITS STRUCTURE

- Minimum benefit age: age 55 from 6 April 2010 (except for incapacity retirement and those with a contractual right to early retirement at age 50 as at 10 December 2003);
- Minimum benefit age also applies to pension credit benefits subject to terms of individual scheme;
- A pensioner can continue working after taking pension benefit;
- From A-Day, all pension schemes are able to pay a tax-free lump sum known as a *pension commencement lump sum* of up to 25% of the fund or value of the benefits subject to an overriding limit of 25% of the LTA. These can be paid at any time after age 55 (even after age 75);
- Income may be taken either as *capped drawdown* (see pensions annuitisation), *flexible drawdown* (see pensions annuitisation) or as a *secured pension* (an annuity or a Scheme Pension – a pension based on the assets of the scheme). Alternatively secured and unsecured pensions (ASPs) were abolished on 6 April 2011.

DEATH BENEFITS

- Under the Finance Act 2011, from 6 April 2011 the tax rate for all lump sum death benefits is set at 55% (previously

Table 28 Pensions Overview

35%) apart from death benefits for those who die before age 75 without having taken a pension, which remain tax-free;
- From 6 April 2011, inheritance tax does not apply to drawdown pension funds remaining under a registered pension scheme, including when the individual dies after reaching age 75;
- Unused drawdown pension funds of a member who dies with no living dependants may be donated to charity tax-free.

PENSIONS ANNUITISATION

- Under the Finance Act 2011, from 6 April 2011, the previous requirement for pension savers to buy an annuity by the age of 75 was removed;
- The maximum income that an individual may withdraw from most drawdown pension funds is capped at 120% (previously 100%) of the equivalent annuity with no minimum (*capped drawdown*);
- The age 75 ceiling was removed for most lump sums to which entitlement arises on or after 6 April 2011;
- Individuals with a lifetime pension income of at least £20,000 p.a. are able to access their surplus pension funds as pension income by way of *flexible drawdown* without any cap on the withdrawals they make (i.e. cash in the whole pension) subject to the individual's marginal tax rate. Care is needed here as not all pensions count towards the £20,000 p.a. minimum.

PENSION SHARING

- Only applies to petitions for divorce or nullity (not judicial separation) issued on or after 1 December 2000;
- Requires an English/Welsh court order: may not be achieved by agreement alone;
- Must be expressed as a percentage (*H v H* [2010] 2 FLR 173) from 1% to 100%;
- A pension in payment may be shared;
- When a person with benefit of pension credit retires at their retirement age (according to terms of scheme) part of his/her pension may be commuted, unless the pension out of which the pension credit was carved has already been the subject of commutation;
- The same rules apply to pension sharing orders made in relation to dissolution and annulment of civil partnerships;
- Forms: P (Pension Inquiry Form); P1 (Pension Sharing Annex);
- Equal division of a Cash Equivalent does not achieve equality of outcome in income terms: appropriate specialist pension or actuarial advice is required.

PENSION PROTECTION FUND

- Established on 6 April 2005 by Pensions Act 2004, Part 2;
- Acts as a form of insurance to pay benefits up to a capped level of certain defined benefit occupational pension schemes, where broadly a *qualifying insolvency event* took place on or after 6 April 2005;
- *Financial Assistance Scheme* may assist some of those ineligible for help from the PPF where, broadly, winding up commenced between 1 January 1997 and 5 April 2005;
- PPF covers by way of *pension compensation* 100% of pension benefits in payment and 90% of accrued pensions for all others with a cap in either case of £34,867.04 p.a. (£31,380.34 p.a. maximum when the 90% level is applied) at age 65 during 2013/14;
- PPF does not pay death-in-service benefits;
- Lump sum commutation of up to 25% of benefits is available;
- ***Pension compensation sharing orders*** and ***pension compensation attachment orders*** available from 6 April 2011 against PPF even where petition issued before that date (Pensions Act 2008 inserting MCA 1973, ss 21B, 21C, 24E, 24F, 24G, 25F, 25G and 40B);
- If the PPF assumes responsibility for a pension scheme, any outstanding pension sharing/attachment orders are implemented by the PPF;
- Forms: PPF (PPF Inquiry Form); PPF1 (Sharing) and PPF2 (Attachment) Annexes.

STATE RETIREMENT PENSION

- Consists of flat-rate *basic pension*, the old *graduated pension* and the *State Second Pension* (**S2P**);
- Subject to contribution requirements, an individual will receive at state pension age a Category A pension which is the flat rate basic pension. A Category B pension is a pension payable to a married woman by virtue of her husband's state pension entitlement in circumstances where she does not have sufficient contributions of her own to obtain a full basic state pension, but has attained state pension age;
- Where a person does not already have a sufficient national insurance contribution of their own to obtain a full basic state pension, the effect of divorce is that a person's claim to a Category A pension may be based upon the contribution record of his/her former spouse/civil partner during the relevant relationship and his/her own contributions before and after that relationship (the *substitution rule*).
- S2P is an earnings-related component payable according to national insurance contributions and was formerly known as the State Earnings Related Pension Scheme (SERPS). SERPS and S2P are collectively referred to as the *Additional State Pension* (**ASP**);
- State retirement age for men is currently 65 and was 60 for women until April 2010. It is to be phased in at 66 for both men and women by 6 April 2020;
- A state pension forecast may be obtained by submitting Form BR19. A capital valuation of ASP may be obtained by submitting Form BR20. Forms BR19 and BR20 may be downloaded from www.direct.gov.uk;
- ASP (but not the basic state pension or graduated pension) may be the subject of a pension sharing order;
- In January 2013, the government published proposals to introduce a simple flat rate state pension scheme to be implemented no earlier than April 2016. Pension sharing will not be applied to the single tier pension, but existing pension sharing orders in relation to ASP will be honoured.

AUTO-ENROLMENT

- A new compulsory pension scheme for employees came into force on 1 October 2012 under the Pensions Act 2008. All eligible employees (but not the self-employed) must be enrolled by their employer in an automatic enrolment scheme, which will be either:
    - their employer's pension scheme (where it is a qualifying scheme); or
    - the new national pension scheme called NEST (National Employment Savings Trust).
- The NEST pension may be shared by a PSO.

Table 29 Exchange Rates

Annual average sterling exchange rates of 24 currencies for the past 10 years

	Argentina *peso*	Australia *dollar*	Brazil *real*	Canada *dollar*	China *yuan*	Denmark *krone*	Europe/EMU *euro*	Hong Kong *dollar*
03	5.17	2.51	5.03	2.29	13.54	10.74	1.45	12.73
04	5.70	2.49	4.43	2.38	15.18	10.97	1.47	14.27
05	5.25	2.39	4.43	2.20	14.93	10.90	1.46	14.15
06	6.01	2.45	4.01	2.09	14.69	10.94	1.47	14.32
07	6.34	2.39	3.91	2.15	15.23	10.89	1.46	15.62
08	5.09	2.19	3.35	1.96	12.92	9.39	1.26	14.43
09	6.18	1.99	3.08	1.78	10.78	8.36	1.12	12.14
10	6.20	1.68	2.72	1.59	10.46	8.69	1.17	12.01
11	6.68	1.55	2.68	1.59	10.38	8.59	1.15	12.48
12	7.21	1.53	3.10	1.58	10.00	9.18	1.23	12.30

	India *rupee*	Israel *shekel*	Japan *yen*	New Zealand *dollar*	Norway *kroner*	Pakistan *rupee*	Poland *zloty*	Russia *rouble*
03	76.18	7.79	189.32	2.81	11.57	99.98	6.34	50.16
04	82.76	8.29	198.10	2.76	12.34	114.22	6.63	52.29
05	79.99	8.16	200.16	2.58	11.71	104.50	5.89	51.06
06	83.41	8.21	214.33	2.84	11.81	119.41	5.71	50.05
07	82.94	8.22	235.71	2.72	11.72	123.33	5.50	51.18
08	80.62	6.62	192.36	2.61	10.34	117.33	4.42	45.82
09	75.64	6.15	146.47	2.48	9.81	136.18	4.85	49.57
10	70.57	5.77	135.46	2.14	9.34	133.73	4.66	46.97
11	74.52	5.74	127.75	2.03	8.99	139.59	4.75	47.12
12	84.67	6.11	126.47	1.96	9.22	212.90	5.16	49.23

	Saudi Arabia *riyal*	Singapore *dollar*	South Africa *rand*	Sweden *krona*	Switzerland *franc*	UAE *dirham*	USA *dollar*	Vietnam *dong*
03	6.13	2.85	12.33	13.19	2.20	6.01	1.64	25384
04	6.87	3.10	11.80	13.45	2.28	6.73	1.83	28743
05	6.82	3.03	11.58	13.58	2.27	6.67	1.82	28797
06	6.91	2.93	12.52	13.57	2.31	6.77	1.84	29473
07	7.50	3.02	14.11	13.52	2.40	7.35	2.00	32174
08	6.95	2.61	15.13	12.09	2.00	6.82	1.85	30452
09	5.88	2.27	13.10	11.93	1.70	5.80	1.57	28008
10	5.80	2.11	11.31	11.12	1.61	5.68	1.55	29542
11	6.01	2.02	11.64	10.41	1.42	5.89	1.60	33020
12	5.94	1.98	13.02	10.73	1.49	5.82	1.59	33210

Table 29 Exchange Rates

The fixed conversion rates adopted when the euro replaced the currencies formerly in use

Country	currency	Rate to •
Austria	schilling	13.7603
Belgium	franc	40.3399
Cyprus**	CYP(£)	0.585274
Estonia****	kroon	15.6466
Finland	mark	5.94573
France	franc	6.55957
Germany	mark	1.95583
Greece	drachma	340.75
Ireland	punt	0.787564
Italy	lira	1936.27
Luxembourg	franc	40.3399
Malta**	lira	0.4293
Netherlands	guilder	2.20371
Portugal	escudo	200.482
Slovakia***	koruna	30.126
Slovenia*	tolar	239.64
Spain	peseta	166.386

The rates fixed on conversion *left* applied when the euro replaced the former currencies of the 12 founding countries (unstarred) on 1 January 2002; followed by Slovenia* (2007), Cyprus** and Malta** (2008), Slovakia*** (2009) and Estonia**** (2011).

The remaining 'acceding countries' (Bulgaria, the Czech Republic, Hungary, Latvia, Lithuania, Poland, and Romania) will adopt the euro when they meet stipulated economic criteria.

The source of the average exchange rates shown on the *facing* page is either the Bank of England (for currencies listed at www.bankofengland.co.uk) or www.ozforex.co.au.

Monthly as well as annual average sterling exchange rates since 1975 for these and other currencies are accessible in @eGlance, as is a versatile calculator.

Table 30 International Living Costs

An index of comparative city living costs in September 2012

City	Index	City	Index	City	Index	City	Index
Tokyo	133	Hong Kong	103	Rome	87	Athens	72
Sydney	122	**London**	100	Istanbul	81	Johannesburg	64
Singapore	119	Vienna	93	Moscow	81	Warsaw	63
Paris	115	Madrid	90	Amsterdam	80	Lagos	60
Geneva	109	Brussels	89	Beijing	78	Cairo	59
Frankfurt	105	New York	89	Rio de Janeiro	76	Mumbai	40
Copenhagen	104	Dublin	87	Prague	75	Karachi	38

Notes:

Centred on London at 100, the index illustrates the cost of living in 27 other cities around the world.

The ratings derive from the Worldwide Cost of Living Survey, published in December 2012 by the Economist Intelligence Unit (EIU). The survey is published 6-monthly.

The survey is based on a range of over 170 goods and services. Full reports for these and a further 107 cities are available from EIU (☎ 020 7576 8181, or visit www.eiu.com).

The index fluctuates readily as cost comparisons are sensitive to exchange rates and inflation.

Table 31 Financial Remedy Procedure

This Table sets out the procedural steps required on applications for a financial remedy (FPR 2010 rule 2.3: see page 66) issued in the High Court or county court on or after 6 April 2011, save in relation to pension sharing (as to which see Table 27) or pension attachment orders (as to which see the Financial Remedy Rules at page 72). For the procedure governing ancillary relief applications issued before 6 April 2011 and the transitional provisions contained in FPR Part 36 and FP(A)R 2012, see @eGlance and previous editions of **At A Glance**.

Note that prior to the commencement of any application for a financial remedy the Court will expect the parties to comply with the **Pre-application Protocol (Annex to PD 9A)** *(see @eGlance). For the procedure to seek* **Transfer to High Court Judge** *see page 74.*

The overriding objective (rules 1.1 to 1.4: see page 66) applies to every stage of financial remedy proceedings.

Phase 1: To end of First Appointment ('FA')

	Step	Party	Timing	FPR / PD
1	Filing of application including, where it relates to land, details of any mortgagee **(Form A – financial orders)** **(Form A1 etc – other financial remedies)**	Either	In an application for a matrimonial / civil partnership order or at any time after such an application has been made At any time	PD 9A para 1.3 9.4(a) and (b) PD 9A para 3.1
2	Fixing of First Appointment **12 to 16 weeks** ahead **(Form C)** NB: No cancellation of date without permission	The Court	When Form A is issued	9.12(1)(a) 9.12(3)
3	Service of copy of applications in Form A / A1 etc and C	The Court OR Applicant	Within **4 days** after Form A / A1 etc filed Within 4 days of receipt of Form A / A1 etc and C from the Court	9.12(1)(b) 9.12(2)(c)(i)
4	Filing of certificate where service effected by Applicant	Applicant	At or before the First Appointment	9.12(2)(c)(ii)
5	Filing and **simultaneous exchange** of **Form E (financial orders / financial relief after overseas divorce etc)** or **Form E1 (other financial remedies)** completed and verified by a statement of truth by each party, and attaching • the documents **required** by the Form • any other documents **necessary** to explain or clarify the information • pension information provided under 9.30 or 9.37(2), (4), or (5) (but no other documents). The **required** documents are • property valuations obtained in last 6 months • most recent mortgage statements • last 12 months' bank statements • latest statement or dividend counterfoil for stocks, shares and similar investments • surrender valuations of insurance policies • last 2 years' business accounts • any available documentation on the basis of which the value of a business is estimated • CE of pension arrangements (in the case of the additional state pension, valuation of rights) / PPF entitlement valuation • last 3 payslips and most recent P60 and P11D • (self employed / partnership) last tax assessment or accountant's letter in default • (self employed / partnership) where next 12 months' estimated income differs significantly from last 12 months', management accounts for period since last accounts	Both	At least **35 days** before FA	9.14(1) 9.14(2)(b)(i) and (ii) 9.14(2)(b)(iii) and (iv) See schedule of documents to accompany Form E
	Bundle of exhibits to Form E must comply with PD 22A (and note in particular paras 11.3 and 13.1)	Both		PD 9A para 5.1

Table 31 Financial Remedy Procedure

	Step	Party	Timing	FPR / PD
6	Service of documents required by but unavoidably not attached to Form E (with explanation).	Either	At earliest opportunity	9.14(3)
	But otherwise **NO general disclosure or inspection before FA**	Neither		9.14(4)
7	Filing and service of		At least **14 days** before FA	9.14(5)
	• Concise statement of issues	Both		
	• Chronology	Both		
	• Questionnaire, **referable to the statement of issues**, seeking further information and documents, or a statement that none are required	Both		
	• Notice (**Form G**) stating whether that party will be able to proceed to FDR at the FA	Both		
	Confirmation of service of persons referred to in rule 9.13(1) to (3)	Applicant		9.14(6)
	Parties should also if possible with a view to identifying and narrowing the issues exchange and file a **case summary, agreed schedule of assets and proposed directions** including name of any proposed expert			PD 9A para 4.1
8	Produce first costs estimate (**Form H**)	Both	At FA	9.27(1) & PD 9A paras 3.1 to 3.2
	Information in Form H must be as full and accurate as possible and set out clearly sums already paid			PD 9A para 3.2
	If a party intends to seek a summary assessment of costs, produce a Woolf costs schedule following **N260** as closely as possible		24 hours before FA	PD 28A para 4.5; CPR PD 44, para 9.5(3) and (4)(b)
9	**THE FIRST APPOINTMENT**	Both parties to attend personally unless otherwise directed	On date fixed 12 to 16 weeks after filing of Form A (Step 2)	9.15(1)
	Objective: to define issues and save costs			9.15(8)
	Directions as to:	The Court		
	• Answering questions and producing documents, and any further **necessary** documentation, **to be verified by a statement of truth**			9.15(2) PD 9A para 5.2
	• Valuations (joint if appropriate)			9.15(3)
	• Obtaining and exchanging expert evidence			
	• Evidence to be adduced by each party			
	• Further chronologies, schedules			
	Consideration may need to be given to possible joinder of a party/parties			9.26B
	Court *must* then:			
	Either: direct FDR, if appropriate		Date for FDR on **Form D**	9.15(4)
	Or (if FDR inappropriate): direct one or more of:			9.15(5)
	• Hearing for further directions			
	• Hearing for interim order			
	• Final hearing (and at which judicial level)			
	• Adjournment for ADR, if appropriate			3.3
	The Court *may* in addition / alternative:			9.15(7)
	• Make interim order, if such application listed for consideration			
	• Having regard to Forms G (see Step 7), treat appointment or part of it as FDR			
	• Direct party with pension rights to file and serve Pension Inquiry Form (Form P) / Pension Protection Fund Inquiry Form (Form PPF)			
	Costs: In considering whether to make a costs order under rule 28.3(6) the Court must have particular regard to the extent to which each party has complied with the requirement to send documents with Form E, and to any breach of the pre-action protocol or PD 9A	The Court		9.15(6) & 28.3(5) PD 9A paras 3.3 and 3.4

Table 31 Financial Remedy Procedure

Phase 2: To end of Financial Dispute Resolution Appointment ('FDR')

	Step	Party	Timing	FPR / PD
10	Comply with all directions made at FA	Both	As per directions order	
	Any further production of documents only with Court permission	Both	Between the FA and FDR	9.16(1)
11	Application for / giving of further directions OR application for / directing FDR	Both / The Court	By application at any stage	9.16(2)
12	Where FDR has been ordered: Notice to Court of all offers, proposals and responses, including without prejudice offers (but excluding offers made during ADR)	Applicant	At least **7 days** before FDR	9.17(3) PD 9A para 6.4
	Produce second costs estimate in Form H	Both	At FDR	9.27(1) & PD 9A para 3.1 to 3.2
	Information in Form H must be as full and accurate as possible and set out clearly sums already paid			PD 9A para 3.2
13	**THE FDR APPOINTMENT** For practical advice on the FDR see the *Financial Dispute Resolution Appointments: Best Practice Guidance* produced by the Family Justice Council in December 2012 (available online and in *@eGlance*). **Objective:** 'parties must use best endeavours to reach agreement' **Ground rules:** • 'A meeting held for the purposes of discussion and negotiation': see *Rose v Rose* [2002] 1 FLR 978 • Parties must approach the occasion openly and without reserve and non-disclosure of the content of the meeting is vital • The Court will expect the parties to make offers and proposals and consider those received • Conducted by a judge who will not have anything else to do with the case save as set out *below* • Legal representatives will be expected to have full knowledge of the case • Offer details lodged are not to be kept on Court file after FDR **DJ *may* then only** (*Myerson* [2009] 1 FLR 826) • Adjourn from time to time • Make appropriate consent order • Give further directions / fix final hearing Note: Where FDR has failed in a substantial case narrative affidavits of the financial history should be ordered: *W v W* [2000] Fam Law 473 per Wilson J **Costs:** The Court may make an order for costs where it is appropriate because of the conduct of a party in relation to the proceedings (see Step 19 for the matters to which the Court must have regard) and having regard to any breach of the pre-action protocol or PD 9A	Both parties to attend personally unless otherwise ordered: 9.17(10)	On date fixed at FA (Step 9)	9.17(6) 9.17(1) and PD 9A para 6.1 PD 9A para 6.2 PD 9A para 6.3 9.17(2) PD 9A para 6.5 9.17(5) 9.17(7) 9.17(8) 9.17(9) 28.3(6), PD 28A paras 4.3 and 4.4 and PD 9A paras 3.3 and 3.4

The dynamic version of this Procedure Table in *@eGlance* provides instant finger-tip access to and fro between each Step and the text of the corresponding Rule and / or Practice Direction, as well as extensive editorial Commentary.

Call ☎ 01652 652222 or visit www.classlegal.com to download your copy now: special rates apply if you have purchased this *At A Glance* directly from The Family Law Bar Association.

AT A GLANCE

Table 31 Financial Remedy Procedure

	Step	Party	Timing	FPR / PD
14	**Application for interim order**	Either	At any time	
	• The Part 18 procedure applies to an application for an interim order, which should be made in form D11		Both	9.7(2)
	• Where the applicant applies before filing of Form E, the written evidence must explain why the application is necessary and give up to date information about his means			9.7(3)
	• Unless he has filed Form E, the respondent must file and serve a statement of means at least **7 days** before the hearing			9.7(4)
	• A party may at any stage apply **without notice** for interim orders apart from maintenance or variation orders		Either	9.7(5)
	• Rule 28.3 (costs) only applies to interim variation applications			28.3(4)(b) and PD 28A paras 4.1 and 4.2

Phase 3: To final hearing

	Step	Party	Timing	FPR / PD
15	**Directions orders made at FDR to be complied with appropriately**	Both	As per directions order	
16	**Further Directions / FDR**	Either party may apply or Court may direct	Any time	9.16(2)
17	**Statement of open proposals, setting out concise details, including the amounts involved**	Applicant	Not less than **14 days** before final hearing	9.28(1)
	Unless Court otherwise directs, file with Court and serve on other party			
		Respondent	Not more than **7 days** after receipt of Applicant's statement	9.28(2)
18	**THE FINAL HEARING**		On date fixed at First Appointment (Step 9) or at FDR (Step 13) or otherwise	
	Unless Court otherwise directs, file and serve a statement of costs in Form H1	Both	Not less than 14 days before final hearing	9.27(2)
	Information in Form H1 must be as full and accurate as possible and set out clearly sums already paid			PD 9A para 3.2
19	**Costs after judgment**			
	• Only open offers to settle are admissible at the final hearing			PD 28A para 4.3
	• The general rule is that the Court will not make an order requiring one party to pay the costs of another; but the Court may make such an order where it considers it appropriate to do so because of the conduct of a party in relation to the proceedings			28.3(5) and PD 9A para 3.3 28.3(6) and PD 28A paras 4.3 and 4.4
	• For the financial remedies to which the general rule applies see 28.3(4)(b) and PD 28A paras 4.1 and 4.2			
	• In deciding what order if any to make under 28.3(6) the Court must have regard to:			28.3(7)
	– failure to comply with the rules, an order or relevant practice direction			
	– any open offer to settle			
	– whether it was reasonable for a party to raise, pursue or contest a particular allegation or issue			
	– the manner in which a party has pursued or responded to the application or a particular allegation or issue			
	– any other aspect of a party's conduct in relation to the proceedings which the Court considers relevant			
	– the financial effect on the parties of any costs order			
	CPR 44.2(1), (4) and (5) are disapplied			28.3(2)
	CPR 44.2(6) to (8) and 44.12 are applied			28.3(3)

Table 32 The IFLA Arbitration Scheme

In February 2012 an innovative financial arbitration procedure for dispute resolution was launched by the Institute of Family Law Arbitrators (IFLA, www.ifla.org.uk). Its stakeholders are Resolution, the FLBA and the Chartered Institute of Arbitrators (CIArb). The Scheme is governed by the Arbitration Act 1996 ('AA 1996') and IFLA's Arbitration Rules ('the Rules': currently the 2012 (2nd edition) Rules).

By art 2.1 of the Rules, the Scheme may be adopted for financial and property disputes arising from: marriage and its breakdown (including financial provision on divorce, judicial separation or nullity); civil partnership and its breakdown; co-habitation and the ending of co-habitation; parenting or those sharing parental responsibility; and provision for dependants from a deceased's estate. The Scheme covers, but is not limited to, claims which would come within the following statutes: MWPA 1882, s. 17; MCA 1973, Pt II; I(PFD)A 1975; MFPA 1984, Pt III (financial relief after overseas divorce); CA 1989, Sch 1; TLATA 1996; and CPA 2004 Sch 5, or Sch 7, Part 1, para 2 (financial relief after overseas dissolution) (art 2.2).

The Scheme can not be used to resolve questions directly concerning: the liberty of individuals; the status either of individuals or of their relationship; the care or parenting of children; bankruptcy or insolvency; or any person or organisation not a party to the arbitration (art 2.3).

By their arbitration application (Form ARB1) the parties either seek the appointment of a nominated arbitrator or request IFLA to select an arbitrator from its Family Panel (art 4.3). Details of Panel members, all of whom are experienced family law practitioners accredited by IFLA who have been trained and been awarded Membership of CIArb, are available on the IFLA website. Accredited arbitrators are regulated by the code and disciplinary procedures of CIArb.

By their ARB1 the parties agree to be bound by the arbitrator's written decision (the award), subject to (a) any right of appeal or other available challenge; (b) (insofar as the subject matter of the award requires it to be embodied in a court order) any changes which the court making that order may require; and (c) (in the case of an award of continuing payments) any future award or order varying the award (para 6.4 and art 13.3). They also agree that they will not, while the arbitration is continuing, apply to court except in connection with the arbitration or to seek relief that is not available in the arbitration (para 6.2); and, if and so far as the subject matter of the award makes it necessary, to apply to an appropriate court for an order in the same or similar terms as the award or the relevant part of the award (para 6.5 and art 13.4).

Disputes under the Scheme are arbitrated in accordance with the mandatory and non-mandatory provisions of AA 1996; the Rules, to the extent that they exclude, replace or modify the non-mandatory provisions of the Act; and the agreement of the parties, to the extent that that excludes, replaces or modifies the non-mandatory provisions of the Act or the Rules (art 1.3). However, the parties may not agree to exclude, replace or modify art 3, which provides that the substance of the dispute is to be arbitrated only in accordance with the law of England and Wales (art 1.3(c)). Thus, subject only to the mandatory provisions of the Act and art 3 of the Rules, the parties possess substantial powers to regulate the process (although once the arbitration has commenced those powers may only be exercised with the agreement of the arbitrator (art 1.4)). This emphasis on party autonomy derives from AA 1996, s. 1(b) which provides that 'the parties should be free to agree how their disputes are resolved, subject only to such safeguards as are necessary in the public interest'.

The arbitrator will generally give procedural directions at the outset of the arbitration, and as necessary during its course. The procedure adopted will depend on the nature of the issues in dispute and will range from determination on paper alone to full hearing with oral evidence. Art 10 ('General procedure') contains a CPR-style procedural régime, while art 12 ('Alternative procedure') provides for a régime similar to the FPR Part 9 financial remedy procedure. But the parties, prior to the commencement of the arbitration (constituted by the arbitrator's formal acceptance letter) or thereafter with their arbitrator's consent, may cut, paste and modify the process to meet their needs and means and the particular characteristics of the issues they bring for adjudication.

The award must be delivered in writing and, unless the parties agree otherwise or the award is by consent, must contain sufficient reasons to show how and why the arbitrator has reached the decisions it contains (art 13.2).

While there are presumptions (unless the parties agree otherwise) that there will be no order for costs *inter partes* and that the parties will be liable for the arbitrator's fees in equal shares (art 14.4), the arbitrator has discretion to impose costs orders on the basis of conduct (art 14.5).

How the award is implemented will depend on the nature of the dispute. In financial remedy cases parties will in general apply to the court for an order confirming the terms of the award. While the jurisdiction of the court may not be ousted, it is anticipated that it will only be in rare circumstances that the court will decline to uphold the award, given the parties' agreement at the outset to be bound by it. It is envisaged that procedural arrangements will be established for the 'fast tracking' of consent orders based on arbitral awards under the IFLA Scheme, as has been done in the case of agreements reached through the collaborative process (*S v P (settlement by collaborative process)* [2008] 2 FLR 2040).

Where, on the other hand, the court does not have a supervisory role (as for instance where the dispute involves a property claim between unmarried couples), the award may be enforced, with leave of the court, as though it were a court judgment or order (AA 1996, s. 66(1)).

Table 32 The IFLA Arbitration Scheme

There is a right of appeal to the court on a point of law, unless the parties have agreed to exclude it (AA 1996, s. 69(1)). The court has power to set aside the award if there has been a serious irregularity which has resulted or may result in substantial injustice (*ibid*, s. 68(1)).

For a more detailed description of the Scheme see the article at [2012] Fam Law 1353 and 1496, available to download at www.FamilyArbitrator.com.

The text of AA 1996, the Rules and a word-processable Form ARB1 are available in *@eGlance*.

Key procedural provisions of the IFLA Scheme for family finance arbitration

	Step	IFLA Rules / AA 96 section
1	Parties check that the dispute falls within the **scope** of the Scheme.	Art 2
2	Parties sign **Form ARB1** (application for family arbitration, available in *@eGlance* and at FamilyArbitrator.com) seeking **EITHER** the appointment of a nominated arbitrator ('**A**')	Art 4.1
	OR that IFLA nominate a Panel arbitrator; and submit to IFLA, c/o Resolution, PO Box 302, Orpington, Kent, BR6 8QX (01689 820272; info@ifla.org.uk).	Art 4.3
3	By their ARB1 parties agree *inter alia*:	
	• to be **bound** by A's award (subject to court-made amendments)	Para 6.4 & art 13.3
	• **not to apply to court** during the arbitration save in connection therewith	Para 6.2
	• if necessary, **to apply to court for an order** in the terms of the award.	Para 6.5 & art 13.4
4	**IFLA sends ARB1 to A** with request to contact the parties. If, after considering ARB1 and any representations from the parties, either IFLA or A considers that the dispute is not suitable for arbitration, then parties will be so advised and their application treated as withdrawn.	Art 4.4
5	A must disclose any actual or potential **conflict of interest** or any matter giving rise to justifiable doubt as to impartiality.	Art 5.1
6	The arbitration **commences** once A communicates to the parties his / her acceptance (i.e., following agreement as to A's terms and conditions). *Note*: while not required by the Rules A may convene, in advance of formal appointment, an **exploratory meeting** at which the parties can raise queries about the process, and A can ensure that they have understood their obligations.	Art 4.5
7	Disputes under the Scheme are arbitrated in accordance with:	Art 1.3
	• the provisions of Arbitration Act 1996 ('**AA96**'), both mandatory and non-mandatory	
	• the **Rules**, to the extent that they exclude, replace or modify the non-mandatory provisions of AA96, and	
	• the parties' **agreement**, to the extent that that excludes, replaces or modifies the non-mandatory provisions of AA96 or the Rules. (Art 3, stipulating that the law of England and Wales be applied, is mandatory.)	Art 1.3(c)
8	On commencement, A is likely to convene a **case management hearing** (in person or by telephone, videolink / Skype or email) and invite submissions as to the nature of the dispute, procedure etc. Directions may be given then or subsequently and at any stage in the arbitration.	Art 10.2 Art 11
9	While the parties are free to agree the **form of procedure**, once the arbitration has commenced A's consent is needed. A has wide discretion and extensive case-management powers.	Arts 1.4, 8.1 & 9; AA 33, 34 & 37
10	The Rules offer two **procedural templates**:	
	• a CPR-type procedure ('general procedure')	Art 10
	• a financial remedy-type procedure ('alternative procedure').	Art 12
	Variants of the above, or a documents-only procedure or some other simplified or expedited procedure may be adopted, depending on the circumstances.	Art 9.1
11	The **court's powers** may be invoked in support of the arbitration.	AA 42 to 45
12	A's **award** to be in writing and contain reasons (unless agreed otherwise or if the award is by consent).	Art 13.2
13	In financial remedy proceedings a **reflective court order** will generally be required to give effect to the award and thus a consent application (or if opposed, notice to show cause) should be issued.	Art 13.4
	In civil proceedings AA96 s. 66 may facilitate **enforcement** of the award.	AA 66
14	Subject to A's overriding discretion to make a conduct-based costs order, there is a **'no order as to costs'** presumption (which may, subject to art 1.4, be disapplied by agreement).	Art 14.4 Art 14.5
15	The arbitration process may be **challenged** only on the following bases:	
	• A's lack of jurisdiction (unlikely to arise under the Scheme given the clarity of ARB1)	AA 67
	• a 'serious irregularity' causing substantial injustice	AA 68
	• by agreement or with court's leave, an appeal on a point of law, unless expressly excluded by the parties.	AA 69

The Table is based on the 2012 (2nd Edition) of the Scheme Rules. Modest revisions envisaged during 2013 are unlikely to impact on this Table. For an overview see *opposite*, and visit FamilyArbitrator.com for general information and current documentation.

Table 33 Useful Websites

@eGlance Update Service	www.classlegal.com/ateglance/get
American Academy of Matrimonial Lawyers	www.aaml.org
Australasian Legal Information Institute	www.austlii.edu.au
Automobile Association	www.theAA.com
Bar Council	www.barcouncil.org.uk
Benefits (general information)	www.gov.uk/browse/benefits
British and Irish Legal Information Institute	www.bailii.org
CGT Indexation Factors	www.hmrc.gov.uk/rates/cgt08.htm#3
Child Support Agency/Child Maintenance Service	www.gov.uk/child-maintenance
Child Support Commissioners' Decisions	www.judiciary.gov.uk/media/tribunal-decisions/osccs-decisions
Chartered Institute of Arbitrators	www.ciarb.org
Civil Procedure Rules	www.justice.gov.uk/courts/procedure-rules/civil
Class Legal	www.classlegal.com
Companies House	www.companies-house.gov.uk
Countries of the world	http://news.bbc.co.uk/1/hi/country_profiles/default.stm
Currency rates worldwide	www.xe.com
Economist Intelligence Unit (EIU)	www.eiu.com
European Court of Human Rights	www.echr.coe.int/echr
European Court of Justice	http://curia.europa.eu/jcms/jcms/j_6/
European Judicial Atlas	http://ec.europa.eu/justice_home/judicialatlascivil/html/index_en.htm
European Judicial Network	http://ec.europa.eu/civiljustice/index_en.htm
European legislation	http://eur-lex.europa.eu/en/index.htm
Family arbitration information resource	www.familyarbitrator.com
Family Law/Jordans	www.familylaw.co.uk
Family Law news	www.familylaw.co.uk/categories/news
FLR (full text)	www.familylaw.co.uk/online-services
Family Law Bar Association	www.flba.co.uk
Family Law Week	www.familylawweek.co.uk
Family Lore	http://news.familylorefocus.com
Financial Times	www.ft.com
Government Actuary's Department	www.gad.gov.uk
Government Information Service	www.gov.uk
Hague Conference on Private International Law	www.hcch.net
Hague Convention on Child Abduction	www.hcch.net/index_en.php?act=text.display&tid=21
1 Hare Court	www.1hc.com
HM Courts and Tribunals Service	www.justice.gov.uk/about/hmcts
Daily Court Lists, Family Division	www.justice.gov.uk/courts/court-lists/list-family
Daily Court Lists, PRFD	www.justice.gov.uk/courts/court-lists/list-pr-family-division
HM Revenue and Customs	www.hmrc.gov.uk
House Prices Indices (Halifax)	www.lloydsbankinggroup.com/media1/economic_insight/halifax_house_price_index_page.asp
ICLR Case Search	http://cases.iclr.co.uk
Independent Schools Council	www.isc.co.uk
Information for Lawyers	www.infolaw.co.uk
Institute of Family Law Arbitrators	www.ifla.org.uk
International Academy of Matrimonial Lawyers	www.iaml.org
Land Registry	www.landregistry.gov.uk
Law Society	www.lawsociety.org.uk
Legal Aid	www.justice.gov.uk/legal-aid
Lexis Nexis Butterworths	www.lexisnexis.co.uk
Life assurance quotes	www.cavendishonline.co.uk/life/step1.php
Ministry of Justice	www.justice.gov.uk
Human Rights	www.justice.gov.uk/human-rights
National Savings and Investments	www.nsandi.com
Office for National Statistics	www.ons.gov.uk
Official Solicitor	www.justice.gov.uk/about/ospt
Pension annuity quotes	www.pensionsorter.co.uk/annuities.cfm
QEB Chambers	www.qeb.co.uk
Resolution	www.resolution.org.uk
RPI (full table)	www.ons.gov.uk/ons/key-figures/index.html
Share prices	www.iii.co.uk
Statutes	www.legislation.gov.uk/ukpga
Statutory Instruments	www.legislation.gov.uk/uksi
Supreme Court (Decided Cases)	www.supremecourt.gov.uk/decided-cases/index.html
Sweet & Maxwell	www.sweetandmaxwell.co.uk
UK Parliament	www.parliament.uk
Hansard: House of Commons Debates	www.parliament.the-stationery-office.co.uk/pa/cm/cmhansrd.htm
House of Lords Debates	www.parliament.the-stationery-office.co.uk/pa/ld/ldhansrd.htm
House of Lords Judgments	www.publications.parliament.uk/pa/ld/ldjudgmt.htm
Upmystreet (regional data)	www.upmystreet.com

Other Financial Remedy Materials

	Page
Matrimonial Causes Act 1973, ss. 21A to 25D, 28, 29, 31, 32, 34, 35 and 37	54
Financial Remedy Rules	66
Transfer to High Court Judge	74
Court Bundles: PD 27A	75
Costs: FPR 2010 Part 28 and PD 28A	78
Costs: Editors' Note	83
Brussels II Revised and FPR 7.27: Extracts	84
Note on the EU Maintenance Regulation	86
Leading Cases	88
Perpetual Calendar	104

Matrimonial Causes Act 1973

21A. Pension sharing orders
(1) For the purposes of this Act, a pension sharing order is an order which –
(a) provides that one party's –
  (i) shareable rights under a specified pension arrangement, or
  (ii) shareable state scheme rights,
  be subject to pension sharing for the benefit of the other party, and
(b) specifies the percentage value to be transferred.
(2) In subsection (1) above –
(a) the reference to shareable rights under a pension arrangement is to rights in relation to which pension sharing is available under Chapter I of Part IV of the Welfare Reform and Pensions Act 1999, or under corresponding Northern Ireland legislation,
(b) the reference to shareable state scheme rights is to rights in relation to which pension sharing is available under Chapter II of Part IV of the Welfare Reform and Pensions Act 1999, or under corresponding Northern Ireland legislation, and
(c) 'party' means a party to a marriage.

Sections 21B and 21C (pension compensation sharing orders) are not reproduced.

Ancillary relief in connection with divorce proceedings, etc

22. Maintenance pending suit
(1) On a petition for divorce, nullity of marriage or judicial separation, the court may make an order for maintenance pending suit, that is to say, an order requiring either party to the marriage to make to the other such periodical payments for his or her maintenance and for such term, being a term beginning not earlier than the date of the presentation of the petition and ending with the date of the determination of the suit, as the court thinks reasonable.
(2) An order under this section may not require a party to a marriage to pay to the other party any amount in respect of legal services for the purposes of the proceedings.
(3) In subsection (2) "legal services" has the same meaning as in section 22ZA.

22ZA. Orders for payment in respect of legal services
(1) In proceedings for divorce, nullity of marriage or judicial separation, the court may make an order or orders requiring one party to the marriage to pay to the other ("the applicant") an amount for the purpose of enabling the applicant to obtain legal services for the purposes of the proceedings.
(2) The court may also make such an order or orders in proceedings under this Part for financial relief in connection with proceedings for divorce, nullity of marriage or judicial separation.
(3) The court must not make an order under this section unless it is satisfied that, without the amount, the applicant would not reasonably be able to obtain appropriate legal services for the purposes of the proceedings or any part of the proceedings.
(4) For the purposes of subsection (3), the court must be satisfied, in particular, that-
(a) the applicant is not reasonably able to secure a loan to pay for the services, and
(b) the applicant is unlikely to be able to obtain the services by granting a charge over any assets recovered in the proceedings.
(5) An order under this section may be made for the purpose of enabling the applicant to obtain legal services of a specified description, including legal services provided in a specified period or for the purposes of a specified part of the proceedings.
(6) An order under this section may-
(a) provide for the payment of all or part of the amount by instalments of specified amounts, and
(b) require the instalments to be secured to the satisfaction of the court.
(7) An order under this section may direct that payment of all or part of the amount is to be deferred.
(8) The court may at any time in the proceedings vary an order made under this section if it considers that there has been a material change of circumstances since the order was made.
(9) For the purposes of the assessment of costs in the proceedings, the applicant's costs are to be treated as reduced by any amount paid to the applicant pursuant to an order under this section for the purposes of those proceedings.
(10) In this section "legal services", in relation to proceedings, means the following types of services-
(a) providing advice as to how the law applies in the particular circumstances,
(b) providing advice and assistance in relation to the proceedings,
(c) providing other advice and assistance in relation to the settlement or other resolution of the dispute that is the subject of the proceedings, and
(d) providing advice and assistance in relation to the enforcement of decisions in the proceedings or as part of the settlement or resolution of the dispute,

Matrimonial Causes Act 1973

and they include, in particular, advice and assistance in the form of representation and any form of dispute resolution, including mediation.

(11) In subsections (5) and (6) "specified" means specified in the order concerned.

22ZB. Matters to which court is to have regard in deciding how to exercise power under section 22ZA
(1) When considering whether to make or vary an order under section 22ZA, the court must have regard to-
(a) the income, earning capacity, property and other financial resources which each of the applicant and the paying party has or is likely to have in the foreseeable future,
(b) the financial needs, obligations and responsibilities which each of the applicant and the paying party has or is likely to have in the foreseeable future,
(c) the subject matter of the proceedings, including the matters in issue in them,
(d) whether the paying party is legally represented in the proceedings,
(e) any steps taken by the applicant to avoid all or part of the proceedings, whether by proposing or considering mediation or otherwise,
(f) the applicant's conduct in relation to the proceedings,
(g) any amount owed by the applicant to the paying party in respect of costs in the proceedings or other proceedings to which both the applicant and the paying party are or were party, and
(h) the effect of the order or variation on the paying party.
(2) In subsection (1)(a) "earning capacity", in relation to the applicant or the paying party, includes any increase in earning capacity which, in the opinion of the court, it would be reasonable to expect the applicant or the paying party to take steps to acquire.
(3) For the purposes of subsection (1)(h), the court must have regard, in particular, to whether the making or variation of the order is likely to-
(a) cause undue hardship to the paying party, or
(b) prevent the paying party from obtaining legal services for the purposes of the proceedings.
(4) The Lord Chancellor may by order amend this section by adding to, omitting or varying the matters mentioned in subsections (1) to (3).
(5) An order under subsection (4) must be made by statutory instrument.
(6) A statutory instrument containing an order under subsection (4) may not be made unless a draft of the instrument has been laid before, and approved by a resolution of, each House of Parliament.
(7) In this section "legal services" has the same meaning as in section 22ZA.

23. Financial provision orders in connection with divorce proceedings, etc
(1) On granting a decree of divorce, a decree of nullity of marriage or a decree of judicial separation or at any time thereafter (whether, in the case of a decree of divorce or of nullity of marriage, before or after the decree is made absolute), the court may make any one or more of the following orders, that is to say –
(a) an order that either party to the marriage shall make to the other such periodical payments, for such term, as may be specified in the order;
(b) an order that either party to the marriage shall secure to the other to the satisfaction of the court such periodical payments, for such term, as may be so specified;
(c) an order that either party to the marriage shall pay to the other such lump sum or sums as may be so specified;
(d) an order that a party to the marriage shall make to such person as may be specified in the order for the benefit of a child of the family, or to such a child, such periodical payments, for such term, as may be so specified;
(e) an order that a party to the marriage shall secure to such person as may be so specified for the benefit of such a child, or to such a child, to the satisfaction of the court, such periodical payments, for such term, as may be so specified;
(f) an order that a party to the marriage shall pay to such person as may be so specified for the benefit of such a child, or to such a child, such lump sum as may be so specified;
subject, however, in the case of an order under paragraph (d), (e) or (f) above, to the restrictions imposed by section 29(1) and (3) below on the making of financial provision orders in favour of children who have attained the age of eighteen.
(2) The court may also, subject to those restrictions, make any one or more of the orders mentioned in subsection (1)(d), (e) and (f) above –
(a) in any proceedings for divorce, nullity of marriage or judicial separation, before granting a decree; and
(b) where any such proceedings are dismissed after the beginning of the trial, either forthwith or within a reasonable period after the dismissal.
(3) Without prejudice to the generality of subsection (1)(c) or (f) above –
(a) an order under this section that a party to a marriage shall pay a lump sum to the other party may be made for the purpose of enabling that other party to meet any liabilities or expenses reasonably incurred by him or her in maintaining himself or herself or any child of the family before making an application for an order under

Matrimonial Causes Act 1973

this section in his or her favour;
- (b) an order under this section for the payment of a lump sum to or for the benefit of a child of the family may be made for the purpose of enabling any liabilities or expenses reasonably incurred by or for the benefit of that child before the making of an application for an order under this section in his favour to be met; and
- (c) an order under this section for the payment of a lump sum may provide for the payment of that sum by instalments of such amount as may be specified in the order and may require the payment of the instalments to be secured to the satisfaction of the court.

(4) The power of the court under subsection (1) or (2)(a) above to make an order in favour of a child of the family shall be exercisable from time to time; and where the court makes an order in favour of a child under subsection (2)(b) above, it may from time to time, subject to the restrictions mentioned in subsection (1) above, make a further order in his favour of any of the kinds mentioned in subsection (1)(d), (e) or (f) above.

(5) Without prejudice to the power to give a direction under section 30 below for the settlement of an instrument by conveyancing counsel, where an order is made under subsection (1)(a), (b) or (c) above on or after granting a decree of divorce or nullity of marriage, neither the order nor any settlement made in pursuance of the order shall take effect unless the decree has been made absolute.

(6) Where the court –
- (a) makes an order under this section for the payment of a lump sum; and
- (b) directs –
  - (i) that payment of that sum or any part of it shall be deferred; or
  - (ii) that that sum or any part of it shall be paid by instalments,

the court may order that the amount deferred or the instalments shall carry interest at such rate as may be specified by the order from such date, not earlier than the date of the order, as may be so specified, until the date when payment of it is due.

24. Property adjustment orders in connection with divorce proceedings, etc

(1) On granting a decree of divorce, a decree of nullity of marriage or a decree of judicial separation or at any time thereafter (whether, in the case of a decree of divorce or of nullity of marriage, before or after the decree is made absolute), the court may make any one or more of the following orders, that is to say –
- (a) an order that a party to the marriage shall transfer to the other party, to any child of the family or to such person as may be specified in the order for the benefit of such a child such property as may be so specified, being property to which the first-mentioned party is entitled, either in possession or reversion;
- (b) an order that a settlement of such property as may be so specified, being property to which a party to the marriage is so entitled, be made to the satisfaction of the court for the benefit of the other party to the marriage and of the children of the family or either or any of them;
- (c) an order varying for the benefit of the parties to the marriage and of the children of the family or either or any of them any ante-nuptial or post-nuptial settlement (including such a settlement made by will or codicil) made on the parties to the marriage, other than one in the form of a pension arrangement (within the meaning of section 25D below);
- (d) an order extinguishing or reducing the interest of either of the parties to the marriage under any such settlement, other than one in the form of a pension arrangement (within the meaning of section 25D below);

subject, however, in the case of an order under paragraph (a) above, to the restrictions imposed by section 29(1) and (3) below on the making of orders for a transfer of property in favour of children who have attained the age of eighteen.

(2) The court may make an order under subsection (1)(c) above notwithstanding that there are no children of the family.

(3) Without prejudice to the power to give a direction under section 30 below for the settlement of an instrument by conveyancing counsel, where an order is made under this section on or after granting a decree of divorce or nullity of marriage, neither the order nor any settlement made in pursuance of the order shall take effect unless the decree has been made absolute.

24A. Orders for sale of property

(1) Where the court makes an order under section 22ZA or makes under section 23 or 24 of this Act a secured periodical payments order, an order for the payment of a lump sum or a property adjustment order, then, on making that order or at any time thereafter, the court may make a further order for the sale of such property as may be specified in the order, being property in which or in the proceeds of sale of which either or both of the parties to the marriage has or have a beneficial interest, either in possession or reversion.

(2) Any order made under subsection (1) above may contain such consequential or supplementary provisions as the court thinks fit and, without prejudice to the generality of the foregoing provision, may include –
- (a) provision requiring the making of a payment out of the proceeds of sale of the property to which the order relates, and
- (b) provision requiring any such property to be offered for sale to a person, or class of persons, specified in the order.

Matrimonial Causes Act 1973

(3) Where an order is made under subsection (1) above on or after the grant of a decree of divorce or nullity of marriage, the order shall not take effect unless the decree has been made absolute.

(4) Where an order is made under subsection (1) above, the court may direct that the order, or such provision thereof as the court may specify, shall not take effect until the occurrence of an event specified by the court or the expiration of a period so specified.

(5) Where an order under subsection (1) above contains a provision requiring the proceeds of sale of the property to which the order relates to be used to secure periodical payments to a party to the marriage, the order shall cease to have effect on the death or re-marriage of, or formation of a civil partnership by, that person.

(6) Where a party to a marriage has a beneficial interest in any property, or in the proceeds of sale thereof, and some other person who is not a party to the marriage also has a beneficial interest in that property or in the proceeds of sale thereof, then, before deciding whether to make an order under this section in relation to that property, it shall be the duty of the court to give that other person an opportunity to make representations with respect to the order; and any representations made by that other person shall be included among the circumstances to which the court is required to have regard under section 25(1) below.

24B. Pension sharing orders in connection with divorce proceedings etc

(1) On granting a decree of divorce or a decree of nullity of marriage or at any time thereafter (whether before or after the decree is made absolute), the court may, on an application made under this section, make one or more pension sharing orders in relation to the marriage.

(2) A pension sharing order under this section is not to take effect unless the decree on or after which it is made has been made absolute.

(3) A pension sharing order under this section may not be made in relation to a pension arrangement which –
(a) is the subject of a pension sharing order in relation to the marriage, or
(b) has been the subject of pension sharing between the parties to the marriage.

(4) A pension sharing order under this section may not be made in relation to shareable state scheme rights if –
(a) such rights are the subject of a pension sharing order in relation to the marriage, or
(b) such rights have been the subject of pension sharing between the parties to the marriage.

(5) A pension sharing order under this section may not be made in relation to the rights of a person under a pension arrangement if there is in force a requirement imposed by virtue of section 25B or 25C below which relates to benefits or future benefits to which he is entitled under the pension arrangement.

24C. Pension sharing orders: duty to stay

(1) No pension sharing order may be made so as to take effect before the end of such period after the making of the order as may be prescribed by regulations made by the Lord Chancellor.

(2) The power to make regulations under this section shall be exercisable by statutory instrument which shall be subject to annulment in pursuance of a resolution of either House of Parliament.

24D. Pension sharing orders: apportionment of charges
If a pension sharing order relates to rights under a pension arrangement, the court may include in the order provision about the apportionment between the parties of any charge under section 41 of the Welfare Reform and Pensions Act 1999 (charges in respect of pension sharing costs), or under corresponding Northern Ireland legislation.

Sections 24E to 24G (pension compensation sharing orders) are not reproduced.

25. Matters to which court is to have regard in deciding how to exercise its powers under ss 23, 24, 24A, 24B and 24E

(1) It shall be the duty of the court in deciding whether to exercise its powers under section 23, 24, 24A, 24B or 24E above and, if so, in what manner, to have regard to all the circumstances of the case, first consideration being given to the welfare while a minor of any child of the family who has not attained the age of eighteen.

(2) As regards the exercise of the powers of the court under section 23(1)(a), (b) or (c), 24, 24A, 24B or 24E above in relation to a party to the marriage, the court shall in particular have regard to the following matters –
(a) the income, earning capacity, property and other financial resources which each of the parties to the marriage has or is likely to have in the foreseeable future, including in the case of earning capacity any increase in that capacity which it would in the opinion of the court be reasonable to expect a party to the marriage to take steps to acquire;
(b) the financial needs, obligations and responsibilities which each of the parties to the marriage has or is likely to have in the foreseeable future;
(c) the standard of living enjoyed by the family before the breakdown of the marriage;
(d) the age of each party to the marriage and the duration of the marriage;
(e) any physical or mental disability of either of the parties to the marriage;
(f) the contributions which each of the parties has made or is likely in the foreseeable future to make to the welfare of the family, including any contribution by looking after the home or caring for the family;

Matrimonial Causes Act 1973

   (g) the conduct of each of the parties, if that conduct is such that it would in the opinion of the court be inequitable to disregard it;
   (h) in the case of proceedings for divorce or nullity of marriage, the value to each of the parties to the marriage of any benefit which, by reason of the dissolution or annulment of the marriage, that party will lose the chance of acquiring.
(3) As regards the exercise of the powers of the court under section 23(1)(d), (e) or (f), (2) or (4), 24 or 24A above in relation to a child of the family, the court shall in particular have regard to the following matters:
   (a) the financial needs of the child;
   (b) the income, earning capacity (if any), property and other financial resources of the child;
   (c) any physical or mental disability of the child;
   (d) the manner in which he was being and in which the parties to the marriage expected him to be educated or trained;
   (e) the considerations mentioned in relation to the parties to the marriage in paragraphs (a), (b), (c) and (e) of subsection (2) above.
(4) As regards the exercise of the powers of the court under section 23(1)(d), (e) or (f), (2) or (4), 24 or 24A above against a party to a marriage in favour of a child of the family who is not the child of that party, the court shall also have regard –
   (a) to whether that party assumed any responsibility for the child's maintenance, and, if so, to the extent to which, and the basis upon which, that party assumed such responsibility and to the length of time for which that party discharged such responsibility;
   (b) to whether in assuming and discharging such responsibility that party did so knowing that the child was not his or her own;
   (c) to the liability of any other person to maintain the child.

25A. Exercise of court's powers in favour of party to marriage on decree of divorce or nullity of marriage
(1) Where on or after the grant of a decree of divorce or nullity of marriage the court decides to exercise its powers under section 23(1)(a), (b) or (c), 24, 24A, 24B or 24E above in favour of a party to the marriage, it shall be the duty of the court to consider whether it would be appropriate so to exercise those powers that the financial obligations of each party towards the other will be terminated as soon after the grant of the decree as the court considers just and reasonable.
(2) Where the court decides in such a case to make a periodical payments or secured periodical payments order in favour of a party to the marriage, the court shall in particular consider whether it would be appropriate to require those payments to be made or secured only for such term as would in the opinion of the court be sufficient to enable the party in whose favour the order is made to adjust without undue hardship to the termination of his or her financial dependence on the other party.
(3) Where on or after the grant of a decree of divorce or nullity of marriage an application is made by a party to the marriage for a periodical payments or secured periodical payments order in his or her favour, then, if the court considers that no continuing obligation should be imposed on either party to make or secure periodical payments in favour of the other, the court may dismiss the application with a direction that the applicant shall not be entitled to make any future application in relation to that marriage for an order under section 23(1)(a) or (b) above.

25B. Pensions
   (1) The matters to which the court is to have regard under section 25(2) above include –
   (a) in the case of paragraph (a), any benefits under a pension arrangement which a party to the marriage has or is likely to have, and
   (b) in the case of paragraph (h), any benefits under a pension arrangement which, by reason of the dissolution or annulment of the marriage, a party to the marriage will lose the chance of acquiring,
and, accordingly, in relation to benefits under a pension arrangement, section 25(2)(a) above shall have effect as if 'in the foreseeable future' were omitted.
   (2) [*repealed*]
   (3) The following provisions apply where, having regard to any benefits under a pension arrangement, the court determines to make an order under section 23 above.
   (4) To the extent to which the order is made having regard to any benefits under a pension arrangement, the order may require the person responsible for the pension arrangement in question, if at any time any payment in respect of any benefits under the arrangement becomes due to the party with pension rights, to make a payment for the benefit of the other party.
   (5) The order must express the amount of any payment required to be made by virtue of subsection (4) above as a percentage of the payment which becomes due to the party with pension rights.
   (6) Any such payment by the person responsible for the arrangement –
   (a) shall discharge so much of his liability to the party with pension rights as corresponds to the amount of the payment, and

Matrimonial Causes Act 1973

(b) shall be treated for all purposes as a payment made by the party with pension rights in or towards the discharge of his liability under the order.

(7) Where the party with pension rights has a right of commutation under the arrangement, the order may require him to exercise it to any extent; and this section applies to any payment due in consequence of commutation in pursuance of the order as it applies to other payments in respect of benefits under the arrangement.

(7A) The power conferred by subsection (7) above may not be exercised for the purpose of commuting a benefit payable to the party with pension rights to a benefit payable to the other party.

(7B) The power conferred by subsection (4) or (7) above may not be exercised in relation to a pension arrangement which –
(a) is the subject of a pension sharing order in relation to the marriage, or
(b) has been the subject of pension sharing between the parties to the marriage.

(7C) In subsection (1) above, references to benefits under a pension arrangement include any benefits by way of pension, whether under a pension arrangement or not.

25C. Pensions: lump sums

(1) The power of the court under section 23 above to order a party to a marriage to pay a lump sum to the other party includes, where the benefits which the party with pension rights has or is likely to have under a pension arrangement include any lump sum payable in respect of his death, power to make any of the following provision by the order.

(2) The court may –
(a) if the person responsible for the pension arrangement in question has power to determine the person to whom the sum, or any part of it, is to be paid, require him to pay the whole or part of that sum, when it becomes due, to the other party,
(b) if the party with pension rights has power to nominate the person to whom the sum, or any part of it, is to be paid, require the party with pension rights to nominate the other party in respect of the whole or part of that sum,
(c) in any other case, require the person responsible for the pension arrangement in question to pay the whole or part of that sum, when it becomes due, for the benefit of the other party instead of to the person to whom, apart from the order, it would be paid.

(3) Any payment by the person responsible for the arrangement under an order made under section 23 above by virtue of this section shall discharge so much of his liability in respect of the party with pension rights as corresponds to the amount of the payment.

(4) The powers conferred by this section may not be exercised in relation to a pension arrangement which –
(a) is the subject of a pension sharing order in relation to the marriage, or
(b) has been the subject of pension sharing between the parties to the marriage.

25D. Pensions: supplementary

(1) Where –
(a) an order made under section 23 above by virtue of section 25B or 25C above imposes any requirement on the person responsible for a pension arrangement ('the first arrangement') and the party with pension rights acquires rights under another pension arrangement ('the new arrangement') which are derived (directly or indirectly) from the whole of his rights under the first arrangement, and
(b) the person responsible for the new arrangement has been given notice in accordance with regulations made by the Lord Chancellor,
the order shall have effect as if it had been made instead in respect of the person responsible for the new arrangement.

(2) The Lord Chancellor may by regulations –
(a) in relation to any provision of sections 25B or 25C above which authorises the court making an order under section 23 above to require the person responsible for a pension arrangement to make a payment for the benefit of the other party, make provision as to the person to whom, and the terms on which, the payment is to be made,
(ab) make, in relation to payment under a mistaken belief as to the continuation in force of a provision included by virtue of section 25B or 25C above in an order under section 23 above, provision about the rights or liabilities of the payer, the payee or the person to whom the payment was due,
(b) require notices to be given in respect of changes of circumstances relevant to such orders which include provision made by virtue of sections 25B and 25C above,
(ba) make provision for the person responsible for a pension arrangement to be discharged in prescribed circumstances from a requirement imposed by virtue of section 25B or 25C above,
(e) make provision about calculation and verification in relation to the valuation of –
(i) benefits under a pension arrangement, or
(ii) shareable state scheme rights,
for the purposes of the court's functions in connection with the exercise of any of its powers under this Part of this Act.

Matrimonial Causes Act 1973

(2A) Regulations under subsection (2)(e) above may include –
(a) provision for calculation or verification in accordance with guidance from time to time prepared by a prescribed person, and
(b) provision by reference to regulations under section 30 or 49(4) of the Welfare Reform and Pensions Act 1999.

(2B) Regulations under subsection (2) above may make different provision for different cases.

(2C) Power to make regulations under this section shall be exercisable by statutory instrument which shall be subject to annulment in pursuance of a resolution of either House of Parliament.

(3) In this section and sections 25B and 25C above –
'occupational pension scheme' has the same meaning as in the Pension Schemes Act 1993;
'the party with pension rights' means the party to the marriage who has or is likely to have benefits under a pension arrangement and 'the other party' means the other party to the marriage;
'pension arrangement' means –
(a) an occupational pension scheme,
(b) a personal pension scheme,
(c) a retirement annuity contract,
(d) an annuity or insurance policy purchased, or transferred, for the purpose of giving effect to rights under an occupational pension scheme or a personal pension scheme, and
(e) an annuity purchased, or entered into, for the purpose of discharging liability in respect of a pension credit under section 29(1)(b) of the Welfare Reform and Pensions Act 1999 or under corresponding Northern Ireland legislation;
'personal pension scheme' has the same meaning as in the Pension Schemes Act 1993;
'prescribed' means prescribed by regulations;
'retirement annuity contract' means a contract or scheme approved under Chapter III of Part XIV of the Income and Corporation Taxes Act 1988;
'shareable state scheme rights' has the same meaning as in section 21A(1) above; and
'trustees or managers', in relation to an occupational pension scheme or a personal pension scheme, means –
(a) in the case of a scheme established under a trust, the trustees of the scheme, and
(b) in any other case, the managers of the scheme.

(4) In this section and sections 25B and 25C above, references to the person responsible for a pension arrangement are –
(a) in the case of an occupational pension scheme or a personal pension scheme, to the trustees or managers of the scheme,
(b) in the case of a retirement annuity contract or an annuity falling within paragraph (d) or (e) of the definition of 'pension arrangement' above, the provider of the annuity, and
(c) in the case of an insurance policy falling within paragraph (d) of the definition of that expression, the insurer.

The former subss. (2)(c) and (2)(d) of section 25D have been repealed. Sections 25E (The Pension Protection Fund), 25F (pension compensation attachment orders) and 25G (supplementary) are not reproduced.

* * * * *

28. Duration of continuing financial provision orders in favour or party to marriage, and effect of remarriage or formation of civil partnership

(1) Subject in the case of an order made on or after the grant of a decree of a divorce or nullity of marriage to the provisions of sections 25A(2) above and 31(7) below, the term to be specified in a periodical payments or secured periodical payments order in favour of a party to a marriage shall be such term as the court thinks fit, except that the term shall not begin before or extend beyond the following limits, that is to say –
(a) in the case of a periodical payments order, the term shall begin not earlier than the date of the making of an application for the order, and shall be so defined as not to extend beyond the death of either of the parties to the marriage or, where the order is made on or after the grant of a decree of divorce or nullity of marriage, the remarriage of, or formation of a civil partnership by, the party in whose favour the order is made; and
(b) in the case of a secured periodical payments order, the term shall begin not earlier than the date of the making of an application for the order, and shall be so defined as not to extend beyond the death or, where the order is made on or after the grant of such a decree, the remarriage of, or formation of a civil partnership by, the party in whose favour the order is made.

(1A) Where a periodical payments or secured periodical payments order in favour of a party to a marriage is made on or after the grant of a decree of divorce or nullity of marriage, the court may direct that that party shall not be entitled to apply under section 31 below for the extension of the term specified in the order.

(2) Where a periodical payments or secured periodical payments order in favour of a party to a marriage is made otherwise than on or after the grant of a decree of divorce or nullity of marriage, and the marriage in question is

Matrimonial Causes Act 1973

subsequently dissolved or annulled but the order continues in force, the order shall, notwithstanding anything in it, cease to have effect on the remarriage of, or formation of a civil partnership by, that party, except in relation to any arrears due under it on the date of the remarriage or formation of the civil partnership.

(3) If after the grant of a decree dissolving or annulling a marriage either party to that marriage remarries whether at any time before or after the commencement of this Act or forms a civil partnership, that party shall not be entitled to apply, by reference to the grant of that decree, for a financial provision order in his or her favour, or for a property adjustment order, against the other party to that marriage.

29. Duration of continuing financial provision orders in favour of children, and age limit on making certain orders in their favour

(1) Subject to subsection (3) below, no financial provision order and no order for a transfer of property under section 24(1)(a) above shall be made in favour of a child who has attained the age of eighteen.

(2) The term to be specified in a periodical payments or secured periodical payments order in favour of a child may begin with the date of the making of an application for the order in question or any later date or a date ascertained in accordance with subsection (5) or (6) below but –
  (a) shall not in the first instance extend beyond the date of the birthday of the child next following his attaining the upper limit of the compulsory school age (construed in accordance with section 8 of the Education Act 1996) unless the court considers that in the circumstances of the case the welfare of the child requires that it should extend to a later date; and
  (b) shall not in any event, subject to subsection (3) below, extend beyond the date of the child's eighteenth birthday.

(3) Subsection (1) above, and paragraph (b) of subsection (2), shall not apply in the case of a child, if it appears to the court that –
  (a) the child is, or will be, or if an order were made without complying with either or both of those provisions would be, receiving instruction at an educational establishment or undergoing training for a trade, profession or vocation, whether or not he is also, or will also be, in gainful employment; or
  (b) there are special circumstances which justify the making of an order without complying with either or both of those provisions.

(4) Any periodical payments order in favour of a child shall, notwithstanding anything in the order, cease to have effect on the death of the person liable to make payments under the order, except in relation to any arrears due under the order on the date of the death.

(5) Where –
(a) a maintenance calculation ('the current calculation') is in force with respect to a child; and
(b) an application is made under Part II of this Act for a periodical payments or secured periodical payments order in favour of that child –
  (i) in accordance with section 8 of the Child Support Act 1991, and
  (ii) before the end of the period of 6 months beginning with the making of the current calculation,
the term to be specified in any such order made on that application may be expressed to begin on, or at any time after, the earliest permitted date.

(6) For the purposes of subsection (5) above, 'the earliest permitted date' is whichever is the later of–
(a) the date 6 months before the application is made; or
(b) the date on which the current calculation took effect or, where successive maintenance calculations have been continuously in force with respect to a child, on which the first of those calculations took effect.

(7) Where –
(a) a maintenance calculation ceases to have effect or is cancelled by or under any provision of the Child Support Act 1991; and
(b) an application is made, before the end of the period of 6 months beginning with the relevant date, for a periodical payments or secured periodical payments order in favour of a child with respect to whom that maintenance calculation was in force immediately before it ceased to have effect or was cancelled,
the term to be specified in any such order made on that application may begin with the date on which that maintenance calculation ceased to have effect or, as the case may be, the date with effect from which it was cancelled, or any later date.

(8) In subsection (7)(b) above –
(a) where the maintenance calculation ceased to have effect, the relevant date is the date on which it so ceased;
(b) [*repealed*].

* * * * *

31. Variation, discharge, etc, of certain orders for financial relief

(1) Where the court has made an order to which this section applies, then, subject to the provisions of this section and of section 28(1A) above, the court shall have power to vary or discharge the order or to suspend any

Matrimonial Causes Act 1973

provision thereof temporarily and to revive the operation of any provision so suspended.

(2) This section applies to the following orders, that is to say –
  (a) any order for maintenance pending suit and any interim order for maintenance;
  (b) any periodical payments order;
  (c) any secured periodical payments order;
  (d) any order made by virtue of section 23(3)(c) or 27(7)(b) above (provision for payment of a lump sum by instalments);
  (dd) any deferred order made by virtue of section 23(1)(c) (lump sums) which includes provision made by virtue of –
    (i) section 25B(4),
    (ii) section 25C, or
    (iii) section 25F(2),
    (provision in respect of pension rights or pension compensation rights);
  (e) any order for a settlement of property under section 24(1)(b) or for a variation of settlement under section 24(1)(c) or (d) above, being an order made on or after the grant of a decree of judicial separation;
  (f) any order made under section 24A(1) above for the sale of property;
  (g) a pension sharing order under section 24B above, or a pension compensation sharing order under section 24E above, which is made at a time before the decree has been made absolute.

(2A) Where the court has made an order referred to in subsection (2)(a), (b) or (c) above, then, subject to the provisions of this section, the court shall have power to remit the payment of any arrears due under the order or of any part thereof.

(2B) Where the court has made an order referred to in subsection (2)(dd)(ii) above, this section shall cease to apply to the order on the death of either of the parties to the marriage.

(3) The powers exercisable by the court under this section in relation to an order shall be exercisable also in relation to any instrument executed in pursuance of the order.

(4) The court shall not exercise the powers conferred by this section in relation to an order for a settlement under section 24(1)(b) or for a variation of settlement under section 24(1)(c) or (d) above except on an application made in proceedings –
  (a) for the rescission of the decree of judicial separation by reference to which the order was made, or
  (b) for the dissolution of the marriage in question.

(4A) In relation to an order which falls within paragraph (g) of subsection (2) above ('the subsection (2) order') –
  (a) the powers conferred by this section may be exercised –
    (i) only on an application made before the subsection (2) order has or, but for paragraph (b) below, would have taken effect; and
    (ii) only if, at the time when the application is made, the decree has not been made absolute; and
  (b) an application made in accordance with paragraph (a) above prevents the subsection (2) order from taking effect before the application has been dealt with.

(4B) No variation of a pension sharing order, or a pension compensation sharing order, shall be made so as to take effect before the decree is made absolute.

(4C) The variation of a pension sharing order, or a pension compensation sharing order, prevents the order taking effect before the end of such period after the making of the variation as may be prescribed by regulations made by the Lord Chancellor.

(5) Subject to subsections (7A) to (7G) below and without prejudice to any power exercisable by virtue of subsection (2)(d), (dd), (e) or (g) above or otherwise than by virtue of this section, no property adjustment order or pension sharing order, or pension compensation sharing order, shall be made on an application for the variation of a periodical payments or secured periodical payments order made (whether in favour of a party to a marriage or in favour of a child of the family) under section 23 above, and no order for the payment of a lump sum shall be made on an application for the variation of a periodical payments or secured periodical payments order in favour of a party to a marriage (whether made under section 23 or under section 27 above).

(6) Where the person liable to make payments under a secured periodical payments order has died, an application under this section relating to that order (and to any order made under section 24A(1) above which requires the proceeds of sale of property to be used for securing those payments) may be made by the person entitled to payments under the periodical payments order or by the personal representatives of the deceased person, but no such application shall, except with the permission of the court, be made after the end of the period of six months from the date on which representation in regard to the estate of that person is first taken out.

(7) In exercising the powers conferred by this section the court shall have regard to all the circumstances of the case, first consideration being given to the welfare while a minor of any child of the family who has not attained the age of eighteen, and the circumstances of the case shall include any change in any of the matters to which the court was required to have regard when making the order to which the application relates, and –
  (a) in the case of a periodical payments or secured periodical payments order made on or after the grant of a decree of divorce or nullity of marriage, the court shall consider whether in all the circumstances and after having regard to any such change it would be appropriate to vary the order so that payments under the order

Matrimonial Causes Act 1973

are required to be made or secured only for such further period as will in the opinion of the court be sufficient (in the light of any proposed exercise by the court, where the marriage has been dissolved, of its powers under subsection (7B) below) to enable the party in whose favour the order was made to adjust without undue hardship to the termination of those payments;

(b) in a case where the party against whom the order was made has died, the circumstances of the case shall also include the changed circumstances resulting from his or her death.

(7A) Subsection (7B) below applies where, after the dissolution of a marriage, the court –

(a) discharges a periodical payments order or secured periodical payments order made in favour of a party to the marriage; or

(b) varies such an order so that payments under the order are required to be made or secured only for such further period as is determined by the court.

(7B) The court has power, in addition to any power it has apart from this subsection, to make supplemental provision consisting of any of –

(a) an order for the payment of a lump sum in favour of a party to the marriage;
(b) one or more property adjustment orders in favour of a party to the marriage;
(ba) one or more pension sharing orders;
(bb) a pension compensation sharing order;
(c) a direction that the party in whose favour the original order discharged or varied was made is not entitled to make any further application for –
  (i) a periodical payments or secured periodical payments order, or
  (ii) an extension of the period to which the original order is limited by any variation made by the court.

(7C) An order for the payment of a lump sum made under subsection (7B) above may –
(a) provide for the payment of that sum by instalments of such amount as may be specified in the order; and
(b) require the payment of the instalments to be secured to the satisfaction of the court.

(7D) Section 23(6) above apply where the court makes an order for the payment of a lump sum under subsection (7B) above as they apply where it makes such an order under section 23 above.

(7E) If under subsection (7B) above the court makes more than one property adjustment order in favour of the same party to the marriage, each of those orders must fall within a different paragraph of section 21(2) above.

(7F) Sections 24A and 30 above apply where the court makes a property adjustment order under subsection (7B) above as they apply where it makes such an order under section 24 above.

(7G) Subsections (3) to (5) of section 24B above apply in relation to a pension sharing order under subsection (7B) above as they apply in relation to a pension sharing order under that section.

(7H) Subsections (3) to (10) of section 24E above apply in relation to a pension compensation sharing order under subsection (7B) above as they apply in relation to a pension compensation sharing order under that section.

(8) The personal representatives of a deceased person against whom a secured periodical payments order was made shall not be liable for having distributed any part of the estate of the deceased after the expiration of the period of six months referred to in subsection (6) above on the ground that they ought to have taken into account the possibility that the court might permit an application under this section to be made after that period by the person entitled to payments under the order; but this subsection shall not prejudice any power to recover any part of the estate so distributed arising by virtue of the making of an order in pursuance of this section.

(9) In considering for the purposes of subsection (6) above the question when representation was first taken out, a grant limited to settled land or to trust property shall be left out of account and a grant limited to real estate or to personal estate shall be left out of account unless a grant limited to the remainder of the estate has previously been made or is made at the same time.

(10) Where the court, in exercise of its powers under this section, decides to vary or discharge a periodical payments or secured periodical payments order, then, subject to section 28(1) and (2) above, the court shall have power to direct that the variation or discharge shall not take effect until the expiration of such period as may be specified in the order.

Subss. (11) to (15) of section 31 have not been reproduced.

32. Payment of certain arrears unenforceable without the leave of the court

(1) A person shall not be entitled to enforce through the High Court or any county court the payment of any arrears due under an order for maintenance pending suit, an interim order for maintenance or any financial provision order without the leave of that court if those arrears became due more than twelve months before proceedings to enforce the payment of them are begun.

(2) The court hearing an application for the grant of leave under this section may refuse leave, or may grant leave subject to such restrictions and conditions (including conditions as to the allowing of time for payment or the making of payment by instalments) as that court thinks proper, or may remit the payment of the arrears or of any part thereof.

(3) An application for the grant of leave under this section shall be made in such manner as may be prescribed by rules of court.

Matrimonial Causes Act 1973

* * * *

34. Validity of maintenance agreements

(1) If a maintenance agreement includes a provision purporting to restrict any right to apply to a court for an order containing financial arrangements, then –
  (a) that provision shall be void; but
  (b) any other financial arrangements contained in the agreement shall not thereby be rendered void or unenforceable and shall, unless they are void or unenforceable for any other reason (and subject to sections 35 and 36 below), be binding on the parties to the agreement.

(2) In this section and in section 35 below –
'maintenance agreement' means any agreement in writing made, whether before or after the commencement of this Act, between the parties to a marriage, being
  (a) an agreement containing financial arrangements, whether made during the continuance or after the dissolution or annulment of the marriage; or
  (b) a separation agreement which contains no financial arrangements in a case where no other agreement in writing between the same parties contains such arrangements;
'financial arrangements' means provisions governing the rights and liabilities towards one another when living separately of the parties to a marriage (including a marriage which has been dissolved or annulled) in respect of the making or securing of payments or the disposition or use of any property, including such rights and liabilities with respect to the maintenance or education of any child, whether or not a child of the family.

35. Alteration of agreements by court during lives of parties

(1) Where a maintenance agreement is for the time being subsisting and each of the parties to the agreement is for the time being either domiciled or resident in England and Wales, then, subject to subsections (1A) and (3) below, either party may apply to the court or to a magistrates' court for an order under this section.

(1A) If an application or part of an application relates to a matter where jurisdiction falls to be determined by reference to the jurisdictional requirements of the Maintenance Regulation and Schedule 6 to the Civil Jurisdiction and Judgments (Maintenance) Regulations 2011—
  (a) the requirement as to domicile or residence in subsection (1) does not apply to the application or that part of it, but
  (b) the court may not entertain the application or that part of it unless it has jurisdiction to do so by virtue of that Regulation and that Schedule.

(2) If the court to which the application is made is satisfied either –
  (a) that by reason of a change in the circumstances in the light of which any financial arrangements contained in the agreement were made or, as the case may be, financial arrangements were omitted from it (including a change foreseen by the parties when making the agreement), the agreement should be altered so as to make different, or, as the case may be, so as to contain, financial arrangements, or
  (b) that the agreement does not contain proper financial arrangements with respect to any child of the family,
then subject to subsections (3), (4) and (5) below, that court may by order make such alterations in the agreement –
    (i) by varying or revoking any financial arrangements contained in it, or
    (ii) by inserting in it financial arrangements for the benefit of one of the parties to the agreement or of a child of the family,
as may appear to that court to be just having regard to all the circumstances, including, if relevant, the matters mentioned in section 25(4) above;
and the agreement shall have effect thereafter as if any alteration made by the order had been made by agreement between the parties and for valuable consideration.

(3) A magistrates' court shall not entertain an application under subsection (1) above unless both the parties to the agreement are resident in England and Wales and the court acts in, or is authorised by the Lord Chancellor to act for, a local justice area in which at least one of the parties is resident, and shall not have power to make any order on such an application except –
  (a) where in a case where the agreement includes no provision for periodical payments by either of the parties, an order inserting provision for the making by one of the parties of periodical payments for the maintenance of the other party or for the maintenance of any child of the family;
  (b) in a case where the agreement includes provision for the making by one of the parties of periodical payments, an order increasing or reducing the rate of, or terminating, any of those payments.

(4) Where a court decides to alter, by order under this section, an agreement by inserting provision for the making or securing by one of the parties to the agreement of periodical payments for the maintenance of the other party or by increasing the rate of the periodical payments which the agreement provides shall be made by one of the parties for the maintenance of the other, the term for which the payments or, as the case may be, the additional payments attributable to the increase are to be made under the agreement as altered by the order shall be such term as the court may specify, subject to the following limits, that is to say –
  (a) where the payments will not be secured, the term shall be so defined as not to extend beyond the death of either

Matrimonial Causes Act 1973

of the parties to the agreement or the remarriage of, or formation of a civil partnership by, the party to whom the payments are to be made;
   (b) where the payments will be secured, the term shall be so defined as not to extend beyond the death or remarriage of, or formation of a civil partnership by, that party.
(5) Where a court decides to alter, by order under this section, an agreement by inserting provision for the making or securing by one of the parties to the agreement of periodical payments for the maintenance of a child of the family or by increasing the rate of the periodical payments which the agreement provides shall be made or secured by one of the parties for the maintenance of such a child, then, in deciding the term for which under the agreement as altered by the order the payments, or as the case may be, the additional payments attributable to the increase are to be made or secured for the benefit of the child, the court shall apply the provisions of section 29(2) and (3) above as to age limits as if the order in question were a periodical payments or secured periodical payments order in favour of the child.
(6) For the avoidance of doubt it is hereby declared that nothing in this section or in section 34 above affects any power of a court before which any proceedings between the parties to a maintenance agreement are brought under any other enactment (including a provision of this Act) to make an order containing financial arrangements or any right of either party to apply for such an order in such proceedings.

* * * * *

37. Avoidance of transactions intended to prevent or reduce financial relief
   (1) For the purposes of this section 'financial relief' means relief under any of the provisions of sections 22, 23, 24, 24B, 27, 31 (except subsection (6)) and 35 above, and any reference in this section to defeating a person's claim for financial relief is a reference to preventing financial relief from being granted to that person, or to that person for the benefit of a child of the family, or reducing the amount of any financial relief which might be so granted, or frustrating or impeding the enforcement of any order which might be or has been made at his instance under any of those provisions.
   (2) Where proceedings for financial relief are brought by one person against another, the court may, on the application of the first-mentioned person –
      (a) if it is satisfied that the other party to the proceedings is, with the intention of defeating the claim for financial relief, about to make any disposition or to transfer out of the jurisdiction or otherwise deal with any property, make such order as it thinks fit for restraining the other party from so doing or otherwise for protecting the claim;
      (b) if it is satisfied that the other party has, with that intention, made a reviewable disposition and that if the disposition were set aside financial relief or different financial relief would be granted to the applicant, make an order setting aside the disposition;
      (c) if it is satisfied, in a case where an order has been obtained under any of the provisions mentioned in subsection (1) above by the applicant against the other party, that the other party has, with that intention, made a reviewable disposition, make an order setting aside the disposition;
   and an application for the purposes of paragraph (b) above shall be made in the proceedings for the financial relief in question.
   (3) Where the court makes an order under subsection (2)(b) or (c) above setting aside a disposition it shall give such consequential directions as it thinks fit for giving effect to the order (including directions requiring the making of any payments or the disposal of any property).
   (4) Any disposition made by the other party to the proceedings for financial relief in question (whether before or after the commencement of those proceedings) is a reviewable disposition for the purposes of subsection (2)(b) and (c) above unless it was made for valuable consideration (other than marriage) to a person who, at the time of the disposition, acted in relation to it in good faith and without notice of any intention on the part of the other party to defeat the applicant's claim for financial relief.
   (5) Where an application is made under this section with respect to a disposition which took place less than three years before the date of the application or with respect to a disposition or other dealing with property which is about to take place and the court is satisfied –
      (a) in a case falling within subsection (2)(a) or (b) above, that the disposition or other dealing would (apart from this section) have the consequence, or
      (b) in a case falling within subsection (2)(c) above, that the disposition has had the consequence,
   of defeating the applicant's claim for financial relief, it shall be presumed, unless the contrary is shown, that the person who disposed of or is about to dispose of or deal with the property did so or, as the case may be, is about to do so, with the intention of defeating the applicant's claim for financial relief.
   (6) In this section 'disposition' does not include any provision contained in a will or codicil but, with that exception, includes any conveyance, assurance or gift of property of any description, whether made by an instrument or otherwise.
   (7) This section does not apply to a disposition made before 1st January 1968.

Financial Remedy Rules

The extracts from FPR 2010 (as amended by the Family Procedure (Amendment) Rules 2011, the Family Procedure (Amendment) Rules 2012 and the Family Procedure (Amendment) (No. 4) and (No. 5) Rules 2012)) and the accompanying PDs here set out mainly derive from Part 9 and PD 9A, but represent only a portion (though intended to be the most significant portion in daily use) of the new rules for financial remedy applications (both for financial orders and the other orders listed in rule 2.3(1)) issued in the High Court or county court on or after 6 April 2011.

For Transitional Provisions (a) see PD 36A re applications launched before 6 April 2011; (b) note that the amendments effected by the Family Procedure (Amendment) Rules 2012 are subject to their own savings and transitional provisions (see ibid., rule 30). This PD and rule are not reproduced here but may be viewed in @eGlance.

The procedural requirements of these rules are set out in tabular form at Table 31 and (in relation to pension sharing) at Table 27.

For comprehensive coverage of all 2010 (and subsequent Amendment) Rules and PDs affecting financial cases use @eGlance, which also contains all variants of the ancillary relief rules in force prior to 6 April 2011.

The overriding objective

1.1.—(1) These rules are a new procedural code with the overriding objective of enabling the court to deal with cases justly, having regard to any welfare issues involved.
(2) Dealing with a case justly includes, so far as is practicable—
   (a) ensuring that it is dealt with expeditiously and fairly;
   (b) dealing with the case in ways which are proportionate to the nature, importance and complexity of the issues;
   (c) ensuring that the parties are on an equal footing;
   (d) saving expense; and
   (e) allotting to it an appropriate share of the court's resources, while taking into account the need to allot resources to other cases.

Application by the court of the overriding objective

1.2. The court must seek to give effect to the overriding objective when it—
(a) exercises any power given to it by these rules; or
(b) interprets any rule.

Duty of the parties

1.3. The parties are required to help the court to further the overriding objective.

Court's duty to manage cases

1.4.—(1) The court must further the overriding objective by actively managing cases.
(2) Active case management includes—
   (a) setting timetables or otherwise controlling the progress of the case;
   (b) identifying at an early stage—
      (i) the issues; and
      (ii) who should be a party to the proceedings;
   (c) deciding promptly—
      (i) which issues need full investigation and hearing and which do not; and
      (ii) the procedure to be followed in the case;
   (d) deciding the order in which issues are to be resolved;
   (e) controlling the use of expert evidence;
   (f) encouraging the parties to use an alternative dispute resolution procedure if the court considers that appropriate and facilitating the use of such procedure;
   (g) helping the parties to settle the whole or part of the case;
   (h) encouraging the parties to co-operate with each other in the conduct of proceedings;
   (i) considering whether the likely benefits of taking a particular step justify the cost of taking it;
   (j) dealing with as many aspects of the case as it can on the same occasion;
   (k) dealing with the case without the parties needing to attend at court;
   (l) making use of technology; and
   (m) giving directions to ensure that the case proceeds quickly and efficiently.

* * * * * *

2.3.—(1) In these rules ...

"financial order" means—
(a) an avoidance of disposition order;
(b) an order for maintenance pending suit;
(c) an order for maintenance pending outcome of proceedings;
(d) an order for periodical payments or lump sum provision as mentioned in section 21(1) of the 1973 Act, except an order under section 27(6) of that Act;
(e) an order for periodical payments or lump sum provision as mentioned in paragraph 2(1) of Schedule 5 to the 2004 Act, made under Part 1 of Schedule 5 to that Act;
(f) a property adjustment order;
(g) a variation order;
(h) a pension sharing order; or
(i) a pension compensation sharing order;

("variation order", "pension compensation sharing order" and "pension sharing order" are defined in rule 9.3.)

"financial remedy" means—
(a) a financial order;
(b) an order under Schedule 1 to the 1989 Act;
(c) an order under Part 3 of the 1984 Act except an application under section 13 of the 1984 Act for permission to apply for a financial remedy;
(d) an order under Schedule 7 to the 2004 Act except an application under paragraph 4 of Schedule 7 to the 2004 Act for permission to apply for an order under paragraph 9 or 13 of that Schedule;
(e) an order under section 27 of the 1973 Act;
(f) an order under Part 9 of Schedule 5 to the 2004 Act;
(g) an order under section 35 of the 1973 Act;
(h) an order under paragraph 69 of Schedule 5 to the 2004 Act;
(i) an order under Part 1 of the 1978 Act;
(j) an order under Schedule 6 to the 2004 Act;
(k) an order under section 10(2) of the 1973 Act; or
(l) an order under section 48(2) of the 2004 Act;

* * * * * *

Application

9.1 The rules in this Part apply to an application for a financial remedy.

("Financial remedy" and "financial order" are defined in rule 2.3)

PD 9A: Introduction

1.1 Part 9 of the Family Procedure Rules sets out the procedure applicable to the financial proceedings that are included in the definition of a "financial remedy".

Financial Remedy Rules

1.2 The procedure is applicable to a limited extent to applications for financial remedies that are heard in magistrates' courts (namely, those under section 35 of the Matrimonial Causes Act 1973, paragraph 69 of Schedule 5 to the Civil Partnership Act 2004, Part I of the Domestic Proceedings and Magistrates' Courts Act 1978, Schedule 1 to the Children Act 1989 and Schedule 6 to the Civil Partnership Act 2004). However, unless the context otherwise requires, this Practice Direction does not apply to proceedings in a magistrates' court.

1.3 Where an application for a financial remedy includes an application relating to land, details of any mortgagee must be included in the application.

Pre-application protocol

2.1 The "pre-application protocol" annexed to this Direction [and reproduced at page 66] outlines the steps parties should take to seek and provide information from and to each other prior to the commencement of any application for a financial remedy. The court will expect the parties to comply with the terms of the protocol.

* * * * * *

When an Application for a financial order may be made

9.4. An application for a financial order may be made—
(a) in an application for a matrimonial or civil partnership order; or
(b) at any time after an application for a matrimonial or civil partnership order has been made.

* * * * * *

Application for an order preventing a disposition

9.6.— The Part 18 procedure applies to an application for an order preventing a disposition.

(2) An application for an order preventing a disposition may be made without notice to the respondent.

("Order preventing a disposition" is defined in rule 9.3.)

Application for interim orders

9.7.—(1) A party may apply at any stage of the proceedings for—
(a) an order for maintenance pending suit;
(b) an order for maintenance pending outcome of proceedings;
(c) an order for interim periodical payments;
(d) an interim variation order; or
(e) any other form of interim order.

(2) The Part 18 procedure applies to an application for an interim order.

(3) Where a party makes an application before filing a financial statement, the written evidence in support must—
(a) explain why the order is necessary; and
(b) give up to date information about that party's financial circumstances.

(4) Unless the respondent has filed a financial statement, the respondent must, at least 7 days before the court is to deal with the application, file a statement of his means and serve a copy on the applicant.

(5) An application for an order mentioned in paragraph (1)(e) may be made without notice.

Application for periodical payments order at same rate as an order for maintenance pending suit

9.8.—(1) This rule applies where there are matrimonial proceedings and—
(a) a decree nisi of divorce or nullity of marriage has been made;
(b) at or after the date of the decree nisi an order for maintenance pending suit is in force; and
(c) the spouse in whose favour the decree nisi was made has made an application for an order for periodical payments.

(2) The spouse in whose favour the decree nisi was made may apply, using the Part 18 procedure, for an order providing for payments at the same rate as those provided for by the order for maintenance pending suit.

Application for periodical payments order at same rate as an order for maintenance pending outcome of proceedings

9.9.—(1) This rule applies where there are civil partnership proceedings and—
(a) a conditional order of dissolution or nullity of civil partnership has been made;
(b) at or after the date of the conditional order an order for maintenance pending outcome of proceedings is in force;
(c) the civil partner in whose favour the conditional order was made has made an application for an order for periodical payments.

(2) The civil partner in whose favour the conditional order was made may apply, using the Part 18 procedure, for an order providing for payments at the same rate as those provided for by the order for maintenance pending the outcome of proceedings.

Application by parent, guardian etc for financial remedy in respect of children

9.10.—(1) The following people may apply for a financial remedy in respect of a child—
(a) a parent, guardian or special guardian of any child of the family;
(b) any person in whose favour a residence order has been made with respect to a child of the family, and any applicant for such an order;
(c) any other person who is entitled to apply for a residence order with respect to a child;
(d) a local authority, where an order has been made under section 31(1)(a) of the 1989 Act placing a child in its care;
(e) the Official Solicitor, if appointed the children's guardian of a child of the family under rule 16.24; and
(f) a child of the family who has been given permission to apply for a financial remedy.

(2) In this rule "residence order" has the meaning given to it by section 8(1) of the 1989 Act.

Children to be separately represented on certain applications

9.11.—(1) Where an application for a financial remedy includes an application for an order for a variation of settlement, the court must, unless it is satisfied that the proposed variation does not adversely affect the rights or interests of any child concerned, direct that the child be separately represented on the application.

(2) On any other application for a financial remedy the court may direct that the child be separately represented on the application.

Financial Remedy Rules

(3) Where a direction is made under paragraph (1) or (2), the court may if the person to be appointed so consents, appoint—
   (a) a person other than the Official Solicitor; or
   (b) the Official Solicitor,
to be a children's guardian and rule 16.24(5) and (6) and rules 16.25 to 16.28 apply as appropriate to such an appointment.

Duties of the court and the applicant upon issuing an application

9.12.—(1) When an application under this Part is issued in the High Court or in a county court—
   (a) the court will fix a first appointment not less than 12 weeks and not more than 16 weeks after the date of the filing of the application; and
   (b) subject to paragraph (2), within 4 days beginning with the date on which the application was filed, a court officer will—
      (i) serve a copy of the application on the respondent; and
      (ii) give notice of the date of the first appointment to the applicant and the respondent.
(2) Where the applicant wishes to serve a copy of the application on the respondent and on filing the application so notifies the court—
   (a) paragraph (1)(b) does not apply;
   (b) a court officer will return to the applicant the copy of the application and the notice of the date of the first appointment; and
   (c) the applicant must,—
      (i) within 4 days beginning with the date on which the copy of the application is received from the court, serve the copy of the application and notice of the date of the first appointment on the respondent; and
      (ii) file a certificate of service at or before the first appointment.
(Rule 6.37 sets out what must be included in a certificate of service.)
(3) The date fixed under paragraph (1), or for any subsequent appointment, must not be cancelled except with the court's permission and, if cancelled, the court must immediately fix a new date.
(4) In relation to an application to which the Maintenance Regulation or the 2007 Hague Convention applies, where the applicant does not already know the address of the respondent at the time the application is issued, paragraph (2) does not apply and the court will serve the application in accordance with paragraph (1).

Service of application on mortgagees, trustees etc

9.13.—(1) Where an application for a financial remedy includes an application for an order for a variation of settlement, the applicant must serve copies of the application on—
   (a) the trustees of the settlement;
   (b) the settlor if living; and
   (c) such other persons as the court directs.
(2) In the case of an application for an avoidance of disposition order, the applicant must serve copies of the application on the person in whose favour the disposition is alleged to have been made.
(3) Where an application for a financial remedy includes an application relating to land, the applicant must serve a copy of the application on any mortgagee of whom particulars are given in the application.
(4) Any person served under paragraphs (1), (2) or (3) may make a request to the court in writing, within 14 days beginning with the date of service of the application, for a copy of the applicant's financial statement or any relevant part of that statement.
(5) Any person who—
   (a) is served with copies of the application in accordance with paragraphs (1), (2) or (3); or
   (b) receives a copy of a financial statement, or a relevant part of that statement, following an application made under paragraph (4),
may within 14 days beginning with the date of service or receipt file a statement in answer.
(6) Where a copy of an application is served under paragraphs (1), (2) or (3), the applicant must file a certificate of service at or before the first appointment.
(7) A statement in answer filed under paragraph (5) must be verified by a statement of truth.

Procedure before the first appointment

9.14.—(1) Not less than 35 days before the first appointment both parties must simultaneously exchange with each other and file with the court a financial statement in the form referred to in Practice Direction 5A.
(2) The financial statement must—
   (a) be verified by a statement of truth; and
   (b) accompanied by the following documents only—
      (i) any documents required by the financial statement;
      (ii) any other documents necessary to explain or clarify any of the information contained in the financial statement; and
      (iii) any documents provided to the party producing the financial statement by a person responsible for a pension arrangement, either following a request under rule 9.30 or as part of a relevant valuation; and
      (iv) any notification or other document referred to in rule 9.37(2), (4) or (5) which has been received by the party producing the financial statement.
(2A) The requirement of paragraph (2)(a) relating to verification by a statement of truth does not apply to the financial statement of either party where the application has been made under—
   (a) Article 56 of the Maintenance Regulation, using the form in Annex VII to that Regulation; or
   (b) Article 10 of the 2007 Hague Convention, using the Financial Circumstances Form,
and the relief sought is limited to a type to which that Regulation or that Convention, as appropriate, applies, but the court may at any time direct that the financial statement of either party shall be verified by a statement of truth.
(3) Where a party was unavoidably prevented from sending any document required by the financial statement, that party must at the earliest opportunity—
   (a) serve a copy of that document on the other party; and
   (b) file a copy of that document with the court, together with a written explanation of the failure to send it with the financial statement.
(4) No disclosure or inspection of documents may be requested or given between the filing of the application for a financial remedy and the first appointment, except—
   (a) copies sent with the financial statement, or in accordance with paragraph (3); or
   (b) in accordance with paragraphs (5) and (6).
(Rule 21.1 explains what is meant by disclosure and inspection.)

Financial Remedy Rules

(5) Not less than 14 days before the hearing of the first appointment, each party must file with the court and serve on the other party—
   (a) a concise statement of the issues between the parties;
   (b) a chronology;
   (c) a questionnaire setting out by reference to the concise statement of issues any further information and documents requested from the other party or a statement that no information and documents are required; and
   (d) a notice stating whether that party will be in a position at the first appointment to proceed on that occasion to a FDR appointment.
(6) Not less than 14 days before the hearing of the first appointment, the applicant must file with the court and serve on the respondent confirmation—
   (a) of the names of all persons served in accordance with rule 9.13(1) to (3); and
   (b) that there are no other persons who must be served in accordance with those paragraphs.

PD 9A: Procedure before the first appointment

4.1 In addition to the matters listed at rule 9.14(5), the parties should, if possible, with a view to identifying and narrowing any issues between the parties, exchange and file with the court—
   (a) a summary of the case agreed between the parties;
   (b) a schedule of assets agreed between the parties; and
   (c) details of any directions that they seek, including, where appropriate, the name of any expert they wish to be appointed.
4.2 Where a party is prevented from sending the details referred to in (c) above, the party should make that information available at the first appointment.

PD 9A: Financial Statements and other documents

5.1 Practice Direction 22A (Written Evidence) applies to any financial statement filed in accordance with rules 9.14 or 9.19 and to any exhibits to a financial statement. In preparing a bundle of documents to be exhibited to or attached to a financial statement, regard must be had in particular to paragraphs 11.1 to 11.3 and 13.1 to 13.4 of that Direction. Where on account of their bulk, it is impracticable for the exhibits to a financial statement to be retained on the court file after the First Appointment, the court may give directions as to their custody pending further hearings.
5.2 Where the court directs a party to provide information or documents by way of reply to a questionnaire or request by another party, the reply must be verified by a statement of truth. Unless otherwise directed, a reply to a questionnaire or request for information and documents shall not be filed with the court.

(Part 17 and Practice Direction 17A make further provision about statements of truth)

Duties of the court at the first appointment

9.15.—(1) The first appointment must be conducted with the objective of defining the issues and saving costs.
(2) At the first appointment the court must determine—
   (a) the extent to which any questions seeking information under rule 9.14(5)(c) must be answered; and
   (b) what documents requested under rule 9.14(5)(c) must be produced,
   and give directions for the production of such further documents as may be necessary.
(3) The court must give directions where appropriate about—
   (a) the valuation of assets (including the joint instruction of joint experts);
   (b) obtaining and exchanging expert evidence, if required;
   (c) the evidence to be adduced by each party; and
   (d) further chronologies or schedules to be filed by each party.
(4) If the court decides that a referral to a FDR appointment is appropriate it must direct that the case be referred to a FDR appointment.
(5) If the court decides that a referral to a FDR appointment is not appropriate it must direct one or more of the following—
   (a) that a further directions appointment be fixed;
   (b) that an appointment be fixed for the making of an interim order;
   (c) that the case be fixed for a final hearing and, where that direction is given, the court must determine the judicial level at which the case should be heard.
(By rule 3.3 the court may also direct that the case be adjourned if it considers that alternative dispute resolution is appropriate.)
(6) In considering whether to make a costs order under rule 28.3(5), the court must have particular regard to the extent to which each party has complied with the requirement to send documents with the financial statement and the explanation given for any failure to comply.
(7) The court may—
   (a) where an application for an interim order has been listed for consideration at the first appointment, make an interim order;
   (b) having regard to the contents of the notice filed by the parties under rule 9.14(5)(d), treat the appointment (or part of it) as a FDR appointment to which rule 9.17 applies;
   (c) in a case where a pension sharing order or a pension attachment order is requested, direct any party with pension rights to file and serve a Pension Inquiry Form, completed in full or in part as the court may direct; and
   (d) in a case where a pension compensation sharing order or a pension compensation attachment order is requested, direct any party with PPF compensation rights to file and serve a Pension Protection Fund Inquiry Form, completed in full or in part as the court may direct.
(8) Both parties must personally attend the first appointment unless the court directs otherwise.

After the first appointment

9.16.—(1) Between the first appointment and the FDR appointment, a party is not entitled to the production of any further documents except—
   (a) in accordance with directions given under rule 9.15(2); or
   (b) with the permission of the court.
(2) At any stage—
   (a) a party may apply for further directions or a FDR appointment;
   (b) the court may give further directions or direct that parties attend a FDR appointment.

The FDR appointment

9.17.—(1) The FDR appointment must be treated as a meeting held for the purposes of discussion and negotiation.
(2) The judge hearing the FDR appointment must have no further involvement with the application, other than to conduct any further FDR appointment or to make a consent order or a further directions order.

Financial Remedy Rules

(3) Not less than 7 days before the FDR appointment, the applicant must file with the court details of all offers and proposals, and responses to them.

(4) Paragraph (3) includes any offers, proposals or responses made wholly or partly without prejudice, but paragraph (3) does not make any material admissible as evidence if, but for that paragraph, it would not be admissible.

(5) At the conclusion of the FDR appointment, any documents filed under paragraph (3), and any filed documents referring to them, must, at the request of the party who filed them, be returned to that party and not retained on the court file.

(6) Parties attending the FDR appointment must use their best endeavours to reach agreement on matters in issue between them.

(7) The FDR appointment may be adjourned from time to time.

(8) At the conclusion of the FDR appointment, the court may make an appropriate consent order.

(9) If the court does not make an appropriate consent order as mentioned in paragraph (8), the court must give directions for the future course of the proceedings including, where appropriate—
  (a) the filing of evidence, including up to date information; and
  (b) fixing a final hearing date.

(10) Both parties must personally attend the FDR appointment unless the court directs otherwise.

PD 9A: Financial Dispute Resolution (FDR) Appointment

6.1 A key element in the procedure is the Financial Dispute Resolution (FDR) appointment. Rule 9.17 provides that the FDR appointment is to be treated as a meeting held for the purposes of discussion and negotiation. Such meetings have been developed as a means of reducing the tension which inevitably arises in family disputes and facilitating settlement of those disputes.

6.2 In order for the FDR to be effective, parties must approach the occasion openly and without reserve. Non-disclosure of the content of such meetings is vital and is an essential prerequisite for fruitful discussion directed to the settlement of the dispute between the parties. The FDR appointment is an important part of the settlement process. As a consequence of **Re D (Minors) (Conciliation: Disclosure of Information)** *[1993] Fam 231, evidence of anything said or of any admission made in the course of an FDR appointment will not be admissible in evidence, except at the trial of a person for an offence committed at the appointment or in the very exceptional circumstances indicated in* **Re D**.

6.3 Courts will therefore expect—
  (a) parties to make offers and proposals;
  (b) recipients of offers and proposals to give them proper consideration; and
  (c) (subject to paragraph 6.4), that parties, whether separately or together, will not seek to exclude from consideration at the appointment any such offer or proposal.

6.4 Paragraph 6.3(c) does not apply to an offer or proposal made during alternative dispute resolution.

6.5 In order to make the most effective use of the first appointment and the FDR appointment, the legal representatives attending those appointments will be expected to have full knowledge of the case.

6.6 The rules do not provide for FDR appointments to take place during proceedings in magistrates' courts.

(Provision relating to experts in financial remedy proceedings is contained in Practice Direction 25D (Financial Remedy Proceedings and Other Family Proceedings (Except Children Proceedings) – The Use of Single Joint Experts and the Process Leading to Expert Evidence Being Put Before The Court.)

Editors' note:

For practical advice on the FDR Appointment see the *Financial Dispute Resolution Appointments: Best Practice Guidance* produced by the Family Justice Council in December 2012 (available online and in *@eGlance*).

* * * * * *

Power to order delivery up of possession etc.

9.24.—(1) This rule applies where the court has made an order under—
  (a) section 24A of the 1973 Act;
  (b) section 17(2) of the 1984 Act;
  (c) Part 3 of Schedule 5 to the 2004 Act; or
  (d) paragraph 9(4) of Schedule 7 to the 2004 Act.

(2) When the court makes an order mentioned in paragraph (1), it may order any party to deliver up to the purchaser or any other person—
  (a) possession of the land, including any interest in, or right over, land;
  (b) receipt of rents or profits relating to it; or
  (c) both.

* * * * * *

Applications for consent orders for financial remedy

9.26.—(1) Subject to paragraph (5) and to rule 35.2, in relation to an application for a consent order—
  (a) the applicant must file two copies of a draft of the order in the terms sought, one of which must be endorsed with a statement signed by the respondent to the application signifying agreement; and
  (b) each party must file with the court and serve on the other party, a statement of information in the form referred to in Practice Direction 5A.

(2) Where each party's statement of information is contained in one form, it must be signed by both the applicant and respondent to certify that they have read the contents of the other party's statement.

(3) Where each party's statement of information is in a separate form, the form of each party must be signed by the other party to certify that they have read the contents of the statement contained in that form.

(4) Unless the court directs otherwise, the applicant and the respondent need not attend the hearing of an application for a consent order.

(5) Where all or any of the parties attend the hearing of an application for a financial remedy the court may—
  (a) dispense with the filing of a statement of information; and
  (b) give directions for the information which would otherwise be required to be given in such a statement in such a manner as it thinks fit.

(6) In relation to an application for a consent order under Part 3 of the 1984 Act or Schedule 7 to the 2004 Act, the application for permission to make the application may be heard at the same time as the application for a financial remedy if evidence of the respondent's consent to the order is filed with the application.

(The following rules contain provision in relation to applications

Financial Remedy Rules

for consent orders - rule 9.32 (pension sharing order), rule 9.34 (pension attachment order), rule 9.41 (pension compensation sharing orders) and rule 9.43 (pension compensation attachment orders.)

PD 9A: Consent orders

7.1 Rule 9.26(1)(a) requires an application for a consent order to be accompanied by two copies of the draft order in the terms sought, one of which must be endorsed with a statement signed by the respondent to the application signifying the respondent's agreement. The rule is considered to have been properly complied with if the endorsed statement is signed by solicitors on record as acting for the respondent; but where the consent order applied for contains undertakings, it should be signed by the party giving the undertakings as well as by that party's solicitor.

(Provision relating to the enforcement of undertakings is contained in the Practice Direction 33A supplementing Part 33 of the FPR)

7.2 Rule 9.26(1)(b) requires each party to file with the court and serve on the other party a statement of information. Where this is contained in one form, both parties must sign the statement to certify that each has read the contents of the other's statement.

7.3 Rule 35.2 deals with applications for a consent order in respect of a financial remedy where the parties wish to have the content of a written mediation agreement to which the Mediation Directive applies made the subject of a consent order.

Questions as to the court's jurisdiction or whether the proceedings should be stayed

9.26A.—(1) This rule applies to applications for maintenance where a question as to jurisdiction arises under—
(a) the 1968 Convention;
(b) the 1988 Convention;
(c) the Lugano Convention;
(d) the Maintenance Regulation; or
(e) Article 18 of the 2007 Hague Convention.
(2) If at any time after the issue of the application it appears to the court that it does not or may not have jurisdiction to hear an application, or that under the instruments referred to in paragraph (1) it is or may be required to stay the proceedings or to decline jurisdiction, the court must—
(a) stay the proceedings, and
(b) fix a date for a hearing to determine jurisdiction or whether there should be a stay or other order.
(3) The court officer will serve notice of the hearing referred to at paragraph (2)(b) on the parties to the proceedings.
(4) The court must, in writing—
(a) give reasons for its decision under paragraph (2), and
(b) where it makes a finding of fact, state such finding.
(5) The court may with the consent of all the parties deal with any question as to the jurisdiction of the court, or as to whether the proceedings should be stayed, without a hearing.
(6) In this rule—
(a) "the 1968 Convention" has the meaning given to it in the Civil Jurisdiction and Judgments Act 1982;
(b) "the 1988 Convention" and "the Lugano Convention" have the meanings given to them in rule 34.1(2).

International Maintenance Obligations: Communication with the Central Authority for England and Wales

9.26AA.—(1) Where the Lord Chancellor requests information or a document from the court officer for the relevant court for the purposes of Article 58 of the Maintenance Regulation or Articles 12 or 25(2) of the 2007 Hague Convention, the court officer shall provide the requested information or document to the Lord Chancellor forthwith.
(2) In this rule, "relevant court" means the court at which an application under Article 56 of the Maintenance Regulation or Article 10 of the 2007 Hague Convention has been filed.

[The Lord Chancellor is the Central Authority for England and Wales in relation to the 2007 Hague Convention and the Maintenance Regulation]

Adding or removing parties

9.26B.—(1) The court may direct that a person or body be added as a party to proceedings for a financial remedy if—
(a) it is desirable to add the new party so that the court can resolve all the matters in dispute in the proceedings; or
(b) there is an issue involving the new party and an existing party which is connected to the matters in dispute in the proceedings, and it is desirable to add the new party so that the court can resolve that issue.
(2) The court may direct that any person or body be removed as a party if it is not desirable for that person or body to be a party to the proceedings.
(3) If the court makes a direction for the addition or removal of a party under this rule, it may give consequential directions about—
(a) the service of a copy of the application form or other relevant documents on the new party; and
(b) the management of the proceedings.
(4) The power of the court under this rule to direct that a party be added or removed may be exercised either on the court's own initiative or on the application of an existing party or a person or body who wishes to become a party.
(5) An application for an order under this rule must be made in accordance with the Part 18 procedure and, unless the court directs otherwise, must be supported by evidence setting out the proposed new party's interest in or connection with the proceedings or, in the case of removal of a party, the reasons for removal.

Estimates of Costs

9.27.—(1) Subject to paragraph (2), at every hearing or appointment each party must produce to the court an estimate of the costs incurred by that party up to the date of that hearing or appointment.
(2) Not less than 14 days before the date fixed for the final hearing of an application for a financial remedy, each party ("the filing party") must (unless the court directs otherwise) file with the court and serve on each other party a statement giving full particulars of all costs in respect of the proceedings which the filing party has incurred or expects to incur, to enable the court to take account of the parties' liabilities for costs when deciding what order (if any) to make for a financial remedy.
(3) This rule does not apply to magistrates' courts.
(Rule 28.3 makes provision for orders for costs in financial remedy proceedings.)

PD 9A: Costs

3.1 Rule 9.27 applies in the High Court and county court. The rule requires each party to produce to the court, at every hearing or appointment, an estimate of the costs incurred by the party up to the date of that hearing or appointment.

3.2 The purpose of this rule is to enable the court to take account

Financial Remedy Rules

of the impact of each party's costs liability on their financial situations. Parties should ensure that the information contained in the estimate is as full and accurate as possible and that any sums already paid in respect of a party's financial remedy costs are clearly set out. Where relevant, any liability arising from the costs of other proceedings between the parties should continue to be referred to in the appropriate section of a party's financial statement; any such costs should not be included in the estimates under rule 9.27.

Duty to make open proposals

9.28.—(1) Not less than 14 days before the date fixed for the final hearing of an application for a financial remedy, the applicant must (unless the court directs otherwise) file with the court and serve on the respondent an open statement which sets out concise details, including the amounts involved, of the orders which the applicant proposes to ask the court to make.

(2) Not more than 7 days after service of a statement under paragraph (1), the respondent must file with the court and serve on the applicant an open statement which sets out concise details, including the amounts involved, of the orders which the respondent proposes to ask the court to make.

Application and interpretation of this Chapter [Chapter 8]

9.29.—(1) This Chapter applies
  (a) where an application for a financial remedy has been made; and
  (b) the applicant or respondent is the party with pension rights.
(2) In this Chapter—
  (a) in proceedings under the 1973 Act and the 1984 Act, all words and phrases defined in sections 25D(3) and (4) of the 1973 Act have the meaning assigned by those subsections;
  (b) in proceedings under the 2004 Act—
    (i) all words and phrases defined in paragraphs 16(4) to (5) and 29 of Schedule 5 to that Act have the meanings assigned by those paragraphs; and
    (ii) "the party with pension rights" has the meaning given to "civil partner with pension rights" by paragraph 29 of Schedule 5 to the 2004 Act;
  (c) all words and phrases defined in section 46 of the Welfare Reform and Pensions Act 1999 have the meanings assigned by that section.

PD 9A: Pensions

10.1 The phrase "party with pension rights" is used in FPR Part 9, Chapter 8. For matrimonial proceedings, this phrase has the meaning given to it by section 25D(3) of the Matrimonial Causes Act 1973 and means "the party to the marriage who has or is likely to have benefits under a pension arrangement". There is a definition of "civil partner with pension rights" in paragraph 29 of Schedule 5 to the Civil Partnership Act 2004 which mirrors the definition of "party with pension rights" in section 25D(3) of the 1973 Act. The phrase "is likely to have benefits" in these definitions refers to accrued rights to pension benefits which are not yet in payment.

What the party with pension rights must do when the court fixes a first appointment

9.30.—(1) Where the court fixes a first appointment as required by rule 9.12(1)(a) the party with pension rights must request the person responsible for each pension arrangement under which the party has or is likely to have benefits to provide the information referred to in regulation 2(2) of the Pensions on Divorce etc (Provision of Information) Regulations 2000.
(The information referred to in regulation 2 of the Pensions on Divorce etc (Provision of Information) Regulations 2000 relates to the valuation of pension rights or benefits.)

(2) The party with pension rights must comply with paragraph (1) within 7 days beginning with the date on which that party receives notification of the date of the first appointment.
(3) Within 7 days beginning with the date on which the party with pension rights receives the information under paragraph (1) that party must send a copy of it to the other party, together with the name and address of the person responsible for each pension arrangement.
(4) A request under paragraph (1) need not be made where the party with pension rights is in possession of, or has requested, a relevant valuation of the pension rights or benefits accrued under the pension arrangement in question.

Applications for pension sharing orders

9.31. Where an application for a financial remedy includes an application for a pension sharing order, or where a request for such an order is added to an existing application for a financial remedy, the applicant must serve a copy of the application on the person responsible for the pension arrangement concerned.

Applications for consent orders for pension sharing

9.32.—(1) This rule applies where—
  (a) the parties have agreed on the terms of an order and the agreement includes a pension sharing order;
  (b) service has not been effected under rule 9.31; and
  (c) the information referred to in paragraph (2) has not otherwise been provided.
(2) The party with pension rights must—
  (a) request the person responsible for the pension arrangement concerned to provide the information set out in Section C of the Pension Inquiry Form; and
  (b) on receipt, send a copy of the information referred to in sub-paragraph (a) to the other party.

Applications for pension attachment orders

9.33.—(1) Where an application for a financial remedy includes an application for a pension attachment order, or where a request for such an order is added to an existing application for a financial remedy, the applicant must serve a copy of the application on the person responsible for the pension arrangement concerned and must at the same time send—
  (a) an address to which any notice which the person responsible is required to serve on the applicant is to be sent;
  (b) an address to which any payment which the person responsible is required to make to the applicant is to be sent; and
  (c) where the address in sub-paragraph (b) is that of a bank, a building society or the Department of National Savings, sufficient details to enable the payment to be made into the account of the applicant.
(2) A person responsible for a pension arrangement who receives a copy of the application under paragraph (1) may, within 21 days beginning with the date of service of the application, request the party with the pension rights to provide that person with the information disclosed in the financial statement

Financial Remedy Rules

relating to the party's pension rights or benefits under that arrangement.

(3) If the person responsible for a pension arrangement makes a request under paragraph (2), the party with the pension rights must provide that person with a copy of the section of that party's financial statement that relates to that party's pension rights or benefits under that arrangement.

(4) The party with the pension rights must comply with paragraph (3)—
  (a) within the time limited for filing the financial statement by rule 9.14(1); or
  (b) within 21 days beginning with the date on which the person responsible for the pension arrangement makes the request,
  whichever is the later.

(5) A person responsible for a pension arrangement who receives a copy of the section of a financial statement as required pursuant to paragraph (4) may, within 21 days beginning with the date on which that person receives it, send to the court, the applicant and the respondent a statement in answer.

(6) A person responsible for a pension arrangement who files a statement in answer pursuant to paragraph (5) will be entitled to be represented at the first appointment, or such other hearing as the court may direct, and the court must within 4 days, beginning with the date on which that person files the statement in answer, give the person notice of the date of the first appointment or other hearing as the case may be.

Applications for consent orders for pension attachment

9.34.—(1) This rule applies where service has not been effected under rule 9.33(1).

(2) Where the parties have agreed on the terms of an order and the agreement includes a pension attachment order, then they must serve on the person responsible for the pension arrangement concerned—
  (a) a copy of the application for a consent order;
  (b) a draft of the proposed order, complying with rule 9.35; and
  (c) the particulars set out in rule 9.33(1).

(3) No consent order that includes a pension attachment order must be made unless either—
  (a) the person responsible for the pension arrangement has not made any objection within 21 days beginning with the date on which the application for a consent order was served on that person; or
  (b) the court has considered any such objection, and for the purpose of considering any objection the court may make such direction as it sees fit for the person responsible to attend before it or to furnish written details of the objection.

Pension sharing orders or pension attachment orders

9.35. An order for a financial remedy, whether by consent or not, which includes a pension sharing order or a pension attachment order, must—
(a) in the body of the order, state that there is to be provision by way of pension sharing or pension attachment in accordance with the annex or annexes to the order; and
(b) be accompanied by a pension sharing annex or a pension attachment annex as the case may require, and if provision is made in relation to more than one pension arrangement there must be one annex for each pension arrangement.

Duty of the court upon making a pension sharing order or a pension attachment order

9.36.—(1) A court which varies or discharges a pension sharing order or a pension attachment order, must send, or direct one of the parties to send—
  (a) to the person responsible for the pension arrangement concerned; or
  (b) where the Board has assumed responsibility for the pension scheme or part of it, the Board;
  the documents referred to in paragraph (4).

(2) A court which makes a pension sharing order or pension attachment order, must send, or direct one of the parties to send to the person responsible for the pension arrangement concerned, the documents referred to in paragraph (4).

(3) Where the Board has assumed responsibility for the pension scheme or part of it after the making of a pension sharing order or attachment order but before the documents have been sent to the person responsible for the pension arrangement in accordance with paragraph (2), the court which makes the pension sharing order or the pension attachment order, must send, or direct one of the parties to send to the Board the documents referred to in paragraph (4).

(4) The documents to be sent in accordance with paragraph (1) to (3) are—
  (a) in the case of—
    (i) proceedings under the 1973 Act, a copy of the decree of judicial separation;
    (ii) proceedings under Schedule 5 to the 2004 Act, a copy of the separation order;
    (iii) proceedings under Part 3 of the 1984 Act, a copy of the document of divorce, annulment or legal separation;
    (iv) proceedings under Schedule 7 to the 2004 Act, a copy of the document of dissolution, annulment or legal separation;
  (b) in the case of divorce or nullity of marriage, a copy of the decree absolute under rule 7.31 or 7.32; or
  (c) in the case of dissolution or nullity of civil partnership, a copy of the order making the conditional order final under rule 7.31 or 7.32; and
  (d) a copy of the pension sharing order or the pension attachment order, or as the case may be of the order varying or discharging that order, including any annex to that order relating to that pension arrangement but no other annex to that order.

(5) The documents referred to in paragraph (4) must be sent—
  (a) in proceedings under the 1973 Act and the 1984 Act, within 7 days beginning with the date on which—
    (i) the relevant pension sharing or pension attachment order, or any order varying or discharging such an order, is made; or
    (ii) the decree absolute of divorce or nullity or decree of judicial separation is made,
  whichever is the later; and
  (b) in proceedings under the 2004 Act, within 7 days beginning with the date on which—
    (i) the relevant pension sharing or pension attachment order, or any order varying or discharging such an order, is made; or
    (ii) the final order of dissolution or nullity or separation order is made,
  whichever is the later.

* * * * * *

Transfer to High Court Judge

President's Guidance: Financial Proceedings, High Court Cases *[Note: remains in force under FPR 2010]*

1. This Guidance takes effect from 1 December 2009 and applies, as far as practicable, to cases commenced before, as well as those commenced on or after, that date.

A. Financial ancillary relief applications pending in the PRFD where notice in Form A or B has been issued and the parties seek transfer to the High Court

2. In considering whether to apply for the transfer of proceedings to the High Court, the parties must have regard to the provisions of the *Practice Direction: Allocation and Transfer of Proceedings*, issued on 3 November 2008 [*see* [2009] 1 FLR 365; *and reproduced in* @eGlance]. An application for ancillary relief will normally only be considered suitable for hearing in the High Court if it is exceptionally complex or there is another substantial ground for the case being heard in the High Court.

3. An application for the transfer of proceedings to the High Court should normally be made to a circuit or district judge at or after the First Appointment in the Principal Registry. Where an order for transfer is then made, the case will be referred to the Clerk of the Rules and allocated to a Judge of the Family Division in accordance with paragraph 8.

4. Where, exceptionally, the parties seek the transfer of the proceedings to the High Court before the date fixed for the First Appointment both Counsel or, if Counsel are not instructed, solicitor(s) for the parties must complete and file a certificate in the form annexed to this Guidance *[see Note at end]*, stating concisely the reasons for certifying that the application is suitable for determination by a Judge of the Family Division. The completed certificate must be filed with the Clerk of the Rules not less than 21 days before the date fixed for the First Appointment in the Principal Registry.

5. The completed certificate will be referred to and considered by a Judge of the Family Division who will determine whether the certificate indicates that *prima facie* the case is suitable for hearing in the High Court. If so determined, the case will be transferred to the High Court and allocated by the Clerk of the Rules to a Judge of the Family Division in accordance with paragraph 8. A date will be fixed for the First Appointment before the allocated Judge and the merits of the certification will be considered at that appointment.

6. If, at the First Appointment, the allocated Judge considers that the certification was not appropriate, the proceedings will be transferred back to be heard at county court level and the allocated Judge may give directions as to case management, including the level of judiciary before whom the case should be listed. The allocated Judge may make such orders as to costs as considered appropriate.

7. Where proceedings are transferred to the High Court under paragraph 4, it is the responsibility of the solicitor for the applicant to ensure that the First Appointment fixed in the Principal Registry is vacated.

B. Financial ancillary relief applications proceeding in the High Court

8. An application for financial ancillary relief considered suitable for hearing in the High Court will be allocated to one Judge ('the allocated Judge'). The allocated Judge will, so far as practicable, manage the case from First Appointment through to final hearing, except that the financial dispute resolution hearing ('FDR') will be listed in an FDR week before a Judge of the Family Division other than the allocated Judge.

9. If the allocated Judge deems it appropriate, the date for the final hearing may be fixed at the First Appointment.

10. The FDR will be listed with a time estimate of 1 day unless (i) the parties certify, giving written reasons, that a lesser period is sufficient and (ii) obtain the written permission of the FDR Judge (before whom the case is listed for hearing) for the reduced time estimate.

11. Any application in the course of the proceedings should be made to the allocated Judge, unless to do so would be impracticable or would cause undue delay.

Neither the Certificate referred to in paragraph 4 (Form A) nor Form B (an internal Court Listing Proforma) are here reproduced but Form A can be accessed and completed with @eGlance.

Court Bundles: PD 27A

FPR 2010 r 27.6 and PD 27A: Family Proceedings: Court Bundles
(Universal Practice To Be Applied In All Courts Other Than The Family Proceedings Court)

1 The President of the Family Division has issued this practice direction to achieve consistency across the country in all family courts (other than the Family Proceedings Court) in the preparation of court bundles and in respect of other related matters.

Application of the practice direction
2.1 Except as specified in para 2.4, and subject to specific directions given in any particular case, the following practice applies to:
  (a) all hearings of whatever nature (including but not limited to hearings in family proceedings, Civil Procedure Rules 1998 Part 7 and Part 8 claims and appeals) before a judge of the Family Division of the High Court wherever the court may be sitting;
  (b) all hearings in family proceedings in the Royal Courts of Justice (RCJ);
  (c) all hearings in the Principal Registry of the Family Division (PRFD) at First Avenue House; and
  (d) all hearings in family proceedings in all other courts except for Family Proceedings Courts.
2.2 'Hearings' includes all appearances before a judge or district judge, whether with or without notice to other parties and whether for directions or for substantive relief.
2.3 This practice direction applies whether a bundle is being lodged for the first time or is being re-lodged for a further hearing (see para 9.2).
2.4 This practice direction does not apply to:
  (a) cases listed for one hour or less at a court referred to in para 2.1(c) or 2.1(d); or
  (b) the hearing of any urgent application if and to the extent that it is impossible to comply with it.
2.5 The designated family judge responsible for any court referred to in paragraph 2.1(c) or 2.1(d) may, after such consultation as is appropriate (but in the case of hearings in the PRFD at First Avenue House only with the agreement of the Senior District Judge), direct that in that court this practice direction shall apply to all family proceedings irrespective of the length of hearing.

Responsibility for the preparation of the bundle
3.1 A bundle for the use of the court at the hearing shall be provided by the party in the position of applicant at the hearing (or, if there are cross-applications, by the party whose application was first in time) or, if that person is a litigant in person, by the first listed respondent who is not a litigant in person.
3.2 The party preparing the bundle shall paginate it. If possible the contents of the bundle shall be agreed by all parties.

Contents of the bundle
4.1 The bundle shall contain copies of all documents relevant to the hearing, in chronological order from the front of the bundle, paginated and indexed, and divided into separate sections (each section being separately paginated) as follows:
  (a) preliminary documents (see para 4.2) and any other case management documents required by any other practice direction;
  (b) applications and orders;
  (c) statements and affidavits (which must be dated in the top right corner of the front page);
  (d) care plans (where appropriate);
  (e) experts' reports and other reports (including those of a guardian, children's guardian or litigation friend); and
  (f) other documents, divided into further sections as may be appropriate.
Copies of notes of contact visits should normally not be included in the bundle unless directed by a judge.
4.2 At the commencement of the bundle there shall be inserted the following documents (the preliminary documents):
  (i) an up to date summary of the background to the hearing confined to those matters which are relevant to the hearing and the management of the case and limited, if practicable, to one A4 page;
  (ii) a statement of the issue or issues to be determined (1) at that hearing and (2) at the final hearing;
  (iii) a position statement by each party including a summary of the order or directions sought by that party (1) at that hearing and (2) at the final hearing;
  (iv) an up to date chronology, if it is a final hearing or if the summary under (i) is insufficient;
  (v) skeleton arguments, if appropriate, with copies of all authorities relied on; and
  (vi) a list of essential reading for that hearing.
4.3 Each of the preliminary documents shall state on the front page immediately below the heading the date when it was prepared and the date of the hearing for which it was prepared.
4.4 The summary of the background, statement of issues, chronology, position statement and any skeleton arguments shall be cross-referenced to the relevant pages of the bundle.
4.5 The summary of the background, statement of issues, chronology and reading list shall in the case of a final hearing, and shall so far as practicable in the case of any other hearing, each consist of a single document in a form agreed by all parties. Where the parties disagree as to the content the fact of their disagreement and their differing contentions shall be set out at the appropriate places in the document.
4.6 Where the nature of the hearing is such that a complete bundle of all documents is unnecessary, the bundle (which need not be repaginated) may comprise only those documents necessary for the hearing, but
  (i) the summary (para 4.2(i)) must commence with a statement that the bundle is limited or incomplete; and
  (ii) the bundle shall if reasonably practicable be in a form agreed by all parties.
4.7 Where the bundle is re-lodged in accordance with para 9.2, before it is re-lodged:
  (a) the bundle shall be updated as appropriate; and
  (b) all superseded documents (and in particular all outdated summaries, statements of issues, chronologies, skeleton arguments and similar documents) shall be removed from the bundle.

Court Bundles: PD 27A

Format of the bundle

5.1 The bundle shall be contained in one or more A4 size ring binders or lever arch files (each lever arch file being limited to 350 pages).

5.2 All ring binders and lever arch files shall have clearly marked on the front and the spine:
(a) the title and number of the case;
(b) the court where the case has been listed;
(c) the hearing date and time;
(d) if known, the name of the judge hearing the case; and
(e) where there is more than one ring binder or lever arch file, a distinguishing letter (A, B, C etc).

Timetable for preparing and lodging the bundle

6.1 The party preparing the bundle shall, whether or not the bundle has been agreed, provide a paginated index to all other parties not less than 4 working days before the hearing (in relation to a case management conference to which the provisions of the *Public Law Protocol* [2003] 2 FLR 719 apply, not less than 5 working days before the case management conference).

6.2 Where counsel is to be instructed at any hearing, a paginated bundle shall (if not already in counsel's possession) be delivered to counsel by the person instructing that counsel not less than 3 working days before the hearing.

6.3 The bundle (with the exception of the preliminary documents if and insofar as they are not then available) shall be lodged with the court not less than 2 working days before the hearing, or at such other time as may be specified by the judge.

6.4 The preliminary documents shall be lodged with the court no later than 11 am on the day before the hearing and, where the hearing is before a judge of the High Court and the name of the judge is known, shall at the same time be sent by email to the judge's clerk.

Lodging the bundle

7.1 The bundle shall be lodged at the appropriate office. If the bundle is lodged in the wrong place the judge may:
(a) treat the bundle as having not been lodged; and
(b) take the steps referred to in para 12.

7.2 Unless the judge has given some other direction as to where the bundle in any particular case is to be lodged (for example a direction that the bundle is to be lodged with the judge's clerk) the bundle shall be lodged:
(a) for hearings in the RCJ, in the office of the Clerk of the Rules, 1st Mezzanine (Rm 1M), Queen's Building, Royal Courts of Justice, Strand, London WC2A 2LL (DX 44450 Strand);
(b) for hearings in the PRFD at First Avenue House, at the List Office counter, 3rd floor, First Avenue House, 42/49 High Holborn, London, WC1V 6NP (DX 396 Chancery Lane); and
(c) for hearings at any other court, at such place as may be designated by the designated family judge or other judge at that court and in default of any such designation at the court office of the court where the hearing is to take place.

7.3 Any bundle sent to the court by post, DX or courier shall be clearly addressed to the appropriate office and shall show the date and place of the hearing on the outside of any packaging as well as on the bundle itself.

Lodging the bundle – additional requirements for cases being heard at First Avenue House or at the RCJ

8.1 In the case of hearings at the RCJ or First Avenue House, parties shall:
(a) if the bundle or preliminary documents are delivered personally, ensure that they obtain a receipt from the clerk accepting it or them; and
(b) if the bundle or preliminary documents are sent by post or DX, ensure that they obtain proof of posting or despatch.

The receipt (or proof of posting or despatch, as the case may be) shall be brought to court on the day of the hearing and must be produced to the court if requested. If the receipt (or proof of posting or despatch) cannot be produced to the court the judge may: (i) treat the bundle as having not been lodged; and (ii) take the steps referred to in para 12.

8.2 For hearings at the RCJ:
(a) bundles or preliminary documents delivered after 11 am on the day before the hearing will not be accepted by the Clerk of the Rules and shall be delivered:
(i) in a case where the hearing is before a judge of the High Court, directly to the clerk of the judge hearing the case;
(ii) in a case where the hearing is before a Circuit Judge, Deputy High Court Judge or Recorder, directly to the messenger at the Judge's entrance to the Queen's Building (with telephone notification to the personal assistant to the Designated Family Judge, 020 7947 7155, that this has been done).
(b) upon learning before which judge a hearing is to take place, the clerk to counsel, or other advocate, representing the party in the position of applicant shall no later than 3 pm the day before the hearing:
(i) in a case where the hearing is before a judge of the High Court, telephone the clerk of the judge hearing the case;
(ii) in a case where the hearing is before a Circuit Judge, Deputy High Court Judge or Recorder, telephone the personal assistant to the Designated Family Judge;
to ascertain whether the judge has received the bundle (including the preliminary documents) and, if not, shall organise prompt delivery by the applicant's solicitor.

Removing and re-lodging the bundle

9.1 Following completion of the hearing the party responsible for the bundle shall retrieve it from the court immediately or, if that is not practicable, shall collect it from the court within 5 working days. Bundles which are not collected in due time may be destroyed.

9.2 The bundle shall be re-lodged for the next and any further hearings in accordance with the provisions of this practice direction and in a form which complies with para 4.7.

Time estimates

10.1 In every case a time estimate (which shall be inserted at the front of the bundle) shall be prepared which shall so far as practicable be agreed by all parties and shall:

Court Bundles: PD 27A

(a) specify separately: (i) the time estimated to be required for judicial pre-reading; and (ii) the time required for hearing all evidence and submissions; and (iii) the time estimated to be required for preparing and delivering judgment; and
(b) be prepared on the basis that before they give evidence all witnesses will have read all relevant filed statements and reports.
10.2 Once a case has been listed, any change in time estimates shall be notified immediately by telephone (and then immediately confirmed in writing):
(a) in the case of hearings in the RCJ, to the Clerk of the Rules;
(b) in the case of hearings in the PRFD at First Avenue House, to the List Officer at First Avenue House; and
(c) in the case of hearings elsewhere, to the relevant listing officer.

Taking cases out of the list
11 As soon as it becomes known that a hearing will no longer be effective, whether as a result of the parties reaching agreement or for any other reason, the parties and their representatives shall immediately notify the court by telephone and by letter. The letter, which shall wherever possible be a joint letter sent on behalf of all parties with their signatures applied or appended, shall include:
(a) a short background summary of the case;
(b) the written consent of each party who consents and, where a party does not consent, details of the steps which have been taken to obtain that party's consent and, where known, an explanation of why that consent has not been given;
(c) a draft of the order being sought; and
(d) enough information to enable the court to decide: (i) whether to take the case out of the list; and (ii) whether to make the proposed order.

Penalties for failure to comply with the practice direction
12 Failure to comply with any part of this practice direction may result in the judge removing the case from the list or putting the case further back in the list and may also result in a 'wasted costs' order in accordance with CPR, Part 48.7 or some other adverse costs order.

Commencement of the practice direction and application of other practice directions
13 This practice direction replaces *Practice Direction (Family Proceedings: Court Bundles) (10 March 2000)* [2000] 1 WLR 737, [2000] 1 FLR 536 and shall have effect from 2 October 2006.

14 Any reference in any other practice direction to *Practice Direction (Family Proceedings: Court Bundles) (10 March 2000)* shall be read as if substituted by a reference to this practice direction.

15 This practice direction should where appropriate be read in conjunction with *Practice Direction (Family Proceedings: Human Rights)* [now re-issued as FPR 2010 PD 29B] [2000] 1 WLR 1782, [2000] 2 FLR 429 and with *Practice Direction (Care Cases: Judicial Continuity and Judicial Case Management)* appended to the *Public Law Protocol* [2003] 2 FLR 719.

In particular, nothing in this practice direction is to be read as removing or altering any obligation to comply with the requirements of the *Public Law Protocol*.

This Practice Direction is issued:
(i) in relation to family proceedings, by the President of the Family Division, as the nominee of the Lord Chief Justice, with the agreement of the Lord Chancellor; and
(ii) to the extent that it applies to proceedings to which s 5 of the Civil Procedure Act 1997 applies, by the Master of the Rolls as the nominee of the Lord Chief Justice, with the agreement of the Lord Chancellor.

Practitioners' Commentary

Strict adherence to paras 4.2 and 4.5 requires six separate preliminary documents to be prepared and lodged by 11 a.m. on the day before the hearing and that the parties should if practicable agree the content of the most potentially contentious of them. There is now a further requirement prior to the First Appointment to agree if possible a case summary and schedule of assets as well as the directions sought: PD 9A para 4.1. Experience in financial remedy cases is that such documents are often repetitive and unmanageable and that attempts to agree content are costly but almost always fail. Judges are generally content to accept a composite note from each side containing the information specified in para 4.2(i) to (vi). However some judges have indicated that the chronology, schedule of assets and bundle of authorities should be agreed. Whilst an agreed bundle of authorities can and should be produced, agreed chronologies and asset schedules remain impracticable for the reasons suggested. Most judges welcome email filing (referred to in para 6.4).

For cases at the RCJ, filing the combined note by 11 a.m. on the day before the hearing can prove fruitless as cases are often not allocated to a judge until later that day. Commonly therefore parties file the preliminary documents at 11 a.m. and obtain the necessary receipt (see para 8.1(a)), and then at 2 p.m. send duplicate copies direct to the allocated judge's clerk (in accordance with para 8.2(b)) without first establishing whether the judge has received the original documents.

Non-compliance with the requirement to file preliminary documents the day before the hearing has become routine but is totally unacceptable. *Judges, individually and collectively, have applied sanctions without, so far, discernible impact. Persistent or blatant offenders risk disallowance of fees and disciplinary complaint to regulatory bodies. For fair warning of the potential sanctions (including naming and shaming) for non-compliance see **Re X and Y (bundles)** [2008] 2 FLR 2058.*

For PRFD hearings listed for longer than one hour at First Avenue House the usual practice is to lodge the preliminary documents immediately after lunch on the day before the hearing, direct to the allocated district judge. In the case of hearings listed there for one hour or less and therefore outside the scope of the PD (para 2.4(a)) advocates generally supply analogous documents immediately prior to the hearing.

Costs: FPR 2010 Part 28 and PD 28A

What follow are **key *but not comprehensive* extracts** from the FPR 2010 costs régime as applicable to all applications for financial remedies. Transitional provisions regulate the costs of any applications launched before 6 April 2011: see PD 36A, para 4.5.

Application of CPR régime

FPR 2010 Part 28 applies swathes (but by no means all) of the CPR costs régime, but a number of parts of the relevant CPR rules are omitted or amended.

On 1 April 2013 the provisions of the CPR were comprehensively overhauled and rewritten in order to implement the recommendations of the Review of Civil Litigation Costs. The old CPR Parts 43 to 48 and the Costs Practice Direction were revoked. The current rules are contained in Parts 44 to 47, each with its own Practice Direction. Part 48 contains the transitional provisions.

By FPR Part 28 the following parts of the CPR as amended are applied: Part 44 – general rules about costs (except rules 44.2(2) and (3) and 44.10(2) and (3)); Rule 45.8 – fixed costs (but not in a magistrates' court); Part 46 – special cases (but not rule 46.7 in a magistrates' court); and Part 47 – procedure for detailed assessment (but not in a magistrates' court). These CPR provisions as amended for FPR use are conveniently accessible in *@eGlance*.

PD 28A applies the CPR Costs PDs with modifications that do no more than reflect that certain parts of the CPR régime have not been applied.

A most important change introduced in the CPR, so far as financial remedy proceedings are concerned, is the requirement of proportionality in the assessment of costs. To this end CPR rule 44.4(5) has been introduced. Further, the old procedure of certifying a case a fit for one or more counsel is now reintroduced by CPR PD 44 para 5.1.

Special treatment of some financial remedy applications

This application of the CPR régime is subject to FPR rule 28.3, retaining the 'no order' principle for a limited class of financial remedy proceedings. The financial remedies subject to rule 28.3 are as follows:

- a financial order, except an order for maintenance pending suit (or an order for maintenance pending outcome of proceedings) or an interim periodical payments order or any other interim order made within financial order proceedings (apart from an interim variation order)
- an order under Part 3 of MFPA 1984 or under Schedule 7 to CPA 2004
- an order under section 10(2) of MCA1973 or under section 48(2) of CPA 2004.

The **financial applications not covered by rule 28.3**, and which are therefore subject to the modified CPR régime are:

- an order for maintenance pending suit (or pending outcome of proceedings)
- an interim periodical payments order
- any other interim order (for example, on a preliminary issue) made within financial order proceedings (apart from an interim variation order)
- an order under Schedule 1 to the Children Act 1989
- an order under section 27 MCA 1973 or under Part 9 of Schedule 5 to CPA 2004 (failure to maintain)
- an order under section 35 MCA 1973 or under paragraph 69 of Schedule 5 to CPA 2004 (variation of maintenance agreement)
- an order under Part 1 DPMCA 1978 or under Schedule 6 to CPA 2004 (maintenance proceedings in magistrates' courts)
- an order under section 36 MCA 1973 or para 73 of Schedule 5 to CPA 2004 (alteration of maintenance agreement after death of one party)
- an order under section 17 MWPA 1882 or section 66 of the CPA 2004 (question as to property to be decided in summary way)
- an order under section 13 MFPA 1984 or para 4 of Schedule 7 to CPA 2004 (permission to apply for a financial remedy after overseas proceedings)
- an order for the transfer of a tenancy under section 53 of and Schedule 7 to FLA 1996
- an order preventing avoidance under CSA 1991, section 32L
- a legal services payment order under sections 22ZA and 22ZB of MCA 1973 or paras 38A and 38B of Schedule 5 to the CPA 2004.

*See also the **Editors' Note** which follows these extracts.*

RELEVANT EXTRACTS

Estimates of Costs

FPR 9.27

(1) Subject to paragraph (2), at every hearing or appointment each party must produce to the court an estimate of the costs incurred by that party up to the date of that hearing or appointment *[in Form H]*.
(2) Not less than 14 days before the date fixed for the final hearing of an application for a financial remedy, each party ('the filing party') must (unless the court directs otherwise) file with the court and serve on each other party a statement giving full particulars of all costs in respect of the proceedings which the filing party has incurred or expects to incur, to enable the court to take account of the parties' liabilities for costs when deciding what order (if any) to make for a financial remedy *[in Form H1]*.
(3) This rule does not apply to magistrates' courts.

* * * * *

Costs in financial remedy proceedings

FPR 28.3

Costs: FPR 2010 Part 28 and PD 28A

(1) This rule applies in relation to financial remedy proceedings
(2) Rule 44.2(1), (4) and (5) of the CPR do not apply to financial remedy proceedings.
(3) Rule 44.2(6) to (8) and 44.12 of the CPR apply to an order made under this rule as they apply to an order made under rule 44.2 of the CPR.
(4) In this rule –
  (a) 'costs' has the same meaning as in rule 44.1(1)(c) of the CPR; and
  (b) 'financial remedy proceedings' means proceedings for –
    (i) a financial order except an order for maintenance pending suit, an order for maintenance pending outcome of proceedings, an interim periodical payments order or any other form of interim order for the purposes of rule 9.7(1)(a), (b), (c) and (e);
    (ii) an order under Part 3 of the 1984 Act;
    (iii) an order under Schedule 7 to the 2004 Act;
    (iv) an order under section 10(2) of the 1973 Act;
    (v) an order under section 48(2) of the 2004 Act.
(5) Subject to paragraph (6), the general rule in financial remedy proceedings is that the court will not make an order requiring one party to pay the costs of another party.
(6) The court may make an order requiring one party to pay the costs of another party at any stage of the proceedings where it considers it appropriate to do so because of the conduct of a party in relation to the proceedings (whether before or during them).
(7) In deciding what order (if any) to make under paragraph (6), the court must have regard to–
  (a) any failure by a party to comply with these rules, any order of the court or any practice direction which the court considers relevant;
  (b) any open offer to settle made by a party;
  (c) whether it was reasonable for a party to raise, pursue or contest a particular allegation or issue;
  (d) the manner in which a party has pursued or responded to the application or a particular allegation or issue;
  (e) any other aspect of a party's conduct in relation to proceedings which the court considers relevant; and
  (f) the financial effect on the parties of any costs order.
(8) No offer to settle which is not an open offer to settle is admissible at any stage of the proceedings, except as provided by rule 9.17.

PD 28A Costs in financial remedy proceedings

4.1 Rule 28.3 relates to the court's power to make costs orders in financial remedy proceedings. For the purposes of rule 28.3,'financial remedy proceedings' are defined in accordance with rule 28.3(4)(b). That definition, which is more limited than the principal definition in rule 2.3(1), includes –

(a) an application for a financial order, except –
  (i) an order for maintenance pending suit or an order for maintenance pending outcome of proceedings;
  (ii) an interim periodical payments order or any other form of interim order for the purposes of rule 9.7(1)(a),(b),(c) and (e);
(b) an application for an order under Part 3 of the Matrimonial and Family Proceedings Act 1984 or Schedule 7 to the Civil Partnership Act 2004; and (c) an application under section 10(2) of the Matrimonial Causes Act 1973 or section 48(2) of the Civil Partnership Act 2004.

4.2 Accordingly, it should be noted that –
(a) while most interim financial applications are excluded from rule 28.3, the rule does apply to an application for an interim variation order within rule 9.7(1)(d),
(b) rule 28.3 does not apply to an application for any of the following financial remedies –
  (i) an order under Schedule 1 to the Children Act 1989;
  (ii) an order under section 27 of the Matrimonial Causes Act 1973 or Part 9 of Schedule 5 to the Civil Partnership Act 2004;
  (iii) an order under section 35 of the Matrimonial Causes Act 1973 or paragraph 69 of Schedule 5 to the Civil Partnership Act 2004; or
  (iv) an order under Part 1 of the Domestic Proceedings and Magistrates' Courts Act 1978 or Schedule 6 to the Civil Partnership Act 2004.

4.3 Under rule 28.3 the court only has the power to make a costs order in financial remedy proceedings when this is justified by the litigation conduct of one of the parties. When determining whether and how to exercise this power the court will be required to take into account the list of factors set out in that rule. The court will not be able to take into account any offers to settle expressed to be'without prejudice' or'without prejudice save as to costs' in deciding what, if any, costs orders to make.

4.4 In considering the conduct of the parties for the purposes of rule 28.3(6) and (7) (including any open offers to settle), the court will have regard to the obligation of the parties to help the court to further the overriding objective (see rules 1.1 and 1.3) and will take into account the nature, importance and complexity of the issues in the case. This may be of particular significance in applications for variation orders and interim variation orders or other cases where there is a risk of the costs becoming disproportionate to the amounts in dispute.

4.5 Parties who intend to seek a costs order against another party in proceedings to which rule 28.3 applies should ordinarily make this plain in open correspondence or in skeleton arguments before the date of the hearing. In any case where summary assessment of costs awarded under rule 28.3 would be appropriate parties are under an obligation to file a statement of costs in CPR Form N260.

Costs: FPR 2010 Part 28 and PD 28A

4.6 [not reproduced as no longer applicable in light of MCA ss. 22ZA and 22ZB]

4.7 By virtue of rule 28.2(1), where rule 28.3 does not apply, the exercise of the court's discretion as to costs is governed by the relevant provisions of the CPR and in particular rule 44.2 (excluding r 44.2(2) and (3)).

* * * * *

Civil Procedure Rules 1998

44.2 Court's discretion as to costs

(1) The court has discretion as to –
   (a) whether costs are payable by one party to another;
   (b) the amount of those costs; and
   (c) when they are to be paid.

[(2) and (3) are disapplied for FPR purposes]

(4) In deciding what order (if any) to make about costs, the court will have regard to all the circumstances, including:
   (a) the conduct of all the parties;
   (b) whether a party has succeeded on part of its case, even if that party has not been wholly successful; and
   (c) any admissible offer to settle made by a party which is drawn to the court's attention, and which is not an offer to which costs consequences under Part 36 apply.

(5) The conduct of the parties includes:
   (a) conduct before, as well as during, the proceedings and in particular the extent to which the parties followed the Practice Direction – Pre-Action Conduct or any relevant pre-action protocol;
   (b) whether it was reasonable for a party to raise, pursue or contest a particular allegation or issue;
   (c) the manner in which a party has pursued or defended its case or a particular allegation or issue; and
   (d) whether a claimant who has succeeded in the claim, in whole or in part, exaggerated its claim.

(6) The orders which the court may make under this rule include an order that a party must pay:
   (a) a proportion of another party's costs;
   (b) a stated amount in respect of another party's costs;
   (c) costs from or until a certain date only;
   (d) costs incurred before proceedings have begun;
   (e) costs relating to particular steps taken in the proceedings;
   (f) costs relating only to a distinct part of the proceedings; and
   (g) interest on costs from or until a certain date, including a date before judgment.

(7) Before the court considers making an order under paragraph (6)(f), it will consider whether it is practicable to make an order under paragraph (6)(a) or (c) instead.

(8) Where the court orders a party to pay costs subject to detailed assessment, it will order that party to pay a reasonable sum on account of costs, unless there is good reason not to do so.

44.3 Basis of assessment

(1) Where the court is to assess the amount of costs (whether by summary or detailed assessment) it will assess those costs:
   (a) on the standard basis; or
   (b) on the indemnity basis,

but the court will not in either case allow costs which have been unreasonably incurred or are unreasonable in amount.

(Rule 44.5 sets out how the court decides the amount of costs payable under a contract.)

(2) Where the amount of costs is to be assessed on the standard basis, the court will:
   (a) only allow costs which are proportionate to the matters in issue. Costs which are disproportionate in amount may be disallowed or reduced even if they were reasonably or necessarily incurred; and
   (b) resolve any doubt which it may have as to whether costs were reasonably and proportionately incurred or were reasonable and proportionate in amount in favour of the paying party.

(Factors which the court may take into account are set out in rule 44.4.)

(3) Where the amount of costs is to be assessed on the indemnity basis, the court will resolve any doubt which it may have as to whether costs were reasonably incurred or were reasonable in amount in favour of the receiving party.

(4) Where:
   (a) the court makes an order about costs without indicating the basis on which the costs are to be assessed; or
   (b) the court makes an order for costs to be assessed on a basis other than the standard basis or the indemnity basis,

the costs will be assessed on the standard basis.

(5) Costs incurred are proportionate if they bear a reasonable relationship to:
   (a) the sums in issue in the proceedings;
   (b) the value of any non-monetary relief in issue in the proceedings;
   (c) the complexity of the litigation;
   (d) any additional work generated by the conduct of the paying party; and
   (e) any wider factors involved in the proceedings, such as reputation or public importance.

…

(7) Paragraphs (2)(a) and (5) do not apply in relation to cases commenced before 1 April 2013 and in relation to such cases, rule 44.4(2)(a) as it was in force immediately before 1 April 2013 will apply instead.

Costs: FPR 2010 Part 28 and PD 28A

44.4 Factors to be taken into account in deciding the amount of costs

(1) The court will have regard to all the circumstances in deciding whether costs were:
- (a) if it is assessing costs on the standard basis:
  - (i) proportionately and reasonably incurred; or
  - (ii) proportionate and reasonable in amount, or
- (b) if it is assessing costs on the indemnity basis:
  - (i) unreasonably incurred; or
  - (ii) unreasonable in amount.

(2) In particular, the court will give effect to any orders which have already been made.

(3) The court will also have regard to:
- (a) the conduct of all the parties, including in particular:
  - (i) conduct before, as well as during, the proceedings; and
  - (ii) the efforts made, if any, before and during the proceedings in order to try to resolve the dispute;
- (b) the amount or value of any money or property involved;
- (c) the importance of the matter to all the parties;
- (d) the particular complexity of the matter or the difficulty or novelty of the questions raised;
- (e) the skill, effort, specialised knowledge and responsibility involved;
- (f) the time spent on the case;
- (g) the place where and the circumstances in which work or any part of it was done; and
- (h) the receiving party's last approved or agreed budget.

(Rule 35.4(4) gives the court power to limit the amount that a party may recover with regard to the fees and expenses of an expert.)

44.6 Procedure for assessing costs

(1) Where the court orders a party to pay costs to another party (other than fixed costs) it may either:
- (a) make a summary assessment of the costs; or
- (b) order detailed assessment of the costs by a costs officer,

unless any rule, practice direction or other enactment provides otherwise.

(Practice Direction 44 – General rules about costs sets out the factors which will affect the court's decision under paragraph (1).)

...

44.7 Time for complying with an order for costs

A party must comply with an order for the payment of costs within 14 days of:
- (a) the date of the judgment or order if it states the amount of those costs;
- (b) if the amount of those costs (or part of them) is decided later in accordance with Part 47, the date of the certificate which states the amount; or
- (c) in either case, such other date as the court may specify.

(Part 47 sets out the procedure for detailed assessment of costs.)

CPR Costs PD 44: Fees of Counsel

5.1

(1) When making an order for costs the court may state an opinion as to whether or not the hearing was fit for the attendance of one or more counsel, and, if it does so, the court conducting a detailed assessment of those costs will have regard to the opinion stated.

(2) The court will generally express an opinion only where:
- *(a) the paying party asks it to do so;*
- *(b) more than one counsel appeared for a party; or*
- *(c) the court wishes to record its opinion that the case was not fit for the attendance of counsel.*

CPR Costs PD 44: Summary Assessment: General Provisions

9.1 Whenever a court makes an order about costs which does not provide only for fixed costs to be paid the court should consider whether to make a summary assessment of costs.

Timing of summary assessment

9.2 The general rule is that the court should make a summary assessment of the costs:

... (b) at the conclusion of any other hearing, which has lasted not more than one day, in which case the order will deal with the costs of the application or matter to which the hearing related. If this hearing disposes of the claim, the order may deal with the costs of the whole claim, unless there is good reason not to do so, for example where the paying party shows substantial grounds for disputing the sum claimed for costs that cannot be dealt with summarily.

Consent orders

9.4 Where an application has been made and the parties to the application agree an order by consent without any party attending, the parties should seek to agree a figure for costs to be inserted in the consent order or agree that there should be no order for costs.

Duty of parties and legal representatives

9.5

(1) It is the duty of the parties and their legal representatives to assist the judge in making a summary assessment of costs in any case to which paragraph 9.2 above applies, in accordance with the following subparagraphs.

(2) Each party who intends to claim costs must prepare a

Costs: FPR 2010 Part 28 and PD 28A

written statement of those costs showing separately in the form of a schedule:
(a) the number of hours to be claimed;
(b) the hourly rate to be claimed;
(c) the grade of fee earner;
(d) the amount and nature of any disbursement to be claimed, other than counsel's fee for appearing at the hearing;
(e) the amount of legal representative's costs to be claimed for attending or
appearing at the hearing;
(f) counsel's fees; and
(g) any VAT to be claimed on these amounts.
(3) The statement of costs should follow as closely as possible Form N260 and must be signed by the party or the party's legal representative. Where a party is:
(a) an assisted person;
(b) a LSC funded client; ... or
(d) represented by a person in the party's employment, the statement of costs need not include the certificate appended at the end of Form N260.
(4) The statement of costs must be filed at court and copies of it must be served on any party against whom an order for payment of those costs is intended to be sought as soon as possible and in any event: ...
(b) for all other hearings, not less than 24 hours before the time fixed for the hearing.

9.6 The failure by a party, without reasonable excuse, to comply with paragraph 9.5 will be taken into account by the court in deciding what order to make about the costs of the claim, hearing or application, and about the costs of any further hearing or detailed assessment hearing that may be necessary as a result of that failure.

No summary assessment by a costs officer

9.7 The court awarding costs cannot make an order for a summary assessment of costs by a costs officer. If a summary assessment of costs is appropriate but the court awarding costs is unable to do so on the day, the court may give directions as to a further hearing before the same judge.

Assisted persons etc

9.8 The court will not make a summary assessment of the costs of a receiving party who is an assisted person or LSC funded client ...

Children or protected parties

9.9
(1) The court will not make a summary assessment of the costs of a receiving party who is a child or protected party within the meaning of Part 21 unless the legal representative acting for the child or protected party has waived the right to further costs (see Practice Direction 46 paragraph 2.1).
(2) The court may make a summary assessment of costs payable by a child or protected party.

Disproportionate or unreasonable costs

9.10 The court will not give its approval to disproportionate or unreasonable costs. When the amount of the costs to be paid has been agreed between the parties the order for costs must state that the order is by consent.

Here is a sample of the @eGlance Commentary on the FPR, updated quarterly:

Costs allowance – the Legal Services Payment Order

28.49 The Legal Services Payment Order (LSPO) is a completely new, *sui generis*, statutory power. But despite the extensive scope of the language used to define and regulate a LSPO it is not considered that these statutory provisions will be interpreted in a materially different way to the judge-made régime they replace. A key structural innovation is the ability to award a single amount (in effect an interim lump sum) as well as an amount payable by instalments. It must be anticipated that the award of a single sum will become commonplace, although the merit of a costs allowance being paid by instalments, or being in part deferred, in order to cater for later changes in the shape of the litigation should not be overlooked.

28.50 It remains to be seen how widely or narrowly the judiciary will interpret and deploy the power to order a sale of property to give effect to a LSPO.

...

28.52 Section 22ZA(10) should also be noted. A LSPO may be made for the purposes, in particular, of advice and assistance in the form of representation and any form of dispute resolution, including mediation. Thus the power may be exercised free-standingly and before any financial remedy proceedings have been commenced in order to finance any form of alternative dispute resolution, which plainly would include arbitration proceedings.

28.53 **At the time of writing no amendments to FPR 2010 or to PD 28A have been promulgated to 'flesh out' and regulate the LSPO régime. Any such amendments will be incorporated in an update to @eGlance.**

Costs: Editors' Note

It should be very clearly noted indeed that CPR rule 44.2(4)(c) makes Calderbank letters admissible in the costs phase of the proceedings listed above **other than** those covered by FPR rule 28.2; and, following well understood principle should then strongly influence if not dictate the outcome of the costs application: see **KS v ND (Schedule 1: Appeal: Costs)** [2013] EWHC 464 (Fam) at [20].

The removal of maintenance pending suit and comparable orders from the 'no order as to costs' régime is a significant change designed to meet the complaint that the 'no order' principle effectively emasculated the economic value of many such orders.

It is somewhat surprising that the same distinction has not been carried through to variation orders, whether interim or final, where similar concerns have been raised, although PD 28A para 4.4 supplies a strong steer in favour of making orders for costs in such proceedings.

Reported cases and practitioners' experience demonstrate that **the 'no order' principle in rule 28.3 is by no means absolute and does not apply across the board**.

The starting point is that at the final hearing unpaid costs will be 'taken off the top' as a debt of the party in question. For this purpose a much more detailed costs estimate in Form H1 is now required at trial. The approach in **Leadbeater v Leadbeater** [1985] FLR 789 (of adding back costs already paid) is now outmoded.

Where there is a striking disparity in the costs each party incurs the court may, when fairly calculating the relevant assets, disregard unpaid costs and/or add back costs already paid: see **RH v RH** [2008] 2 FLR 2142. An alternative technique is to work out the actual net payment of costs as between the parties and to order a compensatory cross-payment: see **LS v JS (Appeal: Costs)** [2012] EWHC 2960 (Fam).

Calderbank offers are not admissible when determining an application for costs in proceedings governed by Rule 28.3. 'Without Prejudice' offers can still be made but can be referred to only at the FDR hearing. The terms of open proposals to settle are however expressly to be considered in determining whether or not litigation misconduct has occurred.

Clearly the court in determining the substantive outcome should not be influenced by the parties' open positions, and should be ready to penalise in costs a party who has adopted an open position that is manifestly unreasonable or who has failed to make an open offer at all: see **Evans v Evans** [2013] EWHC 506 (Fam) at [178] to [204].

An important provision is rule 28.3(7)(f) which requires the court to have regard to the financial effect of a costs order upon a party: for instance where an adverse costs order might undermine the judicial objective of the order, such as to provide secure housing: see **KS v ND (Schedule 1: Appeal: Costs)** at [25] to [27].

In **M v M** [2010] 1 FLR 256 emphasis was again placed on the requirement of reasonableness in litigating particular issues: a party who had behaved unreasonably in relation to a number of issues was condemned to pay approximately 20% of the other party's overall costs of the proceedings.

See also, to like effect, **GS v L (No. 2) (Financial remedies: Costs**) [2011] EWHC 2116 (Fam), [2013] 1 FLR 407 where the court surveyed the relevant authorities on issue-based costs awards in the civil sphere.

The 'no order' principle in rule 28.3 only applies to mainstream ancillary relief applications between the two principal parties. It does not apply to the costs of a person joined to the proceedings against his will (**KSO v MJO and JMO (PSO intervening)** [2009] 1 FLR 1036) or to the costs of a person who intervenes in the proceedings (**Baker v Rowe** [2010] 1 FLR 761). Nor does it apply to the costs of civil proceedings heard together with financial remedy proceedings (**Ben Hashem v Ali Shayif and Radfan Ltd** [2009] 2 FLR 896); nor to an application made to set aside an ancillary relief order on the grounds of mistake and/or non-disclosure (**Judge v Judge** [2009] 1 FLR 1287).

Sections 49 to 54 of the Legal Aid, Sentencing and Punishment of Offenders Act 2012 put the powers of the court to award a costs allowance in relation to divorce proceedings on a statutory footing by introducing new ss. 22ZA and 22ZB into the maintenance pending suit framework of the Matrimonial Causes Act 1973.

Despite the extensive scope of the language used in ss. 22ZA and 22ZB it is not considered that the statutory provisions will be interpreted in a materially different way to the judge-made régime they replace. A key structural innovation however is the ability to award a single amount (in effect an interim lump sum) as well as an amount payable by instalments. It must be anticipated that the award of a single sum will become commonplace, although the merit of a costs allowance being paid by instalments, or being in part deferred, in order to allow for later changes in the shape of the litigation should not be overlooked.

These provisions do not apply to proceedings under Schedule 1 of the Children Act 1989, the Inheritance (Provision for Family and Dependants) Act 1975 or Part III of the Matrimonial and Family Proceedings Act 1984, where the application will continue to be for an interim order for this purpose and the principles in **Currey v Currey (No 2)** [2007] 1 FLR 946, as well as PD 28A para 4.6, will continue to apply as before.

For in-depth coverage on costs, with links to the relevant rules and periodical updating to include new cases and developments, see the Commentary on Part 28 and PD 28A (and the relevant CPR provisions) in *@eGlance*.

Brussels II Revised and FPR 7.27: Extracts

Council Regulation (EC) No 2201/2003 of 27 November 2003 concerning jurisdiction and the recognition and enforcement of judgments in matrimonial matters and the matters of parental responsibility, repealing Regulation (EC) No 1347/2000 *(extract)*

Article 3
General jurisdiction

1. In matters relating to divorce, legal separation or marriage annulment, jurisdiction shall lie with the courts of the Member State
   (a) in whose territory:
   – the spouses are habitually resident, or
   – the spouses were last habitually resident, insofar as one of them still resides there, or
   – the respondent is habitually resident, or
   – in the event of a joint application, either of the spouses is habitually resident, or
   – the applicant is habitually resident if he or she resided there for at least a year immediately before the application was made, or
   – the applicant is habitually resident if he or she resided there for at least six months immediately before the application was made and is either a national of the Member State in question or, in the case of the United Kingdom and Ireland, has his or her 'domicile' there;
   (b) of the nationality of both spouses or, in the case of the United Kingdom and Ireland, of the 'domicile' of both spouses.
2. For the purpose of this Regulation, 'domicile' shall have the same meaning as it has under the legal systems of the United Kingdom and Ireland.

* * * * *

Article 6
Exclusive nature of jurisdiction under Articles 3, 4 and 5

A spouse who:
   (a) is habitually resident in the territory of a Member State; or
   (b) is a national of a Member State, or, in the case of the United Kingdom and Ireland, has his or her 'domicile' in the territory of one of the latter Member States,
may be sued in another Member State only in accordance with Articles 3, 4 and 5.

Article 7
Residual jurisdiction

1. Where no court of a Member State has jurisdiction pursuant to Articles 3, 4 and 5, jurisdiction shall be determined, in each Member State, by the laws of that State.
2. As against a respondent who is not habitually resident and is not either a national of a Member State or, in the case of the United Kingdom and Ireland, does not have his 'domicile' within the territory of one of the latter Member States, any national of a Member State who is habitually resident within the territory of another Member State may, like the nationals of that State, avail himself of the rules of jurisdiction applicable in that State.

* * * * *

Article 16
Seising of a Court

1. A court shall be deemed to be seised:
   (a) at the time when the document instituting the proceedings or an equivalent document is lodged with the court, provided that the applicant has not subsequently failed to take the steps he was required to take to have service effected on the respondent;
   or
   (b) if the document has to be served before being lodged with the court, at the time when it is received by the authority responsible for service, provided that the applicant has not subsequently failed to take the steps he was required to take to have the document lodged with the court.

Article 17
Examination as to jurisdiction

Where a court of a Member State is seised of a case over which it has no jurisdiction under this Regulation and over which a court of another Member State has jurisdiction by virtue of this Regulation, it shall declare of its own motion that it has no jurisdiction.

Brussels II Revised and FPR 7.27: Extracts

Article 18
Examination as to admissibility

1. Where a respondent habitually resident in a State other than the Member State where the action was brought does not enter an appearance, the court with jurisdiction shall stay the proceedings so long as it is not shown that the respondent has been able to receive the document instituting the proceedings or an equivalent document in sufficient time to enable him to arrange for his defence, or that all necessary steps have been taken to this end.

2. Article 19 of Regulation (EC) No 1348/2000 shall apply instead of the provisions of paragraph 1 of this Article if the document instituting the proceedings or an equivalent document had to be transmitted from one Member State to another pursuant to that Regulation.

3. Where the provisions of Regulation (EC) No 1348/2000 are not applicable, Article 15 of the Hague Convention of 15 November 1965 on the service abroad of judicial and extrajudicial documents in civil or commercial matters shall apply if the document instituting the proceedings or an equivalent document had to be transmitted abroad pursuant to that Convention.

Article 19
Lis pendens and dependent actions

1. Where proceedings relating to divorce, legal separation or marriage annulment between the same parties are brought before courts of different Member States, the court second seised shall of its own motion stay its proceedings until such time as the jurisdiction of the court first seised is established.

2. Where proceedings relating to parental responsibility relating to the same child and involving the same cause of action are brought before courts of different Member States, the court second seised shall of its own motion stay its proceedings until such time as the jurisdiction of the court first seised is established.

3. Where the jurisdiction of the court first seised is established, the court second seised shall decline jurisdiction in favour of that court.

In that case, the party who brought the relevant action before the court second seised may bring that action before the court first seised.

Article 20
Provisional, including protective, measures

1. In urgent cases, the provisions of this Regulation shall not prevent the courts of a Member State from taking such provisional, including protective, measures in respect of persons or assets in that State as may be available under the law of that Member State, even if, under this Regulation, the court of another Member State has jurisdiction as to the substance of the matter.

2. The measures referred to in paragraph 1 shall cease to apply when the court of the Member State having jurisdiction under this Regulation as to the substance of the matter has taken the measures it considers appropriate.

* * * * *

Family Procedure Rules 2010 (part)

Note: FPR 2010 rule 7.27(2) provides for stay of the main suit if required (or if it may be) for want of jurisdiction by virtue of Arts 16 to 19 of the Council Regulation (*above*). This may have the effect of staying any pending financial remedy proceedings.

7.27- Stay of proceedings

... (2) Where at any time after the making of an application under this Part it appears to the court in matrimonial proceedings that, under Articles 16 to 19 of the Council Regulation, the court does not have jurisdiction to hear the application and is or may be required to stay the proceedings, the court will -

(a) stay the proceedings; and

(b) fix a date for a hearing to determine the questions of jurisdiction and whether there should be a further stay or other order.

(3) The court must give reasons for its decision under Articles 16 to 19 of the Council Regulation and, where it makes a finding of fact, state such finding of fact.

... (5) The court may, if all parties agree, deal with any question about the jurisdiction of the court without a hearing.

The full text of the Regulation and of the Rules is easily accessed in *@eGlance*.

Note on the EU Maintenance Regulation

With effect from 18 June 2011, subject to **transitional provisions** (art 75; and see FP(A)R 2011, rule 38), Council Regulation (EC) No 4/2009 of 18 December 2008 on jurisdiction, applicable law, recognition and enforcement of decisions and co-operation in matters relating to maintenance obligations ('the Regulation') has replaced the Brussels I Regulation so far as maintenance matters are concerned. It also limits the scope of the European Enforcement Order Regulation ((EC) No 805/2004) to EEOs issued in the UK for enforcement in other Member States apart from Denmark.

This note deals solely with the Regulation's key provisions concerning ambit, jurisdiction, *lis pendens* and the recognition and enforcement of judgments.

The Regulation is highly complex, detailed and in some instances unclear, and this note is no substitute for specialised and case-specific legal advice.

As to the background, the UK, Denmark and Ireland did not opt in to the Regulation at the outset owing to their objection to the 'applicable law' provisions now contained in art 15 and the Hague Protocol of 23 November 2007 on the Law Applicable to Maintenance Obligations (Council Decision 2009/941/EC). The Regulation was subsequently applied to the UK and Denmark by, respectively, Commission Decision 2009/451/EC and the Agreement at (2009) OJ L149/80 (thus superseding recitals 47 and 48 of the Regulation as adopted, which recorded that it does not apply to those States). The UK and Denmark are not bound by the Hague Protocol (recitals 11 and 12). Thus, English and Danish courts will continue to apply their national law. All other Member States including Ireland have opted in to the Hague Protocol, with the consequence that their courts will as a general rule apply the law of the country of the maintenance creditor's habitual residence (Regulation, art 15; Hague Protocol, art 3(1)).

As the Regulation has **direct effect in national law**, no implementing legislation as such is needed. However, substantial amendment of both primary and secondary legislation has been required to ensure consistency with the Regulation, principally by means of the Civil Jurisdiction and Judgments (Maintenance) Regulations 2011 ('CJJMR'). Thus, *inter alia*, MCA 1973, ss 27, 35 and 52; DPMCA 1978, s 30; MFPA 1984, ss 15 and 16; CA 1989, Sch 1, paras 10 and 14; the provisions of the CPA 2004 which correspond to the foregoing; and CSA 1991, s 44 have all been amended to reflect and give priority to the Regulation's rules on jurisdiction.

Like Brussels I and the EEO Regulations, the Regulation does not define **maintenance**. However, for the purpose of EU maintenance legislation that term has its own autonomous meaning, as developed by ECJ jurisprudence (*de Cavel v de Cavel (No 1)* [1979] ECR 1055; *de Cavel v de Cavel (No 2)* [1980] ECR 731; *van den Boogaard v Laumen* [1997] ECR I-1147, [1997] 2 FLR 399).

The principles were summarised in *Moore v Moore* [2007] 2 FLR 339, CA at [80]: the 'label' given to the claim in national law is not decisive. Whether a claim relates to maintenance will depend on its purpose, and in particular whether it is designed to enable one spouse to provide for himself or herself, or if the needs and resources of each of the spouses are taken into consideration in the determination of its amount, or where the capital sum set is designed to ensure a predetermined level of income. Particular care thus needs to be taken where the claim or order is a 'hybrid' one containing both maintenance and non-maintenance provisions: see *Traversa v Freddi* [2011] 2 FLR 272, CA, at [35-36] and [59-64] and the article at [2010] Fam Law 385.

A potential difficulty has been identified where it is sought to obtain a maintenance-based pension sharing order in England under MFPA 1984, Pt III in circumstances where a foreign court is seised of a maintenance claim: see the article at [2012] Fam Law 191.

The main grounds of **jurisdiction** under the Regulation are set out in art 3 (but see also arts 4 to 7) which provides that jurisdiction lies with the court:

(a) for the place where the defendant is habitually resident; or

(b) for the place where the creditor is habitually resident; or

(c) which, according to its own law, has jurisdiction to entertain proceedings concerning the status of a person if the matter relating to maintenance is ancillary to those proceedings, unless that jurisdiction is based solely on the nationality (but in the case of the UK and Ireland, the domicile: art 2(3)) of one of the parties; or

(d) which, according to its own law, has jurisdiction to entertain proceedings concerning parental responsibility if the matter relating to maintenance is ancillary to those proceedings, unless that jurisdiction is based solely on the nationality (or, in the case of the UK and Ireland, domicile) of one of the parties.

The combined effect of recital 15 and art 3(c) appears to be that the divorce court has no jurisdiction in respect of maintenance where the divorce jurisdiction is based on the domicile of one spouse alone, even in those cases where no other EU State has jurisdiction in respect of maintenance. This seems to be so unless the defendant enters an appearance other than to contest jurisdiction (art 5), or where jurisdiction is based on choice (art 4 – see *below*) or *forum necessitatis* (art 7). A 'subsidiary jurisdiction' based on the spouses' *common* domicile is available where none of the grounds of jurisdiction in arts 3 to 5 is made out and where no non-EU Lugano State has jurisdiction under that Convention (art 6).

Competing claims to jurisdiction are resolved by 'first seised' rules familiar from the Brussels I and IIR

Note on the EU Maintenance Regulation

Regulations: art 12 (*lis pendens* – mandatory stay) and art 13 ('related actions' – discretionary stay). See also FPR 9.26A.

It remains an open question whether discretionary stays under the *forum conveniens* doctrine have survived the Regulation in cases to which art 12 applies and where the other forum is a non-EU State. This depends on whether the recent family decisions in *JKN v JCN (divorce: forum)* [2011] 1 FLR 826 (Theis J) and *AB v CB* [2012] EWHC 3841 (Fam) (Bodey J), both distinguishing the controversial ECJ decision in *Owusu v Jackson* [2005] QB 801, are correct; and, if so, whether they apply by analogy to the Regulation. See the discussion at [2012] IFL 436.

Subject to certain criteria being met, art 4 gives the parties **the right to choose forum**: but not in relation to child maintenance (art 4(3)). This may have important implications where a pre-nuptial agreement records agreement as to jurisdiction: see the discussion at [2011] Fam Law 389.

As to **variation applications** (art 8), the basic rule (which is subject to exceptions) is that the maintenance debtor must apply in the country of the maintenance creditor's habitual residence, if that is where the original order was made and the creditor is still habitually resident there. The maintenance creditor's right to apply to vary is not so restricted.

So far as **recognition and enforcement** are concerned, the aim of the Regulation is to permit maintenance decisions, court settlements and authenticated instruments made in one Member State to be recognised and enforced in another Member State without further formality (recital 9). However, as a result of the decision by Denmark and the UK not to opt in to the Hague Protocol, the Regulation has created two distinct régimes. Seen from the UK perspective:

- Outgoing orders etc. to all States require a declaration of enforceability (exequatur) to be obtained in the state of enforcement (Chapter IV, Sections 2 and 3 of the Regulation; FPR 34.39 (magistrates' courts orders) and 34.40 (High Court and county court orders)).

- Incoming orders etc. from 2007 Hague Protocol States (ie all apart from Denmark) are enforceable directly, without the need for registration (Chapter IV, Sections 1 and 3 of the Regulation; CJJMR, reg 3 and Sch 1, Part 2; Magistrates' Courts Rules 1981, rules 59A and 59B).

- Incoming orders etc. from Denmark require registration in the UK (Chapter IV, Sections 2 and 3 of the Regulation; FPR 34.29 to 34.36A, PD 34A (paras 1.1 to 2.3); CJJMR, reg 3 and Sch 1, Part 3).

Note that, subject to the transitional provisions, it is no longer possible to enforce maintenance orders within the EU under Part I of the Reciprocal Enforcement (Maintenance Orders) Act 1972 (CJJMR, Sch 7, paras 25 to 28). The Regulation takes precedence over Part II of the 1972 Act (art 69(2)). For a detailed discussion of the recognition and enforcement provisions see [2012] Fam Law 39 and [2011] International Family Law 187.

A **Central Authority** ('CA') is established for the purpose, *inter alia*, of transmitting applications for maintenance and enforcement under the Regulation. The CA for England and Wales is the Lord Chancellor (CJJMR, reg 3 and Sch 1, para 2(1)(a)), his powers being exercised in practice by the REMO Unit of the Office of the Official Solicitor and Public Trustee. The procedure to be followed on the receipt by REMO of an application from another Member State for a maintenance order or a variation order has now been set out in an entirely new Part 5 of Sch 1 to the CJJMR (inserted by the International Recovery of Maintenance (Hague Convention 2007 etc.) Regulations 2012, reg 9 and Sch 5, para 8). The application will be dealt with in the magistrates' court if that court has jurisdiction under the DPMCA 1978 or the CA 1989, Sch 1. Otherwise, the application will be transferred to the High Court or county court.

FPR Part 34 was amended with effect from 18 June 2011 to ensure procedural conformity with the Regulation. Further minor amendment has been made by the Family Procedure (Amendment No. 4) Rules 2012. A new PD 34C (Applications for Recognition and Enforcement To or From European Union Member States) came into force on 31 October 2011. It clarifies the relationship between the Maintenance Regulation and other international instruments, summarises the rules governing recognition and enforcement and provides useful clarification of the transitional provisions in art 75.

With effect from 12 November 2011 the Child Maintenance and Enforcement Commission (whose functions have now been transferred to the Secretary of State for Work and Pensions) has been added to the list at Annex X of the Regulation as a national authority with competence in maintenance matters, and thus falls within the definition of 'court' for the purpose of the Regulation (art 2.2) (Commission Implementing Regulation (EU) No 1142/2011).

Many of the International Instruments referred to in this Note on the **EU Maintenance Regulation** are directly accessible from

... **as well as** the statute amendments and FPR and PD changes referenced ... **and** transcripts of all the cases cited ... **and so much more**, not least a detailed and regularly-updated Commentary.

Call ☎ 01652 652222 or visit www.classlegal.com to download your copy now: special rates apply if you have purchased this *At A Glance* directly from The Family Law Bar Association.

Leading Cases

Adjournment of claims	*Departure from*	**Money, small**
Agreements	*Principle applied*	**Negligence (by legal advisers and others)**
Appealing out of time	**Experts**	
Appeals	**Farms**	**Non-disclosure/discovery**
Arrears, enforcement/remission	**Financial relief after overseas divorce**	**Non-parties, disclosure by**
Generally	**Forum conveniens**	**Orders over property**
Magistrates	**Inheritance (Provision for Family and Dependants) Act 1975**	**Pensions**
Avoidance of dispositions		*Military*
Bankruptcy	**Injunctions in support of financial remedies**	*Other*
Banks		**Periodical payments**
Children	*Section 37 injunctions*	*Capitalisation of*
Capital provision	*Freezing (Mareva) injunctions*	*Principles of award*
Income provision, marital	*Search (Anton Piller) orders*	*Variation of*
Income provision, non-marital	*Writ ne exeat regno, etc*	**Practice and procedure**
Child Support Act	*Anti-suit injunctions*	**Proceeds of Crime Act**
Clean break/termination	**Interim capital orders/orders for sale**	**Property, beneficial interest in**
Companies	**Jurisdiction**	*Joint names*
Conduct	*EU Regulations*	*Sole name*
Financial misconduct	*Domicile*	**Remarriage and cohabitation**
Misconduct of proceedings	*Habitual residence*	*Prospects*
Sexual	**Legal Aid**	*Actual remarriage*
Violence, etc	*Effect on order*	*Cohabitation*
Other	*Enforcement of costs orders*	**Resources**
Contributions	*Incidence of charge*	*Computation and extent of*
Costs	*Orders against Legal Aid Agency / Legal Services Commission*	*(Il)liquidity of*
Inter partes		**Resources, non-matrimonial**
Orders against legal advisers and others	**Length of marriage**	*Pre-marital*
	Cohabitation before	*Acquired during marriage*
Delay	*Short*	*Acquired post-separation*
Duxbury income capitalisation	**Lump sums**	**Third parties, claims by/against**
Enforcement	**Maintenance pending suit**	**Trusts**
Equality of division	**Media access, etc**	**Variation of final orders**

Adjournment of claims
MT v MT (financial provision: lump sum)   [1992] 1 FLR 362
G (financial claims: liberty to restore application for lump sum), Re   [2004] EWHC 88 (Fam), [2004] 1 FLR 997

Agreements

Hyman v Hyman	[1929] AC 601, [1929] All ER Rep 245, (1929) FLR Rep 342, HL
Dean v Dean	[1978] Fam 161, [1978] 3 All ER 758, [1978] 3 WLR 288, (1978) FLR Rep 234
Edgar v Edgar	[1980] 3 All ER 887, [1980] 1 WLR 1410, (1981) FLR 19, CA
Camm v Camm	(1983) FLR 577, CA
Simister v Simister (No. 2)	[1987] 1 FLR 194
Amey v Amey	[1992] 2 FLR 89
N v N (consent order: variation)	[1993] 2 FLR 868, CA
Pounds v Pounds	[1994] 4 All ER 777, [1994] 1 WLR 1535, [1994] 1 FLR 775, CA
Richardson v Richardson (No. 2)	[1996] 2 FLR 617, CA
Harris (formerly Manahan) v Manahan	[1996] 4 All ER 454, [1997] 1 FLR 205, CA
Xydhias v Xydhias	[1999] 2 All ER 386, [1999] 1 FLR 683, CA
Smith v Smith	[2000] 3 FCR 374, CA
X v X (Y and Z intervening)	[2002] 1 FLR 508
Rose v Rose (No 1)	[2002] EWCA Civ 208, [2002] 1 FLR 978, CA
A v B (financial relief: agreements)	[2005] EWHC 314 (Fam), [2005] 2 FLR 730
NA v MA	[2006] EWHC 2900 (Fam), [2007] 1 FLR 1760
Soulsbury v Soulsbury	[2007] EWCA Civ 969, [2008] Fam 1, [2008] 2 WLR 834, [2008] 1 FLR 90, CA
S v S (ancillary relief)	[2008] EWHC 2038 (Fam), [2009] 1 FLR 254
Crossley v Crossley	[2007] EWCA Civ 1491, [2008] 1 FLR 1467, CA
MacLeod v MacLeod	[2008] UKPC 64, [2010] AC 298, [2009] 1 All ER 851, [2009] 3 WLR 437, [2009] 1 FLR 641, PC
Radmacher (formerly Granatino) v Granatino	[2010] UKSC 42, [2011] 1 All ER 373, [2010] 2 FLR 1900; sub nom Granatino v Radmacher (formerly Granatino) [2011] 1 AC 534, [2010] 3 WLR 1367, SC
Z v Z (No 2) (financial remedy: marriage contract)	[2011] EWHC 2878 (Fam), [2012] 1 FLR 1100
GS v L (financial remedies: pre-acquired assets: needs)	[2011] EWHC 1759 (Fam), [2013] 1 FLR 300
V v V (prenuptial agreement)	[2011] EWHC 3230 (Fam), [2012] 1 FLR 1315
Kremen v Agrest (No 11) (financial remedy: non-disclosure: post-nuptial agreement)	[2012] EWHC 45 (Fam)
B v S (financial remedy: marital property régime)	[2012] EWHC 265 (Fam), [2012] 2 FLR 502
Z v A (financial remedies: overseas divorce)	[2012] EWHC 467 (Fam), [2012] 2 FLR 667

Leading Cases

Appealing out of time
Johnson v Johnson	(1980) FLR 331, CA
Barder v Barder (Caluori intervening)	[1988] AC 20, [1987] 2 All ER 440, [1987] 2 WLR 1350, [1987] 2 FLR 480, HL
Cornick v Cornick	[1994] 2 FLR 530
Benson v Benson (deceased)	[1996] 1 FLR 692
T v T (consent order: procedure to set aside)	[1996] 2 FLR 640
Harris (formerly Manahan) v Manahan	[1996] 4 All ER 454, [1997] 1 FLR 205, CA
Kean v Kean	[2002] 2 FLR 28
S v S (ancillary relief: consent order)	[2002] EWHC 223 (Fam) [2003] Fam 1, [2002] 3 WLR 1372, [2002] 1 FLR 992
Rose v Rose (No 2)	[2003] EWHC 505 (Fam), [2003] 2 FLR 197
Reid v Reid	[2003] EWHC 2878 (Fam), [2004] 1 FLR 736
Williams v Lindley	[2005] EWCA Civ 103, [2005] 2 FLR 710, CA
Den Heyer v Newby	[2005] EWCA Civ 1311, [2006] 1 FLR 1114, CA
Dixon v Marchant	[2008] EWCA Civ 11, [2008] 1 FLR 655, CA
Horne v Horne	[2009] EWCA Civ 487, [2009] 2 FLR 1031, CA
Myerson v Myerson (No 2)	[2009] EWCA Civ 282, [2010] 1 WLR 114, [2009] 2 FLR 147, CA
Walkden v Walkden	[2009] EWCA Civ 627, [2010] 1 FLR 174, CA
S v S (No 2) (ancillary relief: application to set aside order)	[2009] EWHC 2377 (Fam), [2010] 1 FLR 993
Kingdon v Kingdon	[2010] EWCA Civ 1251, [2011] 1 FLR 1409, CA
Richardson v Richardson	[2011] EWCA Civ 79, [2011] 2 FLR 244, CA

Appeals
Ladd v Marshall	[1954] 3 All ER 745, [1954] 1 WLR 1489, (1954) FLR Rep 422, CA
Piglowska v Piglowski	[1999] 3 All ER 632, [1999] 1 WLR 1360, [1999] 2 FLR 763, HL
Cordle v Cordle	[2001] EWCA Civ 1791, [2002] 1 WLR 1441, [2002] 1 FLR 207, CA
Akintola v Akintola	[2001] EWCA Civ 1989, [2002] 1 FLR 701, CA
B v B (Mesher order)	[2002] EWHC 3106 (Fam), [2003] 2 FLR 285
Vaughan v Vaughan	[2007] EWCA Civ 1085, [2008] 1 FLR 1108, CA
Behzadi v Behzadi	[2008] EWCA Civ 1070, [2009] 2 FLR 649, CA
Kaur v Matharu	[2010] EWCA Civ 930, [2011] 1 FLR 698, CA
N v N (financial orders: appellate role)	[2011] EWCA Civ 940, CA, [2012] 1 FLR 622, CA
Alexander v Alexander	[2011] EWCA Civ 1019, CA
NB v Haringey LBC	[2011] EWHC 3544 (Fam), [2012] 2 FLR 125
NLW v ARC	[2012] EWHC 55 (Fam), [2012] 2 FLR 129
AV v RM (appeal)	[2012] EWHC 1173 (Fam), [2012] 2 FLR 709
HH v BLW (appeal: costs: proportionality)	[2012] EWHC 2199 (Fam), [2013] 1 FLR 420
Karim v Musa	[2012] EWCA Civ 1332 (13 July 2012, as yet unreported), CA
TF v FF	[2013] EWHC 390 (Fam) (Peter Jackson J, 26 February 2013, as yet unreported)

Arbitration
AI v MT	[2013] EWHC 100 (Fam) (Baker J, 30 January 2013, as yet unreported)

Arrears, enforcement/remission: generally
Fowler v Fowler	(1981) FLR 141, CA
Russell v Russell	[1986] 1 FLR 465, CA

Arrears, enforcement/remission: magistrates
Bernstein v O'Neill	[1989] 2 FLR 1
B v C (enforcement: arrears)	[1995] 1 FLR 467
R v Bristol Justices, exp. Hodge	[1997] QB 974, [1997] 2 WLR 756, [1997] 1 FLR 88
C v S (maintenance order: enforcement)	[1997] 1 FLR 298
R v Slough Justices, exp. Lindsay	[1997] 1 FLR 695
R v Cardiff Magistrates' Court, exp. Czech	[1999] 1 FLR 95

Avoidance of dispositions
Green v Green	[1981] 1 All ER 97, [1981] 1 WLR 391
K v K	(1983) FLR 31, CA
Kemmis v Kemmis	[1988] 1 WLR 1307, [1988] 2 FLR 223, CA
Sherry v Sherry	[1991] 1 FLR 307, CA
Purba v Purba	[2000] 1 FLR 444, CA
Mubarak v Mubarik (No 6)	[2007] EWHC 220 (Fam), [2007] 2 FLR 364
Ansari v Ansari	[2008] EWCA Civ 1456, [2010] Fam 1, [2009] 3 WLR 1092, [2009] 1 FLR 1121, CA
AC v DC (financial remedy: effect of s37 avoidance order)	[2012] EWHC 2032 (Fam) (Mostyn J, 19 July 2012, as yet unreported)

Bankruptcy
Avis v Turner	[2007] EWCA Civ 748, [2008] Ch 218, [2008] 2 WLR 1, [2008] 1 FLR 1127, CA; sub nom Turner v Avis [2007] 4 All ER 1103
Hill v Haines	[2007] EWCA Civ 1284, [2008] 2 All ER 901, [2008] 2 WLR 1250, [2008] 1 FLR 1192, CA
Turner v Avis and Avis	[2009] 1 FLR 74
Paulin v Paulin	[2009] EWCA Civ 221, [2010] 1 WLR 1057, [2009] 2 FLR 354, CA
Arif v Zar & Anor	[2012] EWCA Civ 986, [2012] All ER (D) 243 (Jul), [2012] WLR(D) 239
Hayes v Hayes	[2012] EWHC 1240 (Ch), [2012] All ER (D) 236 (Mar)
McRoberts v McRoberts	[2012] EWHC 2966 (Ch), [2012] WLR(D) 305

Leading Cases

For other Leading Cases on Bankruptcy see @eGlance and previous editions of At A Glance.

Banks
Barclays Bank plc v O'Brien	[1994] 1 AC 180, [1993] 4 All ER 417, [1993] 3 WLR 786, [1994] 1 FLR 1, HL
CIBC Mortgages plc v Pitt	[1994] 1 AC 200, [1993] 4 All ER 433, [1993] 3 WLR 802, [1994] 1 FLR 17, HL
Barclays Bank plc v Boulter	[1999] 4 All ER 513, [1999] 1 WLR 1919, [1999] 2 FLR 986, HL
Royal Bank of Scotland plc v Etridge (No. 2)	[2001] UKHL 44, [2002] AC 773, [2001] 3 WLR 1021, [2001] 2 FLR 1364, HL

Children: capital provision
Chamberlain v Chamberlain	[1974] 1 All ER 33, [1973] 1 WLR 1557, (1973) FLR Rep 125, CA
Lilford (Lord) v Glynn	[1979] 1 All ER 441, [1979] 1 WLR 78, (1978) FLR Rep 427, CA
Griffiths v Griffiths	[1984] Fam 70, [1984] 2 All ER 626, [1984] 3 WLR 165, [1984] FLR 662, CA
Kiely v Kiely	[1988] 1 FLR 248, CA
K v K	[1992] 2 All ER 727, [1992] 1 WLR 530, [1992] 2 FLR 220, CA
J v J (a minor: property transfer)	[1993] 2 FLR 56
A v A (minor: capital provision)	[1994] 1 FLR 657
T v S (financial provision for children)	[1994] 2 FLR 883
Phillips v Peace	[1996] 2 FLR 230
J v C (child: financial provision)	[1999] 1 FLR 152
V v V (child maintenance)	[2001] 2 FLR 799
P (child: financial provision), Re	[2003] EWCA Civ 837, [2003] 2 FLR 865, CA
W v W (joinder of Trusts of Land and Children Act applications)	[2003] EWCA Civ 924, [2004] 2 FLR 321
F v G (child: financial provision)	[2004] EWHC 1848 (Fam), [2005] 1 FLR 261
Re S (child: financial provision)	[2004] EWCA Civ 1685, [2005] Fam 316, [2005] 2 WLR 895, [2005] 2 FLR 94, CA
Phillips v Peace (No 2)	[2004] EWHC 3180 (Fam), [2005] 1 WLR 3246, [2005] 2 All ER 752, [2005] 2 FLR 1212
Re S (unmarried parents: financial provision)	[2006] EWCA Civ 479, [2006] 2 FLR 950, CA
M-T v T	[2006] EWHC 2494 (Fam), [2007] 2 FLR 925
Morgan v Hill	[2006] EWCA Civ 1602, [2007] 1 FLR 1480; sub nom Hill v Morgan [2007] 1 WLR 855, CA
MT v OT (financial provision: costs)	[2007] EWHC 838 (Fam), [2008] 2 FLR 1311
Re N (payments for benefit of child)	[2009] EWHC 11 (Fam), [2009] 1 FLR 1442; sub nom In re N (a child) (financial provision: dependency) [2009] 1 WLR 1621
H v C	[2009] 2 FLR 1540
B v R	[2009] EWHC 2026 (Fam), [2010] 1 FLR 563
M v V (child maintenance: jurisdiction: Brussels I)	[2010] EWHC 1453 (Fam), [2011] 1 FLR 109
CF v KM (financial provision for child: costs of legal proceedings)	[2010] EWHC 1754 (Fam), [2011] 1 FLR 208
DE v AB (financial provision for child)	[2011] EWHC 3792 (Fam), [2012] 2 FLR 1396
R v F (Schedule 1: child maintenance: mother's costs of contact proceedings)	[2011] 2 FLR 991
O v P (jurisdiction under Children Act 1989 Sch 1)	[2011] EWHC 2425 (Fam), [2012] 1 FLR 329
G v A (financial remedy: enforcement) (No 3)	[2011] EWHC 2377 (Fam), [2012] 1 FLR 415
G v A (financial remedy: enforcement) (No 4)	[2011] EWHC 2377 (Fam), [2012] 1 FLR 427
PK v BC (financial remedies: Schedule 1)	[2012] EWHC 1382 (Fam), [2012] 2 FLR 1426
PG v TW (No 1) (child: financial provision: legal funding)	[2012] EWHC 1892 (Fam) (Theis J, 4 May 2012, as yet unreported)
PG v TW (No 2) (child: financial provision)	(HHJ Horowitz QC, sitting as a High Court Judge, 21 November 2012, as yet unreported)

Children: income provision, marital
GW v RW (financial provision: departure from equality)	[2003] EWHC 611 (Fam), [2003] 2 FLR 108

Children: income provision, non-marital
Haroutunian v Jennings	(1980) FLR 62, Div Ct
Osborn v Sparks	(1982) FLR 90, Div Ct
C v F (disabled child: maintenance orders)	[1998] 2 FLR 1, CA
P (child: financial provision), Re	[2003] EWCA Civ 837, [2003] 2 FLR 865, CA
F v G (child: financial provision)	[2004] EWHC 1848 (Fam), [2005] 1 FLR 261
S (child: financial provision), Re	[2004] EWCA Civ 1685, [2005] Fam 316, [2005] 2 WLR 895, [2005] 2 FLR 94, CA
SW v RC	[2008] EWHC 73 (Fam), [2008] 1 FLR 1703
Cook v Plummer	[2008] EWCA Civ 484, [2008] 2 FLR 989, CA
H v C	[2009] 2 FLR 1540
G v G (child maintenance: interim costs provision)	[2009] EWHC 2080 (Fam), [2010] 2 FLR 1264
B v R	[2009] EWHC 2026 (Fam), [2010] 1 FLR 563
M v V (child maintenance: jurisdiction: Brussels I)	[2010] EWHC 1453 (Fam), [2011] 1 FLR 109
CF v KM (financial provision for child:	

Leading Cases

Children: income provision, non-marital (Cont'd)
costs of legal proceedings) [2010] EWHC 1754 (Fam), [2011] 1 FLR 208
DE v AB (financial provision for child) [2011] EWHC 3792 (Fam), [2012] 2 FLR 1396
R v F (Schedule 1: child maintenance:
 mother's costs of contact proceedings) [2011] 2 FLR 991
O v P (jurisdiction under Children Act
 1989 Sch 1) [2011] EWHC 2425 (Fam), [2012] 1 FLR 329
G v A (financial remedy:
 enforcement) (No 3) [2011] EWHC 2377 (Fam), [2012] 1 FLR 415
PG v TW (No 1) (child: financial
 provision: legal funding) [2012] EWHC 1892 (Fam) (Theis J, 4 May 2012, as yet unreported)
PG v TW (No 2) (child: financial
 provision) (HHJ Horowitz QC, sitting as a High Court Judge, 21 November 2012, as yet unreported)

Child Support Act
Crozier v Crozier [1994] Fam 114, [1994] 2 All ER 362, [1994] 2 WLR 444, [1994] 1 FLR 126
B v M (child support:
 revocation of order) [1994] 1 FLR 342
B v McL (leave to appeal) [1994] Fam Law 182
E (a minor) (child support:
 blood test), Re [1994] 2 FLR 548, [1995] 1 FCR 245
Mawson v Mawson [1994] 2 FLR 985
Smith v McInerney [1994] 2 FLR 1077
C (CSA: disclosure), Re [1995] 1 FLR 201, [1995] 1 FCR 202
Biggin v SSSS [1995] 1 FLR 851
Department of Social Security v Butler [1995] 4 All ER 193, [1995] 1 WLR 1528, [1996] 1 FLR 65, CA
E v C (child maintenance) [1996] 1 FLR 472
SSSS v Shotton [1996] 2 FLR 241
AMS v Child Support Officer [1998] 1 FLR 955, CA
SSSS v Harmon [1999] 1 WLR 163, [1998] 2 FLR 598, CA
R v SSSS exp. Harris [1999] 1 FLR 837
SSSS v Henderson [1999] 1 FLR 496, CA
F v CSA [1999] 2 FLR 244
Huxley v Child Support Commissioner [2000] 1 FLR 898, CA
Dorney-Kingdom v Dorney-Kingdom [2000] 2 FLR 855, CA
V v V (child maintenance) [2001] 2 FLR 799
R (Denson) v CSA [2002] EWHC 154 (Admin), [2002] 1 FLR 938
C v SSWP and B [2002] EWCA Civ 1854, [2003] 1 FLR 829, CA
SSWP v Jones [2003] EWHC 2163 (Fam), [2004] 1 FLR 282
Pabari v SSWP [2004] EWCA Civ 1480, [2005] 1 All ER 287, CA
R (Kehoe) v SSWP [2005] UKHL 48, [2006] 1 AC 42, [2005] 2 FLR 1249, HL
SSWP v M [2006] UKHL 11, [2006] 2 AC 91, [2006] 4 All ER 929, [2006] 2 WLR 637, [2006] 2 FLR 56, HL
Farley v CSA and another [2006] UKHL 31, [2006] 3 All ER 935, [2006] 2 FLR 1243, HL
Smith v SSWP and another [2006] UKHL 35, [2006] 3 All ER 907, [2007] 1 FLR 166, HL
Chandler v SSWP and another [2007] EWCA Civ 1211, [2008] 1 WLR 734, [2008] 1 FLR 638, CA
R (Humphries) v SSWP [2008] EWHC 1585 (Admin), [2008] 2 FLR 2116
CSA v Learad; CSA v Buddles [2008] EWHC 2193 (Admin), [2009] 1 FLR 31

Clean break/termination
Hanlon v Hanlon [1978] 2 All ER 889, [1978] 1 WLR 592, (1977) FLR Rep 297, CA
Pearce v Pearce (1980) FLR 261, CA
Richardson v Richardson [1993] 4 All ER 673, [1994] 1 WLR 186, [1994] 1 FLR 286
N v N (consent order: variation) [1993] 2 FLR 868, CA
Richardson v Richardson (No. 2) [1996] 2 FLR 617, CA
Flavell v Flavell [1997] 1 FLR 353, CA
C v C (financial relief: short marriage) [1997] 2 FLR 26, CA
Jones v Jones [2001] Fam 96, [2000] 3 WLR 1505, [2000] 2 FLR 307, CA
F v F (clean break: balance of fairness) [2003] 1 FLR 847
Fleming v Fleming [2003] EWCA Civ 1841, [2004] 1 FLR 667, CA
D v D (financial provision:
 periodical payments) [2004] EWHC 445 (Fam), [2004] 1 FLR 988
S v S [2008] EWHC 519 (Fam), [2008] 2 FLR 113
Vaughan v Vaughan [2010] EWCA Civ 349, [2010] 3 WLR 1209, [2010] 2 FLR 242, CA
L v L (financial remedies: deferred
 clean break) [2011] EWHC 2207 (Fam), [2012] 1 FLR 1283

Companies
Potter v Potter [1982] 3 All ER 321, [1982] 1 WLR 1255, (1983) FLR 331, CA
Smith v Smith (1983) FLR 154, CA
Re Bird Precision Bellows [1984] Ch 419, [1984] 3 All ER 444, [1984] 2 WLR 869
Nicholas v Nicholas [1984] FLR 285, CA
Buckingham v Francis [1986] 2 All ER 738
Bullock v Bullock [1986] 1 FLR 372, CA
B v B [1989] 1 FLR 119
P v P [1989] 2 FLR 241

Leading Cases

Companies (Cont'd)
Evans v Evans	[1990] 2 All ER 147, [1990] 1 FLR 319
Poon v Poon	[1994] 2 FLR 857
Mubarak v Mubarak (No 1)	[2001] 1 FLR 673
C v C (variation of post-nuptial settlement: company shares)	[2003] EWHC 1222 (Fam), [2003] 2 FLR 493
P v P (financial relief: illiquid assets)	[2004] EWHC 2277 (Fam), [2005] 1 FLR 548
R v R (financial relief: company valuation)	[2005] 2 FLR 365
A v A	[2004] EWHC 2818 (Fam), [2006] 2 FLR 115
Irvine v Irvine	[2006] EWHC 583 (Ch), [2006] 4 All ER 102
H v H	[2008] EWHC 935 (Fam), [2008] 2 FLR 2092
Ben Hashem v Al Shayif	[2008] EWHC 2380 (Fam), [2009] 1 FLR 115
Petrodel Resources Limited & others v Prest & others	[2012] EWCA Civ 1395; sub nom Prest v Prest [2013] 2 WLR 557, [2013] 1 All ER 795, CA [Judgment of Supreme Court awaited]

Conduct: financial misconduct
Martin v Martin	[1976] Fam 335, [1976] 3 All ER 625, [1976] 3 WLR 580, (1976) FLR Rep 436, CA
Primavera v Primavera	[1992] 1 FLR 16, CA
Le Foe v Le Foe	[2001] 2 FLR 970
B v B (financial provision: welfare of child and conduct)	[2002] 1 FLR 555
F v F	[2008] Fam Law 183

Conduct: misconduct of proceedings
B v B (real property: assessment of interests)	[1988] 2 FLR 490
T v T (interception of documents)	[1994] 2 FLR 1083
Tavoulareas v Tavoulareas	[1998] 2 FLR 418, CA
B v B (financial provision: welfare of child and conduct)	[2002] 1 FLR 555
Al-Khatib v Masry	[2002] EWHC 108 (Fam), [2002] 1 FLR 1053

Conduct: sexual
Brett v Brett	[1969] 1 All ER 1007, [1969] 1 WLR 487, (1968) FLR Rep 83, CA
Harnett v Harnett	[1973] Fam 156, [1973] 2 All ER 593, [1973] 3 WLR 1; affd [1974] 1 All ER 764, [1974] 1 WLR 219, (1973) FLR Rep 305, CA
Cuzner v Underdown	[1974] 2 All ER 351, [1974] 1 WLR 641, (1973) FLR Rep 176, CA
Bailey v Tolliday	(1983) FLR 542

Conduct: violence, etc
Jones v Jones	[1976] Fam 8, [1975] 2 All ER 12, [1975] 2 WLR 606, CA
M v M (financial provision: conduct)	(1982) FLR 83
Kyte v Kyte	[1988] Fam 145, [1987] 3 All ER 1041, [1987] 3 WLR 1114, [1988] 1 FLR 469, CA
Evans v Evans	[1989] 1 FLR 351, CA
H v H (financial provision: conduct)	[1994] 2 FLR 801
H v H (financial relief: attempted murder as conduct)	[2005] EWHC 2911 (Fam), [2006] 1 FLR 990

Conduct: other
Robinson v Robinson	(1981) FLR 1, CA
Robinson v Robinson	[1983] Fam 42, [1983] 1 All ER 391, [1983] 2 WLR 146, (1983) FLR 521, CA
Vasey v Vasey	[1985] FLR 596, CA
K v K (conduct)	[1990] 2 FLR 225
Whiston v Whiston	[1995] Fam 198, [1998] 1 All ER 423, [1995] 3 WLR 405, [1995] 2 FLR 268, CA
S-T (formerly J) v J (transsexual: ancillary relief)	[1998] Fam 103, [1998] 1 All ER 431, [1997] 3 WLR 1287, [1997] 1 FLR 402, CA
Clark v Clark	[1999] 2 FLR 498, CA
Rampal v Rampal (No 2)	[2001] EWCA Civ 989, [2002] Fam 85, [2001] 3 WLR 795, [2001] 2 FLR 1179, CA
Al-Khatib v Masry	[2002] EWHC 108 (Fam), [2002] 1 FLR 1053
Miller v Miller; McFarlane v McFarlane	[2006] UKHL 24, [2006] 2 AC 618, [2006] 3 All ER 1, [2006] 2 WLR 1283, [2006] 1 FLR 1186, HL
S v S (non-matrimonial property: conduct)	[2006] EWHC 2793 (Fam), [2007] 1 FLR 1496

Contributions
White v White	[2001] 1 AC 596, [2001] 1 All ER 1, [2000] 3 WLR 1571, [2000] 2 FLR 981, HL
Cowan v Cowan	[2001] EWCA Civ 679, [2002] Fam 97, [2001] 3 WLR 684, [2001] 2 FLR 192, CA
Lambert v Lambert	[2002] EWCA Civ 1685, [2003] Fam 103, [2003] 4 All ER 342, [2003] 2 WLR 631, [2003] 1 FLR 139, CA
Norris v Norris (No 1)	[2002] EWHC 2996 (Fam), [2003] 1 FLR 1142
GW v RW (financial provision: departure from equality)	[2003] EWHC 611 (Fam), [2003] 2 FLR 108
Foster v Foster	[2003] EWCA Civ 565, [2003] 2 FLR 299, CA
Sorrell v Sorrell	[2005] EWHC 1717 (Fam), [2006] 1 FLR 497
Miller v Miller; McFarlane v McFarlane	[2006] UKHL 24, [2006] 2 AC 618, [2006] 3 All ER 1, [2006] 2 WLR 1283, [2006] 1 FLR 1186, HL

Leading Cases

Contributions (Cont'd)
Charman v Charman (No 2)	[2006] EWHC 1879 (Fam), [2007] 1 FLR 593
Charman v Charman (No 3)	[2007] EWCA Civ 503; sub nom Charman v Charman (No 4), [2007] 1 FLR 1246, CA

Costs: inter partes
Calderbank v Calderbank	[1976] Fam 93, [1975] 3 All ER 333, [1975] 3 WLR 586, (1975) FLR Rep 113, CA
Leadbeater v Leadbeater	[1985] FLR 789
Leary v Leary	[1987] 1 All ER 261, [1987] 1 WLR 72, [1987] 1 FLR 384, CA
Gojkovic v Gojkovic (No. 2)	[1992] Fam 40, [1992] 1 All ER 267, [1991] 3 WLR 621, [1991] 2 FLR 233, CA
Sears Tooth (a firm) v Payne Hicks Beach (a firm) and others	[1997] 2 FLR 116
RH v RH	[2008] EWHC 347 (Fam), [2008] 2 FLR 2142
KSO v MJO and JMO (PSO intervening)	[2008] EWHC 3031 (Fam), [2009] 1 FLR 1036
Judge v Judge	[2008] EWCA Civ 1458, [2009] 1 FLR 1287, CA
Ben Hashem v Ali Shayif and Radfan Ltd	[2009] EWHC 864 (Fam), [2009] 2 FLR 896
M v M	[2009] EWHC 1941 (Fam), [2010] 1 FLR 256
Baker v Rowe	[2009] EWCA Civ 1162, [2010] 1 FLR 761, CA
GS v L (No 2) (financial remedies: costs)	[2011] EWHC 2116 (Fam), [2013] 1 FLR 407
LS v JS (appeal: costs)	[2012] EWHC 2960 (Fam) (Mostyn J, 25 January 2012, as yet unreported)
R v R (financial remedies: needs and practicalities)	[2011] EWHC 3093 (Fam), [2013] 1 FLR 120
Ezair v Ezair	[2012] EWCA Civ 893, [2013] 1 FLR 281, CA
HH v BLW (appeal: costs: proportionality)	[2012] EWHC 2199 (Fam), [2013] 1 FLR 420
TF v FF	[2013] EWHC 390 (Fam) (Peter Jackson J, 26 February 2013, as yet unreported)
KS v ND (Schedule 1: appeal: costs)	[2013] 464 (Fam) (Mostyn J, 12 March 2013, as yet unreported)

The current Costs Rules with Commentary are to be found earlier in this edition. For other Leading Cases on the former costs régime see **@eGlance** *and previous editions of* **At A Glance**.

Costs: orders against legal advisers and others
Chrulew v Borm-Reid & Co	[1992] 1 All ER 953, [1992] 1 WLR 176
Ridehalgh v Horsefield	[1994] Ch 205, [1994] 3 All ER 848, [1994] 3 WLR 462, [1994] 2 FLR 194, CA
C v C (wasted costs order)	[1994] 2 FLR 34
Sarra v Sarra	[1994] 2 FLR 880, sub nom S v S [1995] 1 FCR 185
O (costs: liability of Legal Aid Board), Re	[1997] 1 FLR 465, CA
G (minors) (care proceedings: wasted costs), Re	[2000] Fam 104, [1999] 4 All ER 371, [2000] 2 WLR 1007, [2000] 1 FLR 52
CH (family proceedings: court bundles), Re	[2000] 2 FCR 193
Phillips v Symes	[2004] EWHC 2330 (Ch), [2005] 4 All ER 519
D v H (costs)	[2008] EWHC 559 (Fam), [2008] 2 FLR 824
Re X and Y (bundles)	[2008] EWHC 2058 (Fam), [2008] 2 FLR 2053
Fisher Meredith v JH and PH (financial remedy: appeal: wasted costs)	[2012] EWHC 408 (Fam), [2012] 2 FLR 536

Delay
Hill v Hill	[1998] 1 FLR 198, CA
Rossi v Rossi & Rossi	[2006] EWHC 1482 (Fam), [2007] 1 FLR 790
S v S (ancillary relief after lengthy separation)	[2006] EWHC 2339 (Fam), [2007] 1 FLR 2120
Gordon (formerly Stefanou) v Stefanou	[2010] EWCA Civ 1601, [2011] 1 FLR 1582, CA

Duxbury income capitalisation
Duxbury v Duxbury	[1992] Fam 62n, [1990] 2 All ER 77, [1991] 3 WLR 639, [1987] 1 FLR 7, CA
B v B (financial provision)	[1990] 1 FLR 20
Gojkovic v Gojkovic	[1992] Fam 40, [1990] 2 All ER 84, [1991] 3 WLR 621, [1990] 1 FLR 140, CA
F v F (ancillary relief: substantial assets)	[1995] 2 FLR 45
F v F (Duxbury calculation: rate of return)	[1996] 1 FLR 833
A v A (financial provision)	[1998] 2 FLR 180
Fournier v Fournier	[1998] 2 FLR 990, CA
A v A (elderly applicant: lump sum)	[1999] 2 FLR 969
White v White	[2001] 1 AC 596, [2001] 1 All ER 1, [2000] 3 WLR 1571, [2000] 2 FLR 981, HL
Dharamshi v Dharamshi	[2001] 1 FLR 736, CA
GW v RW (financial provision: departure from equality)	[2003] EWHC 611 (Fam), [2003] 2 FLR 108
Pearce v Pearce	[2003] EWCA Civ 1054, [2004] 1 WLR 68, [2003] 2 FLR 1144, CA
W v W (financial provision: Form E)	[2003] EWHC 2254 (Fam), [2004] 1 FLR 494
CO v CO (ancillary relief: pre-marriage cohabitation)	[2004] EWHC 287 (Fam), [2004] 1 FLR 1095
Dixon v Marchant	[2008] EWCA Civ 11, [2008] 1 FLR 655, CA
McCartney v Mills-McCartney	[2008] EWHC 401 (Fam), [2008] 1 FLR 1508

Enforcement
McGladdery v McGladdery	[1999] 2 FLR 1102, CA
Mubarak v Mubarak (No 2)	[2001] 1 FLR 698, CA
Quinn v Cuff	[2001] EWCA Civ 36, [2001] All ER (D) 49 (Jan), CA
Mubarak v Mubarak (No 3)	[2002] EWHC 2171 (Fam), [2003] 2 FLR 553
Corbett v Corbett	[2003] EWCA Civ 559, [2003] 2 FLR 385, CA

Leading Cases

Enforcement (Cont'd)
Mubarak v Mubarik (No 4)	[2004] EWHC 1158 (Fam), [2004] 2 FLR 932
Ellis v Ellis	[2005] EWCA Civ 853, [2005] All ER (D) 288 (Jun), CA
Mubarak v Mubarik (No 5)	[2006] EWHC 1260 (Fam): sub nom Mubarak v Mubarik (No 2) [2007] 1 WLR 271; sub nom Mubarak v Mubarik (contempt in failure to pay lump sum: standard of proof) [2007] 1 FLR 722
Mubarak v Mubarik (No 6)	[2007] EWHC 220 (Fam), [2007] 2 FLR 364
Mubarak v Mubarik	[2008] JRC 136, [2009] 1 FLR 664, Royal Court of Jersey
O'Farrell v O'Farrell	[2012] EWHC 123 (QB), [2013] 1 FLR 77
Bhura v Bhura	[2012] EWHC 3633 (Fam), FLR Fast Reporting
Blight and others v Brewster	[2012] EWHC 165 (Ch), [2012] All ER (D) 190 (Feb), [2012] 1 WLR 2841
Hope v Krejci and others	[2012] EWHC 1780 (Fam), [2013] 1 FLR 182
Tasarruf Mevduati Sigorta Fonu v Merrill Lynch Bank & Trust Co (Cayman) Ltd	[2011] UKPC 17, [2011] 4 All ER 704, [2012] 1 WLR 1721, PC

Equality of division: departure from
White v White	[2001] 1 AC 596, [2001] 1 All ER 1, [2000] 3 WLR 1571, [2000] 2 FLR 981, HL
Dharamshi v Dharamshi	[2001] 1 FLR 736, CA
Elliott v Elliott	[2001] 1 FCR 477, CA
N v N (financial provision: sale of company)	[2001] 2 FLR 69
S v S (financial provision: departing from equality)	[2001] 2 FLR 246
Cowan v Cowan	[2001] EWCA Civ 679, [2002] Fam 97, [2001] 3 WLR 684, [2001] 2 FLR 192, CA
B v B (financial provision: welfare of child and conduct)	[2002] 1 FLR 555
H-J v H-J (financial provision: equality)	[2002] 1 FLR 415
Cordle v Cordle	[2001] EWCA Civ 1791, [2002] 1 WLR 1441, [2002] 1 FLR 207, CA
Al-Khatib v Masry	[2002] EWHC 108 (Fam), [2002] 1 FLR 1053
Wells v Wells	[2002] EWCA Civ 476, [2002] 2 FLR 97, CA
G v G (financial provision: equal division)	[2002] EWHC 1339 (Fam), [2002] 2 FLR 1143
Lambert v Lambert	[2002] EWCA Civ 1685, [2003] Fam 103, [2003] 4 All ER 342, [2003] 2 WLR 631, [2003] 1 FLR 139, CA
Norris v Norris (No 1)	[2002] EWHC 2996 (Fam), [2003] 1 FLR 1142
F v F (clean break: balance of fairness)	[2003] 1 FLR 847
Parra v Parra	[2002] EWCA Civ 1886, [2003] 1 FLR 942, CA
GW v RW (financial provision: departure from equality)	[2003] EWHC 611 (Fam), [2003] 2 FLR 108
Foster v Foster	[2003] EWCA Civ 565, [2003] 2 FLR 299, CA
C v C (variation of post-nuptial settlement: company shares)	[2003] EWHC 1222 (Fam), [2003] 2 FLR 493
R v R (lump sum repayments)	[2003] EWHC 3197 (Fam), [2004] 1 FLR 928
McFarlane v McFarlane; Parlour v Parlour	[2004] EWCA Civ 872, [2005] Fam 171, [2004] 3 WLR 1480, [2004] 3 All ER 921, [2004] 2 FLR 893, CA
P v P (inherited property)	[2004] EWHC 1364 (Fam), [2005] 1 FLR 576
P v P (financial relief: illiquid assets)	[2004] EWHC 2277 (Fam), [2005] 1 FLR 548
R v R (financial relief: company valuation)	[2005] 2 FLR 365
Q v Q (ancillary relief: periodical payments)	[2005] EWHC 402 (Fam), [2005] 2 FLR 640
V v V (financial relief)	[2005] 2 FLR 697
Sorrell v Sorrell	[2005] EWHC 1717 (Fam), [2006] 1 FLR 497
Miller v Miller	[2005] EWCA Civ 984, [2006] 1 FLR 151, CA
Miller v Miller; McFarlane v McFarlane	[2006] UKHL 24, [2006] 2 AC 618, [2006] 3 All ER 1, [2006] 2 WLR 1283, [2006] 1 FLR 1186, HL
Rossi v Rossi & Rossi	[2006] EWHC 1482 (Fam), [2007] 1 FLR 790
Charman v Charman (No 2)	[2006] EWHC 1879 (Fam), [2007] 1 FLR 593
S v S (ancillary relief after lengthy separation)	[2006] EWHC 2339 (Fam), [2007] 1 FLR 2120
S v S (non-matrimonial property: conduct)	[2006] EWHC 2793 (Fam), [2007] 1 FLR 1496
RP v RP	[2006] EWHC 3409 (Fam), [2007] 1 FLR 2105
H v H	[2007] EWHC 459 (Fam), [2007] 2 FLR 548
Smith v Smith	[2007] EWCA 454, [2007] 2 FLR 1103, CA
Charman v Charman (No 3)	[2007] EWCA Civ 503; sub nom Charman v Charman (No 4), [2007] 1 FLR 1246, CA
CR v CR	[2007] EWHC 3206 (Fam), [2008] 1 FLR 323
L v L (ancillary relief)	[2008] EWHC 882 (Fam), [2008] 1 FLR 142
C v C	[2007] EWHC 2033 (Fam), [2009] 1 FLR 8
P v P (post separation accruals and earning capacity)	[2007] EWHC 2877 (Fam), [2008] 2 FLR 1135
RH v RH	[2008] EWHC 347 (Fam), [2008] 2 FLR 2142
McCartney v Mills-McCartney	[2008] EWHC 401 (Fam), [2008] 1 FLR 1508
B v B (ancillary relief: distribution of assets)	[2008] EWCA Civ 284, [2008] 1 WLR 2362, [2008] 1 FLR 1627, CA
H v H	[2008] EWHC 935 (Fam), [2008] 2 FLR 2092
Behzadi v Behzadi	[2008] EWCA Civ 1070, [2009] 2 FLR 649, CA
SK v WL (ancillary relief: post-	

Leading Cases

Equality of division: departure from (Cont'd)
  separation accrual)   [2010] EWHC 457 (Fam), [2011] 1 FLR 1471
N v N (ancillary relief)   [2010] EWHC 717 (Fam), [2010] 2 FLR 1093
FZ v SZ (ancillary relief: conduct: valuations) [2010] EWHC 1630 (Fam), [2011] 1 FLR 64
Robson v Robson   [2010] EWCA Civ 1171, [2011] 1 FLR 751, CA
Jones v Jones   [2011] EWCA Civ 41, [2012] Fam 1, [2011] 3 WLR 582, [2011] 1 FLR 1723, CA
N v F (financial orders: pre-acquired
  wealth)   [2011] EWHC 586 (Fam), [2011] 2 FLR 533
J v J (financial orders: wife's long
  term needs)   [2011] EWHC 1010 (Fam), [2011] 2 FLR 1280
K v L   [2011] EWCA Civ 550, [2011] 3 All ER 733, [2012] 1 WLR 306; sub nom K v L
                                                (non-matrimonial property: special contribution) [2011] 2 FLR 980, CA
Mansfield v Mansfield   [2011] EWCA Civ 1056, [2012] 1 FLR 117, CA
AR v AR (treatment of inherited wealth) [2011] EWHC 2717 (Fam), [2012] 2 FLR 1
S v AG (financial remedy: lottery prize) [2011] EWHC 2637 (Fam), [2012] 1 FLR 651
A v L (departure from equality: needs) [2011] EWHC 3150 (Fam), [2012] 1 FLR 985
Lawrence v Gallagher   [2012] EWCA Civ 394, [2012] 2 FLR 643, CA
Y v Y   [2012] EWHC 2063 (Fam), FLR Fast Reporting
R v R (financial remedies: needs
  and practicalities)   [2011] EWHC 3093 (Fam), [2013] 1 FLR 120

Equality of division: principle applied
White v White   [2001] 1 AC 596, [2001] 1 All ER 1, [2000] 3 WLR 1571, [2000] 2 FLR 981, HL
H-J v H-J (financial provision: equality) [2002] 1 FLR 415
G v G (financial provision: equal division) [2002] EWHC 1339 (Fam), [2002] 2 FLR 1143
Lambert v Lambert   [2002] EWCA Civ 1685, [2003] Fam 103, [2003] 4 All ER 342,
                                               [2003] 2 WLR 631, [2003] 1 FLR 139, CA
Norris v Norris (No 1)   [2002] EWHC 2996 (Fam), [2003] 1 FLR 1142
Parra v Parra   [2002] EWCA Civ 1886, [2003] 1 FLR 942, CA
C v C (variation of post-nuptial
  settlement: company shares)   [2003] EWHC 1222 (Fam), [2003] 2 FLR 493
P v P (financial relief: illiquid assets)   [2004] EWHC 2277 (Fam), [2005] 1 FLR 548
R v R (financial relief: company valuation) [2005] 2 FLR 365
Miller v Miller; McFarlane v McFarlane   [2006] UKHL 24, [2006] 2 AC 618, [2006] 3 All ER 1, [2006] 2 WLR 1283,
                                               [2006] 1 FLR 1186, HL
E v E (shared residence: financial relief:
  yardstick of equality)   [2006] EWCA Civ 843), [2006] 2 FLR 1228, CA
S v S (ancillary relief: importance of FDR) [2007] EWHC 1975 (Fam), [2008] 1 FLR 944
CR v CR   [2007] EWHC 3206 (Fam), [2008] 1 FLR 323

Experts
F v F (ancillary relief: substantial assets) [1995] 2 FLR 45
N v C (property adjustment order:
  surveyor's negligence)   [1998] 1 FLR 63, CA
Daniels v Walker   [2000] 1 WLR 1382, CA
Peet v Mid-Kent Healthcare NHS Trust   [2001] EWCA Civ 1703, [2002] 3 All ER 688, [2002] 1 WLR 210, CA
Vasilou v Hajigeorgiou   [2005] EWCA Civ 236, [2005] 3 All ER 17, [2005] 1 WLR 2195, CA
K v K (financial relief:
  management of difficult cases)   [2005] EWHC 1070 (Fam), [2005] 2 FLR 1137
Toth v Jarman   [2006] EWCA Civ 1028, [2006] 4 All ER 1276, CA
Stallwood v David   [2006] EWHC 2600 (QB), [2007] 1 All ER 206

Farms
P v P   [1978] 3 All ER 70, [1978] 1 WLR 483, (1977) FLR Rep 546, CA
S v S   (1980) 10 Fam Law 240
White v White   [2001] 1 AC 596, [2001] 1 All ER 1, [2000] 3 WLR 1571, [2000] 2 FLR 981, HL
R v R (lump sum repayments)   [2003] EWHC 3197 (Fam), [2004] 1 FLR 928
P v P (inherited property)   [2004] EWHC 1364 (Fam), [2005] 1 FLR 576

Financial relief after overseas divorce
Jordan v Jordan   [2000] 1 WLR 210, [1999] 2 FLR 1069, CA
Agbaje v Agbaje   [2010] UKSC 13, [2010] AC 628, [2010] 2 All ER 877, [2010] 2 WLR 709,
                                                [2010] 1 FLR 1813, SC
M v M   [2011] EWHC 3574 (Fam) and [2010] EWHC 2817 (Fam), [2011] 1 FLR 1773
Schofield v Schofield   [2011] EWCA Civ 174, [2011] 1 FLR 2129, CA
Traversa v Freddi   [2011] EWCA Civ 81, [2011] 2 FLR 272, CA
Golubovich v Golubovich   [2011] EWCA Civ 479, [2011] 2 FLR 1193, CA
Z v A   [2012] EWHC 1434 (Fam) (Coleridge J, 9 May 2012, as yet unreported)

Forum conveniens
Spiliada Maritime Corpn v
  Cansulex Ltd, The Spiliada   [1987] AC 460, [1986] 3 All ER 843, [1986] 3 WLR 972, HL
de Dampierre v de Dampierre   [1988] AC 92, [1987] 2 All ER 1, [1987] 2 FLR 300, HL
W v W (financial relief: appropriate forum) [1997] 1 FLR 257
S v S (divorce: staying proceedings)   [1997] 1 WLR 1200, [1997] 2 FLR 100
Butler v Butler (Nos 1 and 2)   [1997] 2 All ER 822, [1998] 1 WLR 1208, [1997] 2 FLR 311, CA
Connelly v RTZ Corporation plc   [1998] AC 854, [1997] 4 All ER 335, [1997] 3 WLR 373, HL
D v P (forum conveniens)   [1998] 2 FLR 25, CA

Leading Cases

Forum conveniens (Cont'd)
Krenge v Krenge	[1999] 1 FLR 969
Otobo v Otobo	[2002] EWCA Civ 949, [2003] 1 FLR 192, CA
Armstrong v Armstrong	[2003] EWHC 777 (Fam), [2003] 2 FLR 375
Owusu v Jackson (Case C-281/02)	[2005] QB 801, [2005] 2 All ER (Comm) 577, [2005] 2 WLR 942, ECJ
Cook v Plummer	[2008] EWCA Civ 484, [2008] 2 FLR 989, CA
JKN v JCN (divorce: forum)	[2010] EWHC 843 (Fam), [2011] 1 FLR 826
T v P (jurisdiction: Lugano Convention and forum conveniens)	[2012] EWHC 1627 (Fam), [2013] 1 FLR 478
AB v CB (divorce: jurisdiction)	[2012] EWHC 3841 (Fam), FLR Fast Reporting

Inheritance (Provision for Family and Dependants) Act 1975
Coventry, Coventry v Coventry, Re	[1980] Ch 461, [1979] 3 All ER 815, [1979] 3 WLR 802, (1979) FLR Rep 142, CA
Besterman (deceased), Re	[1984] Ch 458, [1984] 2 All ER 656, [1984] 3 WLR 280, [1984] FLR 503, CA
Bishop v Plumley	[1991] 1 All ER 236, [1991] 1 WLR 582, [1991] 1 FLR 121, CA
Moody v Stevenson	[1992] Ch 486, [1992] 2 All ER 524, [1992] 2 WLR 640, [1992] 1 FLR 494, CA
Jessop v Jessop	[1992] 1 FLR 591, CA
Powell v Osbourne	[1993] 1 FLR 1001, CA
Davis v Davis	[1993] 1 FLR 54, CA
Jennings (deceased), Re	[1994] Ch 286, [1994] 3 All ER 27, [1994] 3 WLR 67, [1994] 1 FLR 536, CA
Abram (deceased), Re	[1996] 2 FLR 379
Krubert (deceased), Re	[1997] Ch 97, [1996] 3 WLR 959, [1997] 1 FLR 42, CA
Cameron v Treasury Solicitor	[1996] 2 FLR 716, CA
Pearce (deceased), Re	[1998] 2 FLR 705, CA
Espinosa v Bourke	[1999] 1 FLR 747, CA
Watson (deceased), Re	[1999] 1 FLR 878
B (deceased), In re	[2000] Ch 662, [2000] 2 All ER 665, CA; sub nom Bouette v Rose [2000] 1 FLR 363, CA
Dix (deceased), In re	[2004] EWCA Civ 139, [2004] Fam 141, [2004] 1 WLR 1399, CA; sub nom Gully v Dix [2004] 1 FLR 918
Kotke v Saffarini	[2005] EWCA Civ 221, [2005] 2 FLR 517, CA
Fielden v Cunliffe	[2005] EWCA Civ 1508, [2006] Ch 361, [2006] 2 All ER 115, [2006] 2 WLR 481, [2006] 1 FLR 745, CA
Dingmar v Dingmar	[2006] EWCA Civ 942, [2007] 2 All ER 382, CA
Baynes v Hedger	[2009] EWCA Civ 374, [2009] 2 FLR 767, CA
Ilott v Mitson and others	[2011] EWCA Civ 346, [2012] 2 FLR 170, CA
Smith v Smith	[2011] EWHC 2133 (Ch), [2012] 2 FLR 230
Iqbal v Ahmed	[2011] EWCA Civ 900, [2012] 1 FLR 31, CA
Lilleyman v Lilleyman	[2012] EWHC 821 (Ch), [2013] Ch 225, [2013] 1 All ER 302, [2012] 3 WLR 754, [2013] 1 FLR 87
Lilleyman v Lilleyman (costs)	[2012] EWHC 1056 (Ch), [2013] 1 FLR 69; sub nom Lilleyman v Lilleyman (No 2) [2013] 1 All ER 325, [2012] 1 WLR 2801

Injunctions in support of financial remedies: section 37 injunctions
Jordan v Jordan	(1965) Sol Jo 353
Smith v Smith	(1974) 4 Fam Law 80
Jackson v Jackson	(1979) 9 Fam Law 56, CA
Hamlin v Hamlin	[1986] Fam 11, [1985] 2 All ER 1037, [1985] 3 WLR 629, [1986] 1 FLR 61, CA
Crittenden v Crittenden	[1990] 2 FLR 361, CA
Shipman v Shipman	[1991] 1 FLR 250
Bater v Bater	[1999] 4 All ER 944, [1999] 2 FLR 993, CA
Khreino v Khreino (No 2) (court's power to grant injunctions)	[2000] 1 FCR 80, CA
ND v KP (freezing order: ex parte application)	[2011] EWHC 457 (Fam), [2011] 2 FLR 662

Injunctions in support of financial remedies: freezing (Mareva) injunctions
Mareva Cia Naviera SA v International Bulkcarriers SA	[1980] 1 All ER 213, CA
Shipman v Shipman	[1991] 1 FLR 250
Ghoth v Ghoth	[1992] 2 All ER 920, [1992] 2 FLR 300, CA
Crédit Suisse Fides Trust SA v Cuoghi	[1997] 3 All ER 724, [1997] 3 WLR 871, CA
Khreino v Khreino (No 2) (court's power to grant injunctions)	[2000] 1 FCR 80, CA
W v H (Family Division: without notice orders)	[2001] 1 All ER 300, [2000] 2 FLR 927
S (a child) (Family Division: without notice orders), Re	[2001] 1 All ER 362, [2001] 1 WLR 211, [2001] 1 FLR 308
Rhode v Rhode and Pembroke Square Ltd	[2007] EWHC 496 (Fam), [2007] 2 FLR 971
N v R (injunction)	[2008] EWHC 1347 (Fam), [2009] 2 FLR 342
ND v KP (freezing order: ex parte application)	[2011] EWHC 457 (Fam), [2011] 2 FLR 662
KY v DD (injunctions)	[2011] EWHC 1277 (Fam), [2012] 2 FLR 200
JSC BTA Bank v Solodchenko & Ors	[2011] EWHC 2163 (Ch), [2012] 1 All ER 735

For other Leading Cases on freezing injunctions see **@eGlance** *and previous editions of* **At A Glance**.

Leading Cases

Injunctions in support of financial remedies: search (Anton Piller) orders
Anton Piller KG v
  Manufacturing Processes Ltd [1976] Ch 55, [1976] 1 All ER 779, CA
Burgess v Burgess [1996] 2 FLR 34, CA
Araghchinchi v Araghchinchi [1997] 2 FLR 142, CA

For other Leading Cases on search orders see @eGlance and previous editions of **At A Glance**.

Injunctions in support of financial remedies: writ ne exeat regno, etc
B v B (injunction:
  restraint on leaving jurisdiction) [1997] 3 All ER 258, [1998] 1 WLR 329, [1997] 2 FLR 148
Young v Young [2012] EWHC 138 (Fam), [2012] Fam 198, [2012] 3 WLR 266, [2012] 2 FLR 470

For other Leading Cases on writ ne exeat regno, etc see @eGlance and previous editions of **At A Glance**.

Injunctions in support of financial remedies: anti-suit / Hemain injunctions
Société Nationale Industrielle
  Aérospatiale v Lee Kui Jak [1987] AC 871, [1987] 3 All ER 510, [1987] 3 WLR 59, PC
Hemain v Hemain [1988] 2 FLR 388, CA
Bloch v Bloch [2002] EWHC 1711 (Fam), [2003] 1 FLR 1
R v R (divorce: Hemain injunction) [2003] EWHC 2113 (Fam), [2005] 1 FLR 386
Turner v Grovit (Case C-159/02) [2005] 1 AC 101, [2004] 3 WLR 1193, ECJ
Golubovich v Golubovich [2010] EWCA Civ 810, [2011] Fam 88, [2010] 3 WLR 1607,
  [2010] 2 FLR 1614, CA

Interim capital orders/orders for sale
Wicks v Wicks [1998] 1 All ER 977, [1998] 3 WLR 277, [1998] 1 FLR 470, CA
Miller-Smith v Miller-Smith [2009] EWCA Civ 1297, [2010] 1 FLR 1402, CA

Jurisdiction: EU Regulations
de Cavel v de Cavel (Case 143/78) [1979] ECR 1055, ECJ
de Cavel v de Cavel (No 2) (Case 120/79) [1980] ECR 731, [1980] 3 CMLR 1, ECJ
K v B (Brussels Convention) [1994] 1 FLR 267
Van den Boogaard v Laumen [1997] QB 759, [1997] 3 WLR 284, [1997] 2 FLR 399, ECJ
Farrell v Long [1997] QB 842, [1997] All ER (EC) 449, [1998] 1 FLR 559, ECJ
D v P (forum conveniens) [1998] 2 FLR 25, CA
Canada Trust Co v Stolzenberg (No 2) [2000] 4 All ER 481, [2000] 3 WLR 1376, HL
Wermuth v Wermuth (No 1) [2002] EWHC 3049 (Fam), [2003] 1 FLR 1022
Wermuth v Wermuth (No 2) [2002] EWCA Civ 50, [2003] 4 All ER 531, [2003] 1 WLR 942,
  [2003] 1 FLR 1029, CA
Rogers-Headicar v Headicar [2004] EWCA Civ 1867, [2005] 2 FCR 1, CA
Chorley v Chorley [2005] EWCA Civ 68, [2005] 1 WLR 1469, [2005] 2 FLR 38, CA
L-K v K (Brussels II revised:
  maintenance pending suit) [2006] EWHC (Fam) 153, [2006] 2 FLR 1114
Prazic v Prazic [2006] EWCA Civ 497, [2006] 2 FLR 1128, CA
Bentinck v Bentinck [2007] EWCA Civ 175, [2007] 2 FLR 1
Moore v Moore [2007] EWCA Civ 361, [2007] 2 FLR 339, CA
L-K v K (No 2) [2006] EWHC 3280 (Fam), [2007] 2 FLR 729
L-K v K (No 3) [2006] EWHC 3281 (Fam), [2007] 2 FLR 741
Re N (jurisdiction) [2007] EWHC 1274 (Fam), [2007] 2 FLR 1196
Leman-Klammers v Klammers [2007] EWCA Civ 919, [2008] 1 FLR 692, CA
Marinos v Marinos [2007] EWHC 2047 (Fam), [2007] 2 FLR 1018
Sundelind Lopez v Lopez Lizazo
  (Case C-68/07) [2008] Fam 21, [2008] 3 WLR 338, [2008] 1 FLR 582, ECJ
Munro v Munro [2007] EWHC 3315 (Fam), [2008] 1 FLR 1613
Olafisoye v Olafisoye [2010] EWHC 3539 (Fam), [2011] 2 FLR 553
C v S (divorce: jurisdiction) [2010] EWHC 2676 (Fam), [2011] 2 FLR 19
V v V (divorce: jurisdiction) [2011] EWHC 1190 (Fam), [2011] 2 FLR 778

Jurisdiction: domicile
Irvin v Irvin [2001] 1 FLR 178
Mark v Mark [2005] UKHL 42, [2006] 1 AC, [2005] 3 All ER 912, [2005] 3 WLR 111,
  [2005] 2 FLR 1193, HL
R v R (divorce jurisdiction: domicile) [2006] 1 FLR 389
Cyganik v Agulian [2006] EWCA Civ 129, [2006] 1 FCR 406, CA
Munro v Munro [2007] EWHC 3315 (Fam), [2008] 1 FLR 1613
Henwood v Barlow Clowes
  International Ltd (in liquidation) and others [2008] EWCA Civ 577, [2008] All ER (D) 330 (May), CA
F v F (divorce: jurisdiction) [2009] EWHC 1448 (Fam), [2009] 2 FLR 1496, CA
M v M (divorce: domicile) [2010] EWHC 982 (Fam), [2011] 1 FLR 919
Holliday v Musa [2010] EWCA Civ 335, [2010] 2 FLR 702, CA
Olafisoye v Olafisoye [2010] EWHC 3539 (Fam), [2011] 2 FLR 553

Jurisdiction: habitual residence
Mark v Mark [2005] UKHL 42, [2006] 1 AC, [2005] 3 All ER 912, [2005] 3 WLR 111,
  [2005] 2 FLR 1193, HL
L-K v K (No 2) [2006] EWHC 3280 (Fam), [2007] 2 FLR 729
Marinos v Marinos [2007] EWHC 2047 (Fam), [2007] 2 FLR 1018
Munro v Munro [2007] EWHC 3315 (Fam), [2008] 1 FLR 1613

Leading Cases

Jurisdiction: habitual residence (Cont'd)
Z v Z (divorce: jurisdiction)	[2009] EWHC 2626 (Fam), [2010] 1 FLR 694
Olafisoye v Olafisoye	[2010] EWHC 3539 (Fam), [2011] 2 FLR 553
C v S (divorce: jurisdiction)	[2010] EWHC 2676 (Fam), [2011] 2 FLR 19
V v V (divorce: jurisdiction)	[2011] EWHC 1190 (Fam), [2011] 2 FLR 778

Legal Aid: effect on order
Collins v Collins	[1987] 1 FLR 226, CA
Scallon v Scallon	[1990] 1 FLR 194, CA

Legal Aid: enforcement of costs orders
Parr v Smith	[1995] 2 All ER 1031, [1996] 1 FLR 490, CA
Chaggar v Chaggar	[1997] 1 All ER 104, [1997] 1 FLR 566, CA
Wraith v Wraith	[1997] 1 WLR 1540, [1997] 2 FLR 415, CA
Waterford Wedgwood plc v David Nagli Ltd	[1999] 3 All ER 185
Jones v Congregational and General Insurance plc	[2003] EWHC 1027 (QB), [2003] 1 WLR 3001

Legal Aid: incidence of charge
Till v Till	[1974] 1 QB 558, [1974] 1 All ER 1096, [1974] 2 WLR 447, (1974) FLR Rep 703, CA
Hanlon v Law Society	[1981] AC 124, [1980] 2 All ER 199, [1980] 2 WLR 756, HL
Draskovic v Draskovic	(1981) 11 Fam Law 87
Manley v Law Society	[1981] 1 All ER 401, [1981] 1 WLR 335, CA
Van Hoorn v Law Society	[1985] QB 106, [1984] 3 All ER 136, [1984] 3 WLR 199, [1984] FLR 203
Curling v Law Society	[1985] 1 All ER 705, [1985] 1 WLR 470, [1985] FLR 831, CA
Stewart v Law Society	[1987] 1 FLR 223
Watkinson v Legal Aid Board	[1991] 2 All ER 953, [1991] 1 WLR 419, [1991] 2 FLR 26, CA
Parkes v Legal Aid Board	[1996] 4 All ER 271, [1997] 1 WLR 1547, [1997] 1 FLR 77, CA
Morgan v Legal Aid Board	[2000] 3 All ER 974, [2000] 1 WLR 1657

Legal Aid: orders against Legal Aid Agency / Legal Services Commission
Nowotnik v Nowotnik	[1967] P 83, [1965] 3 All ER 167, [1965] 3 WLR 920, CA
Hanning v Maitland (No. 2)	[1970] 1 QB 580, [1970] 1 All ER 812, [1970] 2 WLR 151, CA
Povey v Povey	[1972] Fam 40, [1972] 3 All ER 612, [1971] 2 WLR 381, Div Ct
Middleton v Middleton	[1994] 1 FLR 557, CA
Keller v Keller	[1995] 1 FLR 259, CA
O (costs: liability of Legal Aid Board), Re	[1997] 1 FLR 465, CA
Kelly v South Manchester Health Authority	[1997] 3 All ER 274, [1998] 1 WLR 244
R v Secretary of State for the Home Dept exp. Gunn	[2001] EWCA Civ 891, [2001] 3 All ER 481, [2001] 1 WLR 1634, CA
Legal Services Commission v F, A & V	[2011] EWHC 899 (QB), [2011] 2 FLR 1105

Length of marriage: cohabitation before
Campbell v Campbell	[1976] Fam 347, [1977] 1 All ER 1, [1976] 3 WLR 572
Kokosinski v Kokosinski	[1980] Fam 72, [1980] 1 All ER 1106, [1980] 3 WLR 55, (1980) FLR 205
Foley v Foley	[1981] Fam 160, [1981] 2 All ER 857, [1981] 3 WLR 284, (1981) FLR 215, CA
GW v RW (financial provision: departure from equality)	[2003] EWHC 611 (Fam), [2003] 2 FLR 108
CO v CO (ancillary relief: pre-marriage cohabitation)	[2004] EWHC 287 (Fam), [2004] 1 FLR 1095

Length of marriage: short
Miller v Miller	[2005] EWCA Civ 984, [2006] 1 FLR 151, CA
Miller v Miller; McFarlane v McFarlane	[2006] UKHL 24, [2006] 2 AC 618, [2006] 3 All ER 1, [2006] 2 WLR 1283, [2006] 1 FLR 1186, HL
MD v D	[2008] EWHC 1929 (Fam), [2009] 1 FLR 810

Lump sums
Tilley v Tilley	(1980) 10 Fam Law 89, CA
L v L (lump sum: interest)	[1994] 2 FLR 324
Penrose v Penrose	[1994] 2 FLR 621, CA
Masefield v Alexander (lump sum: extension of time)	[1995] 1 FLR 100, CA
M v B (ancillary proceedings: lump sum)	[1998] 1 FLR 53, CA
R v R (lump sum repayments)	[2003] EWHC 3197 (Fam), [2004] 1 FLR 928
Hamilton v Hamilton	[2013] EWCA Civ 13, [2013] All ER (D) 201 (Jan), FLR Fast Reporting, CA

Maintenance pending suit
F v F (maintenance pending suit)	(1983) FLR 382
F v F (ancillary relief: substantial assets)	[1995] 2 FLR 45
A v A (maintenance pending suit: payment of legal fees)	[2001] 1 WLR 605, [2001] 1 FLR 377
G v G (maintenance pending suit: legal costs)	[2002] EWHC 306 (Fam), [2003] 2 FLR 71
M v M (maintenance pending suit)	[2002] EWHC 317 (Fam), [2002] 2 FLR 123
Moses-Taiga v Taiga	[2005] EWCA Civ 1013, [2006] 1 FLR 1074, CA
TL v ML and others (ancillary relief: claim against assets of extended family)	[2005] EWHC 2860 (Fam), [2006] 1 FLR 1263
Currey v Currey (No 2)	[2006] EWCA Civ 1338, [2006] All ER (D) 218 (Oct), [2007] 1 FLR 946, CA
Moore v Moore	[2010] EWCA Civ 1427, [2010] 1 FLR 1413, CA

Leading Cases

Media access, etc
Clibbery v Allen	[2001] 2 FLR 819
Clibbery v Allen (No 2)	[2002] EWCA Civ 45, [2002] Fam 261, [2002] 1 All ER 865, [2002] 2 WLR 1511, [2002] 1 FLR 565, CA
Re S (a child) (identification: restriction on publication)	[2004] UKHL 47, [2005] 1 AC 593, [2004] 4 All ER 683, [2004] 3 WLR 1129, [2005] 1 FLR 591, HL
D v D (divorce: media presence)	[2009] EWHC 946 (Fam), [2009] 2 FLR 324
Spencer v Spencer	[2009] EWHC 1529 (Fam), [2009] 2 FLR 1416
Re X (a child) (residence and contact: rights of media attendance)	[2009] EWHC 1728 (Fam), [2009] 2 FLR 1467
Lykiardopulo v Lykiardopulo	[2010] EWCA Civ 1315, [2011] 1 FLR 1427, CA
A v A (reporting restriction)	[2012] EWHC B17 (Fam), FLR Fast Reporting
W v M (TOLATA proceedings: anonymity)	[2012] EWHC 1679 (Fam) (Mostyn J, 25 June 2012, as yet unreported)

Money: small
Barnes v Barnes	[1972] 3 All ER 872, [1972] 1 WLR 1381, CA
Peacock v Peacock	[1984] 1 All ER 1069, [1984] 1 WLR 532, [1984] FLR 263
Freeman v Swatridge	[1984] FLR 762, CA
Ashley v Blackman	[1988] Fam 85, [1988] 3 WLR 222, [1988] 2 FLR 278
Delaney v Delaney	[1990] 2 FLR 457, CA
SRJ v DWJ (financial provision)	[1999] 2 FLR 176, CA

Negligence (by legal advisers and others)
Dutfield v Gilbert H Stevens & Sons	(1988) 18 Fam Law 473
White v Jones	[1993] 3 All ER 481, [1993] 3 WLR 730, CA
Griffiths v Dawson & Co	[1993] 2 FLR 315
Dickinson v Jones Alexander & Co	[1993] 2 FLR 521
Young v Purdy	[1996] 2 FLR 795, CA
B v Miller & Co	[1996] 2 FLR 23
Kelley v Corston	[1998] QB 686, [1997] 4 All ER 466, [1998] 3 WLR 246, [1998] 1 FLR 986, CA
N v C (property adjustment order: surveyor's negligence)	[1998] 1 FLR 63, CA
Hall & Co v Simons	[2000] 3 All ER 673, [2000] 3 WLR 543, [2000] 2 FLR 545, HL
Westbury v Sampson	[2001] EWCA Civ 407, [2002] 1 FLR 166, CA
Williams v Thompson Leatherdale and Francis	[2008] EWHC 2574 (QB), [2009] 2 FLR 730

Non-disclosure/discovery
J v J	[1955] P 215, [1955] 2 All ER 617, [1955] 3 WLR 72, (1955) FLR Rep 402, CA
Livesey v Jenkins	[1985] AC 424, [1985] 1 All ER 106, [1985] 2 WLR 47, [1985] FLR 813, HL
P v P (financial relief: non-disclosure)	[1994] 2 FLR 381
Baker v Baker	[1995] 2 FLR 829, CA
A v A; B v B	[2000] 1 FLR 701
Al-Khatib v Masry	[2002] EWHC 108 (Fam), [2002] 1 FLR 1053
W v W (financial provision: Form E)	[2003] EWHC 2254 (Fam), [2004] 1 FLR 494
OS v DS (oral disclosure: preliminary hearing)	[2004] EWHC 2376 (Fam), [2005] 1 FLR 675
Minwalla v Minwalla & others	[2004] EWHC 2823 (Fam), [2005] 1 FLR 771
Behzadi v Behzadi	[2008] EWCA Civ 1070, [2009] 2 FLR 649, CA
Bokor-Ingram v Bokor-Ingram	[2009] EWCA Civ 412, [2009] 2 FLR 922, CA
Imerman v Tchenguiz	[2010] EWCA Civ 908, [2011] Fam 116, [2011] 1 All ER 555, [2011] 2 WLR 592, [2010] 2 FLR 814, CA
NG v SG (appeal: non-disclosure)	[2011] EWHC 3270 (Fam), [2012] 1 FLR 1211
Kremen v Agrest (financial remedy: non-disclosure: post-nuptial agreement)	[2012] EWHC 45 (Fam), [2012] 2 FLR 414

Non-parties, disclosure by
Morgan v Morgan	[1977] Fam 122, [1977] 2 All ER 515, [1977] 2 WLR 712, (1976) FLR Rep 473
Wynne v Wynne & Jeffers	[1980] 3 All ER 659, [1981] 1 WLR 69, (1980) 10 Fam Law 241, CA
W v W (disclosure by third party)	(1981) FLR 291
H v H (disclosure by third party)	(1981) FLR 303
Re T (divorce: interim maintenance: discovery)	[1990] 1 FLR 1
Frary v Frary	[1993] 2 FLR 696, CA
B v B (production appointment: procedure)	[1995] 1 FLR 913
D v D (production appointment)	[1995] 2 FLR 497
Charman v Charman	[2005] EWCA Civ 1606, [2006] 2 FLR 422, CA

Orders over property
Mesher v Mesher & Hall	[1980] 1 All ER 126n, CA
Martin v Martin	[1978] Fam 12, [1977] 3 All ER 762, [1977] 3 WLR 101, (1977) FLR Rep 444, CA
Dunford v Dunford	[1980] 1 All ER 122, [1980] 1 WLR 5, (1980) FLR 22, CA
Harvey v Harvey	[1982] Fam 83, [1982] 1 All ER 693, [1982] 2 WLR 283, (1982) FLR 141, CA
Thompson v Thompson	[1986] Fam 38, [1985] 2 All ER 243, [1985] 3 WLR 17, [1985] FLR 863, CA
Mortimer v Mortimer-Griffin	[1986] 2 FLR 315, CA
Clutton v Clutton	[1991] 1 All ER 340, [1991] 1 WLR 359, [1991] 1 FLR 242, CA

Leading Cases

Orders over property (Cont'd)
Popat v Popat	[1991] 2 FLR 163, CA
N v N (valuation: charge-back order)	[1996] 1 FLR 361
Omielan v Omielan	[1996] 2 FLR 306, CA
Jones v Jones	[1997] Fam 59, [1997] 2 WLR 373, [1997] 1 FLR 27, CA
B v B (Mesher order)	[2002] EWHC 3106 (Fam), [2003] 2 FLR 285
TL v ML and others (ancillary relief: claim against assets of extended family)	[2005] EWHC 2860 (Fam), [2006] 1 FLR 1264
Rossi v Rossi & Rossi	[2006] EWHC 1482 (Fam), [2007] 1 FLR 790
Fisher-Aziz v Aziz	[2010] EWCA Civ 673, [2010] 2 FLR 1053, CA

Pensions: military
Walker v Walker	[1983] Fam 68, [1983] 2 All ER 909, [1983] 3 WLR 421, (1983) FLR 779, CA
Ranson v Ranson	[1988] 1 WLR 183, [1988] 1 FLR 292, CA
Legrove v Legrove	[1994] 2 FLR 119, CA
R (Smith) v Secretary of State for Defence and Secretary of State for Work and Pensions	[2004] EWHC 1797 (Admin), [2005] 1 FLR 97

Pensions: other
Cowan v Cowan	[2001] EWCA Civ 679, [2002] Fam 97, [2001] 3 WLR 684, [2001] 2 FLR 192, CA
Rye v Rye	[2002] EWHC 956 (Fam), [2002] 2 FLR 981
Maskell v Maskell	[2002] EWCA Civ 858, [2003] 1 FLR 1138
Norris v Norris (No 1)	[2002] EWHC 2996 (Fam), [2003] 1 FLR 1142
Martin-Dye v Martin-Dye	[2006] EWCA Civ 681, [2006] 4 All ER 779, [2006] 2 FLR 901, CA
H v H	[2009] EWHC 3739 (Fam), [2010] 2 FLR 173
Blight and others v Brewster	[2012] EWHC 165 (Ch), [2012] All ER (D) 190 (Feb), [2012] 1 WLR 2841

For other Leading Cases on Pensions: other see @eGlance and previous editions of At A Glance.

Periodical payments: capitalisation of
Boylan v Boylan	[1988] 1 FLR 282
Harris v Harris	[2001] 1 FCR 68, CA
Cornick v Cornick (No 3)	[2001] 2 FLR 1240
Pearce v Pearce	[2003] EWCA Civ 1054, [2004] 1 WLR 68, [2003] 2 FLR 1144, CA
W v W (financial provision: Form E)	[2003] EWHC 2254 (Fam), [2004] 1 FLR 494
CO v CO (ancillary relief: pre-marriage cohabitation)	[2004] EWHC 287 (Fam), [2004] 1 FLR 1095
Lauder v Lauder	[2007] EWHC 1227 (Fam), [2007] 2 FLR 802
Dixon v Marchant	[2008] EWCA Civ 11, [2008] 1 FLR 655, CA
Vaughan v Vaughan	[2010] EWCA Civ 349, [2011] Fam 46, [2010] 3 WLR 1209, [2010] 2 FLR 242, CA

Periodical payments: principles of award
V v V (financial relief)	[2005] 2 FLR 697
Miller v Miller; McFarlane v McFarlane	[2006] UKHL 24, [2006] 2 AC 618, [2006] 3 All ER 1, [2006] 2 WLR 1283, [2006] 1 FLR 1186, HL
Q v Q (ancillary relief: periodical payments)	[2005] EWHC 402 (Fam), [2005] 2 FLR 640
RP v RP	[2006] EWHC 3409 (Fam), [2007] 1 FLR 2105
Lauder v Lauder	[2007] EWHC 1227 (Fam), [2007] 2 FLR 802
CR v CR	[2007] EWHC 3206 (Fam), [2008] 1 FLR 323
VB v JP	[2008] EWHC 112 (Fam), [2008] 1 FLR 742
H v H	[2008] EWHC 935 (Fam), [2008] 1 FLR 2092
B v S (financial remedy: marital property régime)	[2012] EWHC 265 (Fam), [2012] 2 FLR 502

Periodical payments: variation of
Primavera v Primavera	[1992] 1 FLR 16, CA
Garner v Garner	[1992] 1 FLR 573, CA
Flavell v Flavell	[1997] 1 FLR 353, CA
Jones v Jones	[2001] Fam 96, [2000] 3 WLR 1505, [2000] 2 FLR 307, CA
Harris v Harris	[2001] 1 FCR 68, CA
Mubarak v Mubarik (No 4)	[2004] EWHC 1158 (Fam), [2004] 2 FLR 932
Laing v Laing	[2005] EWHC 3152 (Fam), [2007] 2 FLR 199
North v North	[2007] EWCA Civ 760, [2007] All ER (D) 386 (Jul), [2008] 2 FLR 158, CA
VB v JP	[2008] EWHC 112 (Fam), [2008] 1 FLR 742
McFarlane v McFarlane	[2009] EWHC 891 (Fam), [2009] 2 FLR 1322
Hvorostovsky v Hvorostovsky	[2009] EWCA Civ 791, [2009] 2 FLR 1574, CA

Practice and procedure
W v W (ancillary relief: practice)	[2000] Fam Law 473
Rose v Rose (No 1)	[2002] EWCA Civ 208, [2002] 1 FLR 978, CA
OS v DS (oral disclosure: preliminary hearing)	[2004] EWHC 2376 (Fam), [2005] 1 FLR 675
K v K (financial relief: management of difficult cases)	[2005] EWHC 1070 (Fam), [2005] 2 FLR 1137
S v S (ancillary relief: importance of FDR)	[2007] EWHC 1975 (Fam), [2008] 1 FLR 944

Leading Cases

Practice and procedure (Cont'd)

S v P (settlement by collaborative law process)	[2008] 2 FLR 2040
Re X and Y (bundles)	[2008] EWHC 2058 (Fam), [2008] 2 FLR 2053
P v P (financial relief: procedure)	[2008] EWHC 2953 (Fam), [2009] 1 FLR 696
Myerson v Myerson	[2008] EWCA Civ 1376, [2009] 1 FLR 826, CA
P v P	[2010] 1 FLR 1126
White v Withers LLP and Dearle	[2009] EWCA Civ 1122, [2010] 1 FLR 859, CA
Imerman v Tchenguiz	[2010] EWCA Civ 908, [2011] Fam 116, [2011] 1 All ER 555, [2011] 2 WLR 592, [2010] 2 FLR 814, CA
G v G (financial remedies: strike out)	FLR Fast Reporting (Bodey J, 23 January 2012, neutral citation as yet unavailable)
Fisher Meredith v JH and PH (financial remedy: appeal: wasted costs)	[2012] EWHC 408 (Fam), [2012] 2 FLR 536
X v X (financial remedies: preparation and presentation)	[2012] EWHC 538 (Fam), [2012] 2 FLR 590
HMRC v Charman and Charman	[2012] EWHC 1448 (Fam), [2012] 2 FLR 1119
Arif v Zar & Anor	[2012] EWCA Civ 986, [2012] All ER (D) 243 (Jul), [2012] WLR(D) 239, CA
CPS and SSHD v Gohil	[2012] EWCA Civ 1550, [2013] 1 FLR 1095, CA
Vince v Wyatt	[2013] EWCA Civ 495 (11 April 2013, as yet unreported), CA

Proceeds of Crime Act

Bowman v Fels	[2005] EWCA (Civ) 226, [2005] 2 FLR 247, CA

Property, beneficial interest in: joint names

Stack v Dowden	[2007] UKHL 17, [2007] 2 AC 432, [2007] 2 All ER 929, [2007] 2 WLR 831, [2007] 1 FLR 1858, HL
Murphy v Gooch	[2007] EWCA Civ 603, [2007] 2 FLR 934, CA
Holman v Howes	[2007] EWCA Civ 877, [2008] 1 FLR 1217, CA
Laskar v Laskar	[2008] EWCA Civ 347, [2008] 1 WLR 2695, [2008] 2 FLR 589, CA
Jones v Kernott	[2011] UKSC 53, [2012] AC 776, [2012] 1 All ER 1265, [2011] 3 WLR 1121, [2012] 1 FLR 45, SC
Davis v Smith	[2011] EWCA Civ 1603, [2012] 1 FLR 1177, CA
Gallarotti v Sebastianelli	[2012] EWCA Civ 865, [2012] 2 FLR 1231, CA
Pankhania v Chandegra	[2012] EWCA Civ 1438, [2012] All ER (D) 132 (Nov), CA

For other Leading Cases on Property, beneficial interest in: joint names see **@eGlance** *and previous editions of* **At A Glance**.

Property, beneficial interest in: sole name

Oxley v Hiscock	[2004] EWCA Civ 546, [2005] Fam 211, [2004] 3 WLR 715, [2004] 3 All ER 703, [2004] 2 FLR 669, CA
Abbott v Abbott	[2007] UKPC 53, [2008] 1 FLR 1451, PC

For other Leading Cases on Property, beneficial interest in: sole name see **@eGlance** *and previous editions of* **At A Glance**.

Remarriage and cohabitation: prospects

Wachtel v Wachtel	[1973] Fam 72, [1973] 1 All ER 829, [1973] 2 WLR 366, CA
Smith v Smith	[1976] Fam 18n, [1975] 2 WLR 615n, [1975] 2 All ER 19n; sub nom S v S (1973) FLR Rep 649n
Livesey v Jenkins	[1985] AC 424, [1985] 1 All ER 106, [1985] 2 WLR 47, [1985] FLR 813, HL

Remarriage and cohabitation: actual remarriage

H v H	[1975] Fam 9, [1975] 1 All ER 367, [1975] 2 WLR 124
Stockford v Stockford	(1982) FLR 58, CA
Slater v Slater	(1982) FLR 364, CA
Prow (formerly Brown) v Brown	(1983) FLR 352, CA
Camm v Camm	(1983) FLR 577, CA

Remarriage and cohabitation: cohabitation

Suter v Suter and Jones	[1987] Fam 111, [1987] 2 All ER 336, [1987] 3 WLR 9, [1987] 2 FLR 232, CA
Atkinson v Atkinson	[1988] Fam 93, [1987] 3 All ER 849, [1988] 2 WLR 204, [1988] 2 FLR 353, CA
R v R	[1988] 1 FLR 89, CA
Hepburn v Hepburn	[1989] 1 FLR 373, CA
Duxbury v Duxbury	[1992] Fam 62n, [1990] 2 All ER 77, [1991] 3 WLR 639, [1987] 1 FLR 7, CA
Atkinson v Atkinson	[1995] 2 FLR 356
Atkinson v Atkinson (No 2)	[1996] 1 FLR 51, CA
Hill v Hill	[1998] 1 FLR 198, CA
Fleming v Fleming	[2003] EWCA Civ 1841, [2004] 1 FLR 667, CA
Grey v Grey	[2009] EWCA Civ 1424, [2010] 1 FLR 1764, CA
Grey v Grey (No 3)	[2010] EWHC 1055 (Fam), [2010] 2 FLR 1848

Resources: computation and extent of

Thomas v Thomas	[1995] 2 FLR 668, CA
White v White	[2001] 1 AC 596, [2001] 1 All ER 1, [2000] 3 WLR 1571, [2000] 2 FLR 981, HL
Norris v Norris (No 1)	[2002] EWHC 2996 (Fam), [2003] 1 FLR 1142
TL v ML and others (ancillary relief: claim against assets of extended family)	[2005] EWHC 2860 (Fam), [2006] 1 FLR 1264
G v G (matrimonial property: rights of extended family)	[2005] EWHC 1560 (Fam), [2006] 1 FLR 62
Miller v Miller; McFarlane v McFarlane	[2006] UKHL 24, [2006] 2 AC 618, [2006] 3 All ER 1, [2006] 2 WLR 1283, [2006] 1 FLR 1186, HL

Leading Cases

Resources: computation and extent of (Cont'd)
A v A	[2007] EWHC 99 (Fam), [2007] 2 FLR 467
Vaughan v Vaughan	[2007] EWCA Civ 1085, [2008] 1 FLR 1108, CA
McCartney v Mills-McCartney	[2008] EWHC 401 (Fam), [2008] 1 FLR 1508
SR v CR (ancillary relief: family trusts)	[2008] EWHC 2329 (Fam), [2009] 2 FLR 1083
Behzadi v Behzadi	[2008] EWCA Civ 1070, [2009] 2 FLR 649, CA
Marano v Marano	[2010] EWCA Civ 119, [2010] 1 FLR 1903, CA
B v B (ancillary relief)	[2009] EWHC 3422 (Fam), [2010] 2 FLR 887
Marano v Marano	[2010] EWCA Civ 119, [2010] 1 FLR 1903, CA
M v W (ancillary relief)	[2010] EWHC 1155 (Fam), [2010] 2 FLR 1484
Whaley v Whaley	[2011] EWCA Civ 617, [2012] 1 FLR 735, CA
BJ v MJ (financial remedy: overseas trusts)	[2011] EWHC 2708 (Fam), [2012] 1 FLR 667
RK v RK (financial resources: trust assets)	[2011] EWHC 3910 (Fam), [2013] 1 FLR 329
Petrodel Resources Limited & others v Prest & others	[2012] EWCA Civ 1395; sub nom Prest v Prest [2013] 2 WLR 557, [2013] 1 All ER 795, CA [Judgment of Supreme Court awaited]

Resources: (il)liquidity of
Newton v Newton	[1990] 1 FLR 33, CA
Wells v Wells	[2002] EWCA Civ 476, [2002] 2 FLR 97, CA
N v N (financial provision: sale of company)	[2001] 2 FLR 69
G v G (financial provision: equal division)	[2002] EWHC 1339 (Fam), [2002] 2 FLR 1143
F v F (clean break: balance of fairness)	[2003] 1 FLR 847
GW v RW (financial provision: departure from equality)	[2003] EWHC 611 (Fam), [2003] 2 FLR 108
C v C (variation of post-nuptial settlement: company shares)	[2003] EWHC 1222 (Fam), [2003] 2 FLR 493
R v R (lump sum repayments)	[2003] EWHC 3197 (Fam), [2004] 1 FLR 928
P v P (inherited property)	[2004] EWHC 1364 (Fam), [2005] 1 FLR 576
P v P (financial relief: illiquid assets)	[2004] EWHC 2277 (Fam), [2005] 1 FLR 548
R v R (financial relief: company valuation)	[2005] 2 FLR 365
V v V (financial relief)	[2005] 2 FLR 697
Miller v Miller; McFarlane v McFarlane	[2006] UKHL 24, [2006] 2 AC 618, [2006] 3 All ER 1, [2006] 2 WLR 1283, [2006] 1 FLR 1186, HL
Re C (divorce: financial relief)	[2007] EWHC 1911 (Fam), [2008] 1 FLR 625

Resources, non-matrimonial: pre-marital
P v P (financial provision)	[1978] 3 All ER 70, [1978] 1 WLR 483, (1977) FLR Rep 546, CA
White v White	[2001] 1 AC 596, [2001] 1 All ER 1, [2000] 3 WLR 1571, [2000] 2 FLR 981, HL
Dharamshi v Dharamshi	[2001] 1 FLR 736, CA
Miller v Miller; McFarlane v McFarlane	[2006] UKHL 24, [2006] 2 AC 618, [2006] 3 All ER 1, [2006] 2 WLR 1283, [2006] 1 FLR 1186, HL
S v S (non-matrimonial property: conduct)	[2006] EWHC 2793 (Fam), [2007] 1 FLR 1496
A v A	[2007] EWHC 99 (Fam), [2007] 2 FLR 467
Smith v Smith	[2007] EWCA 454, [2007] 2 FLR 1103, CA
C v C	[2007] EWHC 2033 (Fam), [2009] 1 FLR 8
McCartney v Mills-McCartney	[2008] EWHC 401 (Fam), [2008] 1 FLR 1508
L v L (ancillary relief)	[2008] EWHC 882 (Fam), [2008] 1 FLR 142
B v B (ancillary relief: distribution of assets)	[2008] EWCA Civ 284, [2008] 1 WLR 2362, [2008] 1 FLR 1627, CA
N v N (ancillary relief)	[2010] EWHC 717 (Fam), [2010] 2 FLR 1093
FZ v SZ (ancillary relief: conduct: valuations)	[2010] EWHC 1630 (Fam), [2011] 1 FLR 64
Robson v Robson	[2010] EWCA Civ 1171, [2011] 1 FLR 751, CA
Jones v Jones	[2011] EWCA Civ 41, [2012] Fam 1, [2011] 3 WLR 582, [2011] 1 FLR 1723, CA
N v F (financial orders: pre-acquired wealth)	[2011] EWHC 586 (Fam), [2011] 2 FLR 533
J v J (financial orders: wife's long term needs)	[2011] EWHC 1010 (Fam), [2011] 2 FLR 1280
K v L	[2011] EWCA Civ 550, [2011] 3 All ER 733, [2012] 1 WLR 306; sub nom K v L (non-matrimonial property: special contribution) [2011] 2 FLR 980, CA
Mansfield v Mansfield	[2011] EWCA Civ 1056, [2012] 1 FLR 117, CA
AR v AR (treatment of inherited wealth)	[2011] EWHC 2717 (Fam), [2012] 2 FLR 1
V v V (prenuptial agreement)	[2011] EWHC 3230 (Fam), [2012] 1 FLR 1315
B v B (assessment of assets: pre-marital property)	[2012] EWHC 314 (Fam), [2012] 2 FLR 22
Y v Y	[2012] EWHC 2063 (Fam), FLR Fast Reporting

Resources, non-matrimonial: acquired during marriage
Daubney v Daubney	[1976] Fam 267, [1976] 2 All ER 453, [1976] 2 WLR 959, (1976) FLR Rep 214, CA
Wagstaff v Wagstaff	[1992] 1 All ER 275, [1992] 1 WLR 320, [1992] 1 FLR 333, CA
C v C (financial provision: personal damages)	[1995] 2 FLR 171
White v White	[2001] 1 AC 596, [2001] 1 All ER 1, [2000] 3 WLR 1571, [2000] 2 FLR 981, HL
Norris v Norris (No 1)	[2002] EWHC 2996 (Fam), [2003] 1 FLR 1142
Miller v Miller; McFarlane v McFarlane	[2006] UKHL 24, [2006] 2 AC 618, [2006] 3 All ER 1, [2006] 2 WLR 1283, [2006] 1 FLR 1186, HL
S v AG (financial remedy: lottery prize)	[2011] EWHC 2637 (Fam), [2012] 1 FLR 651

Resources, non-matrimonial: acquired post-separation
Lombardi v Lombardi	[1973] 3 All ER 625, [1973] 1 WLR 1276, CA

Leading Cases

Resources, non-matrimonial: acquired post-separation (Cont'd)
Pearce v Pearce	(1980) FLR 261, CA
Schuller v Schuller	[1990] 2 FLR 193, CA
White v White	[2001] 1 AC 596, [2001] 1 All ER 1, [2000] 3 WLR 1571, [2000] 2 FLR 981, HL
A v B (financial relief: agreements)	[2005] EWHC 314 (Fam), [2005] 2 FLR 730
Miller v Miller; McFarlane v McFarlane	[2006] UKHL 24, [2006] 2 AC 618, [2006] 3 All ER 1, [2006] 2 WLR 1283, [2006] 1 FLR 1186, HL
Rossi v Rossi & Rossi	[2006] EWHC 1482 (Fam), [2007] 1 FLR 790
S v S (ancillary relief after lengthy separation)	[2006] EWHC 2339 (Fam), [2007] 1 FLR 2120
H v H	[2007] EWHC 459 (Fam), [2007] 2 FLR 548
CR v CR	[2007] EWHC 3206 (Fam), [2008] 1 FLR 323
P v P (post separation accruals and earning capacity)	[2007] EWHC 2877 (Fam), [2008] 2 FLR 1135
H v H (financial provision)	[2009] EWHC 494 (Fam), [2009] 2 FLR 795
B v B (ancillary relief: post separation income)	[2010] EWHC 193 (Fam), [2010] 2 FLR 1214
SK v WL (ancillary relief: post-separation accrual)	[2010] EWHC 457 (Fam), [2011] 1 FLR 1471
Gordon (formerly Stefanou) v Stefanou	[2010] EWCA Civ 1601, [2011] 1 FLR 1582, CA

Third parties, claims by/against
Tebbutt v Haynes	[1981] 2 All ER 238, CA
Harwood v Harwood	[1991] 2 FLR 274, CA
T v T (joinder of third parties)	[1996] 2 FLR 357
Laird v Laird	[1999] 1 FLR 791, CA
TL v ML and others (ancillary relief: claim against assets of extended family)	[2005] EWHC 2860 (Fam), [2006] 1 FLR 1264
Rossi v Rossi & Rossi	[2006] EWHC 1482 (Fam), [2007] 1 FLR 790
A v A (No 2) (ancillary relief: costs)	[2007] EWHC 1810 (Fam), [2008] 1 FLR 1428
Ben Hashem v Al Shayif	[2008] EWHC 2380 (Fam), [2009] 1 FLR 115
Gourisaria v Gourisaria	[2010] EWCA Civ 1019, [2011] 1 FLR 262, CA
Goldstone v Goldstone	[2011] EWCA Civ 39, [2011] 1 FLR 1926, CA
Edgerton v Edgerton and Zaffirili Shaikh	[2012] EWCA Civ 181, [2012] 2 FLR 273, CA
Fisher Meredith v JH and PH (financial remedy: appeal: wasted costs)	[2012] EWHC 408 (Fam), [2012] 2 FLR 536

Trusts
Howard v Howard	[1945] P 1, [1945] 1 All ER 91, (1944) FLR Rep 337, CA
Londonderry's Settlement, Re	[1965] Ch 918, [1964] 3 All ER 855, [1965] 2 WLR 229, CA
B v B	(1982) FLR 298, CA
Browne v Browne	[1989] 1 FLR 291, CA
E v E	[1990] 2 FLR 233
T v T (joinder of third parties)	[1996] 2 FLR 357
Murphy's Settlements, Re	[1999] 1 WLR 282, [1998] 3 All ER 1
Fuller v Evans	[2000] 1 All ER 636, [2000] 2 FLR 13
Schmidt v Rosewood Trust Ltd	[2003] UKPC 26, [2003] 3 All ER 76
Charalambous v Charalambous	[2004] EWCA Civ 1030, [2004] 2 FLR 1093, CA; sub nom C v C (ancillary relief: nuptial settlement) [2005] Fam 250, [2005] 2 WLR 241, CA
Minwalla v Minwalla & others	[2004] EWHC 2823 (Fam), [2005] 1 FLR 771
A v A	[2007] EWHC 99 (Fam), [2007] 2 FLR 467
K v K (ancillary relief: deed of appointment)	[2007] EWHC 3485 (Fam), [2009] 2 FLR 936
Breakspear v Ackland	[2008] EWHC 220 (Ch), [2009] Ch 32, [2008] 3 WLR 698
Mubarak v Mubarik	[2008] JRC 136, [2009] 1 FLR 664, Royal Court of Jersey
B v B (ancillary relief)	[2009] EWHC 3422 (Fam), [2010] 2 FLR 887
C v C (ancillary relief: trust fund)	[2009] EWHC 1491 (Fam), [2010] 1 FLR 337
D v D and others and the I Trust	[2009] EWHC 3062 (Fam), [2011] 2 FLR 29
M v W (ancillary relief)	[2010] EWHC 1155 (Fam), [2010] 2 FLR 148
Whaley v Whaley	[2011] EWCA Civ 617, [2012] 1 FLR 735, CA
BJ v MJ (financial remedy: overseas trusts)	[2011] EWHC 2708 (Fam), [2012] 1 FLR 667
G v G (financial remedies: short marriage: trust assets)	[2012] EWHC 167 (Fam), [2012] 2 FLR 48
Hope v Krejci and others	[2012] EWHC 1780 (Fam), [2013] 1 FLR 182
RK v RK (financial resources: trust assets)	[2011] EWHC 3910 (Fam), [2013] 1 FLR 329
DR v GR and ors (financial remedy: variation of overseas trust)	[2013] EWHC 1196 (Fam) (Mostyn J, 10 May 2013, as yet unreported)

Variation of final orders
Tilley v Tilley	(1980) 10 Fam Law 89, CA
Carson v Carson	[1983] 1 All ER 478, [1983] 1 WLR 285, (1981) FLR 352, CA
Sandford v Sandford	[1986] 1 FLR 412, CA
Thompson v Thompson	[1986] Fam 38, [1985] 2 All ER 243, [1985] 3 WLR 17, [1985] FLR 863, CA
Dinch v Dinch	[1987] 1 All ER 818, [1987] 1 WLR 252, [1987] 2 FLR 162, HL
Peacock v Peacock	[1991] 1 FLR 324
Popat v Popat	[1991] 2 FLR 163, CA
Omielan v Omielan	[1996] 2 FLR 306, CA
Mubarak v Mubarik (No 6)	[2007] EWHC 220 (Fam), [2007] 2 FLR 364

Perpetual Calendar

The number opposite each of the years in the list below indicates which of the calendars on the following pages is the one for that year. Thus the number opposite 2013 is 3, so calendar 3 can be used as a 2013 calendar.

Leap years
Years divisible by four without remainder are leap years with 366 days instead of 365 (29 days in February instead of 28). However, the last year of a century is not a leap year except when divisible by 400.

Easter Sunday
These dates apply unless there is a change to a fixed Easter. For other years see *@eGlance*.

Year	Date	Year	Date	Year	Date
2005	27 March	2012	8 April	2019	21 April
2006	16 April	2013	31 March	2020	12 April
2007	8 April	2014	20 April	2021	4 April
2008	23 March	2015	5 April	2022	17 April
2009	12 April	2016	27 March	2023	9 April
2010	4 April	2017	16 April	2024	31 March
2011	24 April	2018	1 April	2025	20 April

Year	Calendar	Year	Calendar	Year	Calendar	Year	Calendar	Year	Calendar	Year	Calendar
1926	6	1951	2	1976	12	2001	2	2026	5	2051	1
1927	7	1952	10	1977	7	2002	3	2027	6	2052	9
1928	8	1953	5	1978	1	2003	4	2028	14	2053	4
1929	3	1954	6	1979	2	2004	12	2029	2	2054	5
1930	4	1955	7	1980	10	2005	7	2030	3	2055	6
1931	5	1956	8	1981	5	2006	1	2031	4	2056	14
1932	13	1957	3	1982	6	2007	2	2032	12	2057	2
1933	1	1958	4	1983	7	2008	10	2033	7	2058	3
1934	2	1959	5	1984	8	2009	5	2034	1	2059	4
1935	3	1960	13	1985	3	2010	6	2035	2	2060	12
1936	11	1961	1	1986	4	2011	7	2036	10	2061	7
1937	6	1962	2	1987	5	2012	8	2037	5	2062	1
1938	7	1963	3	1988	13	2013	3	2038	6	2063	2
1939	1	1964	11	1989	1	2014	4	2039	7	2064	10
1940	9	1965	6	1990	2	2015	5	2040	8	2065	5
1941	4	1966	7	1991	3	2016	13	2041	3	2066	6
1942	5	1967	1	1992	11	2017	1	2042	4	2067	7
1943	6	1968	9	1993	6	2018	2	2043	5	2068	8
1944	14	1969	4	1994	7	2019	3	2044	13	2069	3
1945	2	1970	5	1995	1	2020	11	2045	1	2070	4
1946	3	1971	6	1996	9	2021	6	2046	2	2071	5
1947	4	1972	14	1997	4	2022	7	2047	3	2072	13
1948	12	1973	2	1998	5	2023	1	2048	11	2073	1
1949	7	1974	3	1999	6	2024	9	2049	6	2074	2
1950	1	1975	4	2000	14	2025	4	2050	7	2075	3

1

January
M	2	9	16	23	30
T	3	10	17	24	31
W	4	11	18	25	
T	5	12	19	26	
F	6	13	20	27	
S	7	14	21	28	
S	1	8	15	22	29

February
	6	13	20	27
	7	14	21	28
1	8	15	22	
2	9	16	23	
3	10	17	24	
4	11	18	25	
5	12	19	26	

March
	6	13	20	27
	7	14	21	28
1	8	15	22	29
2	9	16	23	30
3	10	17	24	31
4	11	18	25	
5	12	19	26	

April
3	10	17	24	
4	11	18	25	
5	12	19	26	
6	13	20	27	
7	14	21	28	
1	8	15	22	29
2	9	16	23	30

May
M	1	8	15	22	29
T	2	9	16	23	30
W	3	10	17	24	31
T	4	11	18	25	
F	5	12	19	26	
S	6	13	20	27	
S	7	14	21	28	

June
	5	12	19	26
	6	13	20	27
	7	14	21	28
1	8	15	22	29
2	9	16	23	30
3	10	17	24	
4	11	18	25	

July
3	10	17	24	31
4	11	18	25	
5	12	19	26	
6	13	20	27	
7	14	21	28	
1	8	15	22	29
2	9	16	23	30

August
7	14	21	28	
1	8	15	22	29
2	9	16	23	30
3	10	17	24	31
4	11	18	25	
5	12	19	26	
6	13	20	27	

September
M	4	11	18	25	
T	5	12	19	26	
W	6	13	20	27	
T	7	14	21	28	
F	1	8	15	22	29
S	2	9	16	23	30
S	3	10	17	24	

October
2	9	16	23	30
3	10	17	24	31
4	11	18	25	
5	12	19	26	
6	13	20	27	
7	14	21	28	
1	8	15	22	29

November
6	13	20	27	
7	14	21	28	
1	8	15	22	29
2	9	16	23	30
3	10	17	24	
4	11	18	25	
5	12	19	26	

December
4	11	18	25	
5	12	19	26	
6	13	20	27	
7	14	21	28	
1	8	15	22	29
2	9	16	23	30
3	10	17	24	31

2

January
M	1	8	15	22	29
T	2	9	16	23	30
W	3	10	17	24	31
T	4	11	18	25	
F	5	12	19	26	
S	6	13	20	27	
S	7	14	21	28	

February
	5	12	19	26
	6	13	20	27
	7	14	21	28
1	8	15	22	
2	9	16	23	
3	10	17	24	
4	11	18	25	

March
	5	12	19	26
	6	13	20	27
	7	14	21	28
1	8	15	22	29
2	9	16	23	30
3	10	17	24	31
4	11	18	25	

April
2	9	16	23	30
3	10	17	24	
4	11	18	25	
5	12	19	26	
6	13	20	27	
7	14	21	28	
1	8	15	22	29

May
M		7	14	21	28
T	1	8	15	22	29
W	2	9	16	23	30
T	3	10	17	24	31
F	4	11	18	25	
S	5	12	19	26	
S	6	13	20	27	

June
4	11	18	25	
5	12	19	26	
6	13	20	27	
7	14	21	28	
1	8	15	22	29
2	9	16	23	30
3	10	17	24	

July
2	9	16	23	30
3	10	17	24	31
4	11	18	25	
5	12	19	26	
6	13	20	27	
7	14	21	28	
1	8	15	22	29

August
6	13	20	27	
7	14	21	28	
1	8	15	22	29
2	9	16	23	30
3	10	17	24	31
4	11	18	25	
5	12	19	26	

September
M	3	10	17	24	
T	4	11	18	25	
W	5	12	19	26	
T	6	13	20	27	
F	7	14	21	28	
S	1	8	15	22	29
S	2	9	16	23	30

October
1	8	15	22	29
2	9	16	23	30
3	10	17	24	31
4	11	18	25	
5	12	19	26	
6	13	20	27	
7	14	21	28	

November
5	12	19	26	
6	13	20	27	
7	14	21	28	
1	8	15	22	29
2	9	16	23	30
3	10	17	24	
4	11	18	25	

December
3	10	17	24	31
4	11	18	25	
5	12	19	26	
6	13	20	27	
7	14	21	28	
1	8	15	22	29
2	9	16	23	30

AT A GLANCE

Perpetual Calendar

3

January	February	March	April
M 7 14 21 28	4 11 18 25	4 11 18 25	1 8 15 22 29
T 1 8 15 22 29	5 12 19 26	5 12 19 26	2 9 16 23 30
W 2 9 16 23 30	6 13 20 27	6 13 20 27	3 10 17 24
T 3 10 17 24 31	7 14 21 28	7 14 21 28	4 11 18 25
F 4 11 18 25	1 8 15 22	1 8 15 22 29	5 12 19 26
S 5 12 19 26	2 9 16 23	2 9 16 23 30	6 13 20 27
S 6 13 20 27	3 10 17 24	3 10 17 24 31	7 14 21 28

May	June	July	August
M 6 13 20 27	3 10 17 24	1 8 15 22 29	5 12 19 26
T 7 14 21 28	4 11 18 25	2 9 16 23 30	6 13 20 27
W 1 8 15 22 29	5 12 19 26	3 10 17 24 31	7 14 21 28
T 2 9 16 23 30	6 13 20 27	4 11 18 25	1 8 15 22 29
F 3 10 17 24 31	7 14 21 28	5 12 19 26	2 9 16 23 30
S 4 11 18 25	1 8 15 22 29	6 13 20 27	3 10 17 24 31
S 5 12 19 26	2 9 16 23 30	7 14 21 28	4 11 18 25

September	October	November	December
M 2 9 16 23 30	7 14 21 28	4 11 18 25	2 9 16 23 30
T 3 10 17 24	1 8 15 22 29	5 12 19 26	3 10 17 24 31
W 4 11 18 25	2 9 16 23 30	6 13 20 27	4 11 18 25
T 5 12 19 26	3 10 17 24 31	7 14 21 28	5 12 19 26
F 6 13 20 27	4 11 18 25	1 8 15 22 29	6 13 20 27
S 7 14 21 28	5 12 19 26	2 9 16 23 30	7 14 21 28
S 1 8 15 22 29	6 13 20 27	3 10 17 24	1 8 15 22 29

4

January	February	March	April
M 6 13 20 27	3 10 17 24	3 10 17 24 31	7 14 21 28
T 7 14 21 28	4 11 18 25	4 11 18 25	1 8 15 22 29
W 1 8 15 22 29	5 12 19 26	5 12 19 26	2 9 16 23 30
T 2 9 16 23 30	6 13 20 27	6 13 20 27	3 10 17 24
F 3 10 17 24 31	7 14 21 28	7 14 21 28	4 11 18 25
S 4 11 18 25	1 8 15 22	1 8 15 22 29	5 12 19 26
S 5 12 19 26	2 9 16 23	2 9 16 23 30	6 13 20 27

May	June	July	August
M 5 12 19 26	2 9 16 23 30	7 14 21 28	4 11 18 25
T 6 13 20 27	3 10 17 24	1 8 15 22 29	5 12 19 26
W 7 14 21 28	4 11 18 25	2 9 16 23 30	6 13 20 27
T 1 8 15 22 29	5 12 19 26	3 10 17 24 31	7 14 21 28
F 2 9 16 23 30	6 13 20 27	4 11 18 25	1 8 15 22 29
S 3 10 17 24 31	7 14 21 28	5 12 19 26	2 9 16 23 30
S 4 11 18 25	1 8 15 22 29	6 13 20 27	3 10 17 24 31

September	October	November	December
M 1 8 15 22 29	6 13 20 27	3 10 17 24	1 8 15 22 29
T 2 9 16 23 30	7 14 21 28	4 11 18 25	2 9 16 23 30
W 3 10 17 24	1 8 15 22 29	5 12 19 26	3 10 17 24 31
T 4 11 18 25	2 9 16 23 30	6 13 20 27	4 11 18 25
F 5 12 19 26	3 10 17 24 31	7 14 21 28	5 12 19 26
S 6 13 20 27	4 11 18 25	1 8 15 22 29	6 13 20 27
S 7 14 21 28	5 12 19 26	2 9 16 23 30	7 14 21 28

5

January	February	March	April
M 5 12 19 26	2 9 16 23	2 9 16 23 30	6 13 20 27
T 6 13 20 27	3 10 17 24	3 10 17 24 31	7 14 21 28
W 7 14 21 28	4 11 18 25	4 11 18 25	1 8 15 22 29
T 1 8 15 22 29	5 12 19 26	5 12 19 26	2 9 16 23 30
F 2 9 16 23 30	6 13 20 27	6 13 20 27	3 10 17 24
S 3 10 17 24 31	7 14 21 28	7 14 21 28	4 11 18 25
S 4 11 18 25	1 8 15 22	1 8 15 22 29	5 12 19 26

May	June	July	August
M 4 11 18 25	1 8 15 22 29	6 13 20 27	3 10 17 24 31
T 5 12 19 26	2 9 16 23 30	7 14 21 28	4 11 18 25
W 6 13 20 27	3 10 17 24	1 8 15 22 29	5 12 19 26
T 7 14 21 28	4 11 18 25	2 9 16 23 30	6 13 20 27
F 1 8 15 22 29	5 12 19 26	3 10 17 24 31	7 14 21 28
S 2 9 16 23 30	6 13 20 27	4 11 18 25	1 8 15 22 29
S 3 10 17 24 31	7 14 21 28	5 12 19 26	2 9 16 23 30

September	October	November	December
M 7 14 21 28	5 12 19 26	2 9 16 23 30	7 14 21 28
T 1 8 15 22 29	6 13 20 27	3 10 17 24	1 8 15 22 29
W 2 9 16 23 30	7 14 21 28	4 11 18 25	2 9 16 23 30
T 3 10 17 24	1 8 15 22 29	5 12 19 26	3 10 17 24 31
F 4 11 18 25	2 9 16 23 30	6 13 20 27	4 11 18 25
S 5 12 19 26	3 10 17 24 31	7 14 21 28	5 12 19 26
S 6 13 20 27	4 11 18 25	1 8 15 22 29	6 13 20 27

6

January	February	March	April
M 4 11 18 25	1 8 15 22	1 8 15 22 29	5 12 19 26
T 5 12 19 26	2 9 16 23	2 9 16 23 30	6 13 20 27
W 6 13 20 27	3 10 17 24	3 10 17 24 31	7 14 21 28
T 7 14 21 28	4 11 18 25	4 11 18 25	1 8 15 22 29
F 1 8 15 22 29	5 12 19 26	5 12 19 26	2 9 16 23 30
S 2 9 16 23 30	6 13 20 27	6 13 20 27	3 10 17 24
S 3 10 17 24 31	7 14 21 28	7 14 21 28	4 11 18 25

May	June	July	August
M 3 10 17 24 31	7 14 21 28	5 12 19 26	2 9 16 23 30
T 4 11 18 25	1 8 15 22 29	6 13 20 27	3 10 17 24 31
W 5 12 19 26	2 9 16 23 30	7 14 21 28	4 11 18 25
T 6 13 20 27	3 10 17 24	1 8 15 22 29	5 12 19 26
F 7 14 21 28	4 11 18 25	2 9 16 23 30	6 13 20 27
S 1 8 15 22 29	5 12 19 26	3 10 17 24 31	7 14 21 28
S 2 9 16 23 30	6 13 20 27	4 11 18 25	1 8 15 22 29

September	October	November	December
M 6 13 20 27	4 11 18 25	1 8 15 22 29	6 13 20 27
T 7 14 21 28	5 12 19 26	2 9 16 23 30	7 14 21 28
W 1 8 15 22 29	6 13 20 27	3 10 17 24	1 8 15 22 29
T 2 9 16 23 30	7 14 21 28	4 11 18 25	2 9 16 23 30
F 3 10 17 24	1 8 15 22 29	5 12 19 26	3 10 17 24 31
S 4 11 18 25	2 9 16 23 30	6 13 20 27	4 11 18 25
S 5 12 19 26	3 10 17 24 31	7 14 21 28	5 12 19 26

7

January	February	March	April
M 3 10 17 24 31	7 14 21 28	7 14 21 28	4 11 18 25
T 4 11 18 25	1 8 15 22	1 8 15 22 29	5 12 19 26
W 5 12 19 26	2 9 16 23	2 9 16 23 30	6 13 20 27
T 6 13 20 27	3 10 17 24	3 10 17 24 31	7 14 21 28
F 7 14 21 28	4 11 18 25	4 11 18 25	1 8 15 22 29
S 1 8 15 22 29	5 12 19 26	5 12 19 26	2 9 16 23 30
S 2 9 16 23 30	6 13 20 27	6 13 20 27	3 10 17 24

May	June	July	August
M 2 9 16 23 30	6 13 20 27	4 11 18 25	1 8 15 22 29
T 3 10 17 24 31	7 14 21 28	5 12 19 26	2 9 16 23 30
W 4 11 18 25	1 8 15 22 29	6 13 20 27	3 10 17 24 31
T 5 12 19 26	2 9 16 23 30	7 14 21 28	4 11 18 25
F 6 13 20 27	3 10 17 24	1 8 15 22 29	5 12 19 26
S 7 14 21 28	4 11 18 25	2 9 16 23 30	6 13 20 27
S 1 8 15 22 29	5 12 19 26	3 10 17 24 31	7 14 21 28

September	October	November	December
M 5 12 19 26	3 10 17 24 31	7 14 21 28	5 12 19 26
T 6 13 20 27	4 11 18 25	1 8 15 22 29	6 13 20 27
W 7 14 21 28	5 12 19 26	2 9 16 23 30	7 14 21 28
T 1 8 15 22 29	6 13 20 27	3 10 17 24	1 8 15 22 29
F 2 9 16 23 30	7 14 21 28	4 11 18 25	2 9 16 23 30
S 3 10 17 24	1 8 15 22 29	5 12 19 26	3 10 17 24 31
S 4 11 18 25	2 9 16 23 30	6 13 20 27	4 11 18 25

8

January	February	March	April
M 2 9 16 23 30	6 13 20 27	5 12 19 26	2 9 16 23 30
T 3 10 17 24 31	7 14 21 28	6 13 20 27	3 10 17 24
W 4 11 18 25	1 8 15 22 29	7 14 21 28	4 11 18 25
T 5 12 19 26	2 9 16 23	1 8 15 22 29	5 12 19 26
F 6 13 20 27	3 10 17 24	2 9 16 23 30	6 13 20 27
S 7 14 21 28	4 11 18 25	3 10 17 24 31	7 14 21 28
S 1 8 15 22 29	5 12 19 26	4 11 18 25	1 8 15 22 29

May	June	July	August
M 7 14 21 28	4 11 18 25	2 9 16 23 30	6 13 20 27
T 1 8 15 22 29	5 12 19 26	3 10 17 24 31	7 14 21 28
W 2 9 16 23 30	6 13 20 27	4 11 18 25	1 8 15 22 29
T 3 10 17 24 31	7 14 21 28	5 12 19 26	2 9 16 23 30
F 4 11 18 25	1 8 15 22 29	6 13 20 27	3 10 17 24 31
S 5 12 19 26	2 9 16 23 30	7 14 21 28	4 11 18 25
S 6 13 20 27	3 10 17 24	1 8 15 22 29	5 12 19 26

September	October	November	December
M 3 10 17 24	1 8 15 22 29	5 12 19 26	3 10 17 24 31
T 4 11 18 25	2 9 16 23 30	6 13 20 27	4 11 18 25
W 5 12 19 26	3 10 17 24 31	7 14 21 28	5 12 19 26
T 6 13 20 27	4 11 18 25	1 8 15 22 29	6 13 20 27
F 7 14 21 28	5 12 19 26	2 9 16 23 30	7 14 21 28
S 1 8 15 22 29	6 13 20 27	3 10 17 24	1 8 15 22 29
S 2 9 16 23 30	7 14 21 28	4 11 18 25	2 9 16 23 30

Perpetual Calendar

9

	January	February	March	April
M	1 8 15 22 29	5 12 19 26	4 11 18 25	1 8 15 22 29
T	2 9 16 23 30	6 13 20 27	5 12 19 26	2 9 16 23 30
W	3 10 17 24 31	7 14 21 28	6 13 20 27	3 10 17 24
T	4 11 18 25	1 8 15 22 29	7 14 21 28	4 11 18 25
F	5 12 19 26	2 9 16 23	1 8 15 22 29	5 12 19 26
S	6 13 20 27	3 10 17 24	2 9 16 23 30	6 13 20 27
S	7 14 21 28	4 11 18 25	3 10 17 24 31	7 14 21 28

	May	June	July	August
M	6 13 20 27	3 10 17 24	1 8 15 22 29	5 12 19 26
T	7 14 21 28	4 11 18 25	2 9 16 23 30	6 13 20 27
W	1 8 15 22 29	5 12 19 26	3 10 17 24 31	7 14 21 28
T	2 9 16 23 30	6 13 20 27	4 11 18 25	1 8 15 22 29
F	3 10 17 24 31	7 14 21 28	5 12 19 26	2 9 16 23 30
S	4 11 18 25	1 8 15 22 29	6 13 20 27	3 10 17 24 31
S	5 12 19 26	2 9 16 23 30	7 14 21 28	4 11 18 25

	September	October	November	December
M	2 9 16 23 30	7 14 21 28	4 11 18 25	2 9 16 23 30
T	3 10 17 24	1 8 15 22 29	5 12 19 26	3 10 17 24 31
W	4 11 18 25	2 9 16 23 30	6 13 20 27	4 11 18 25
T	5 12 19 26	3 10 17 24 31	7 14 21 28	5 12 19 26
F	6 13 20 27	4 11 18 25	1 8 15 22 29	6 13 20 27
S	7 14 21 28	5 12 19 26	2 9 16 23 30	7 14 21 28
S	1 8 15 22 29	6 13 20 27	3 10 17 24	1 8 15 22 29

10

	January	February	March	April
M	7 14 21 28	4 11 18 25	3 10 17 24 31	7 14 21 28
T	1 8 15 22 29	5 12 19 26	4 11 18 25	1 8 15 22 29
W	2 9 16 23 30	6 13 20 27	5 12 19 26	2 9 16 23 30
T	3 10 17 24 31	7 14 21 28	6 13 20 27	3 10 17 24
F	4 11 18 25	1 8 15 22 29	7 14 21 28	4 11 18 25
S	5 12 19 26	2 9 16 23	1 8 15 22 29	5 12 19 26
S	6 13 20 27	3 10 17 24	2 9 16 23 30	6 13 20 27

	May	June	July	August
M	5 12 19 26	2 9 16 23 30	7 14 21 28	4 11 18 25
T	6 13 20 27	3 10 17 24	1 8 15 22 29	5 12 19 26
W	7 14 21 28	4 11 18 25	2 9 16 23 30	6 13 20 27
T	1 8 15 22 29	5 12 19 26	3 10 17 24 31	7 14 21 28
F	2 9 16 23 30	6 13 20 27	4 11 18 25	1 8 15 22 29
S	3 10 17 24 31	7 14 21 28	5 12 19 26	2 9 16 23 30
S	4 11 18 25	1 8 15 22 29	6 13 20 27	3 10 17 24 31

	September	October	November	December
M	1 8 15 22 29	6 13 20 27	3 10 17 24	1 8 15 22 29
T	2 9 16 23 30	7 14 21 28	4 11 18 25	2 9 16 23 30
W	3 10 17 24	1 8 15 22 29	5 12 19 26	3 10 17 24 31
T	4 11 18 25	2 9 16 23 30	6 13 20 27	4 11 18 25
F	5 12 19 26	3 10 17 24 31	7 14 21 28	5 12 19 26
S	6 13 20 27	4 11 18 25	1 8 15 22 29	6 13 20 27
S	7 14 21 28	5 12 19 26	2 9 16 23 30	7 14 21 28

11

	January	February	March	April
M	6 13 20 27	3 10 17 24	2 9 16 23 30	6 13 20 27
T	7 14 21 28	4 11 18 25	3 10 17 24 31	7 14 21 28
W	1 8 15 22 29	5 12 19 26	4 11 18 25	1 8 15 22 29
T	2 9 16 23 30	6 13 20 27	5 12 19 26	2 9 16 23 30
F	3 10 17 24 31	7 14 21 28	6 13 20 27	3 10 17 24
S	4 11 18 25	1 8 15 22 29	7 14 21 28	4 11 18 25
S	5 12 19 26	2 9 16 23	1 8 15 22 29	5 12 19 26

	May	June	July	August
M	4 11 18 25	1 8 15 22 29	6 13 20 27	3 10 17 24 31
T	5 12 19 26	2 9 16 23 30	7 14 21 28	4 11 18 25
W	6 13 20 27	3 10 17 24	1 8 15 22 29	5 12 19 26
T	7 14 21 28	4 11 18 25	2 9 16 23 30	6 13 20 27
F	1 8 15 22 29	5 12 19 26	3 10 17 24 31	7 14 21 28
S	2 9 16 23 30	6 13 20 27	4 11 18 25	1 8 15 22 29
S	3 10 17 24 31	7 14 21 28	5 12 19 26	2 9 16 23 30

	September	October	November	December
M	7 14 21 28	5 12 19 26	2 9 16 23 30	7 14 21 28
T	1 8 15 22 29	6 13 20 27	3 10 17 24	1 8 15 22 29
W	2 9 16 23 30	7 14 21 28	4 11 18 25	2 9 16 23 30
T	3 10 17 24	1 8 15 22 29	5 12 19 26	3 10 17 24 31
F	4 11 18 25	2 9 16 23 30	6 13 20 27	4 11 18 25
S	5 12 19 26	3 10 17 24 31	7 14 21 28	5 12 19 26
S	6 13 20 27	4 11 18 25	1 8 15 22 29	6 13 20 27

12

	January	February	March	April
M	5 12 19 26	2 9 16 23	1 8 15 22 29	5 12 19 2
T	6 13 20 27	3 10 17 24	2 9 16 23 30	6 13 20 2
W	7 14 21 28	4 11 18 25	3 10 17 24 31	7 14 21 2
T	1 8 15 22 29	5 12 19 26	4 11 18 25	1 8 15 22 2
F	2 9 16 23 30	6 13 20 27	5 12 19 26	2 9 16 23 3
S	3 10 17 24 31	7 14 21 28	6 13 20 27	3 10 17 24
S	4 11 18 25	1 8 15 22 29	7 14 21 28	4 11 18 25

	May	June	July	August
M	3 10 17 24 31	7 14 21 28	5 12 19 26	2 9 16 23 3
T	4 11 18 25	1 8 15 22 29	6 13 20 27	3 10 17 24 3
W	5 12 19 26	2 9 16 23 30	7 14 21 28	4 11 18 25
T	6 13 20 27	3 10 17 24	1 8 15 22 29	5 12 19 26
F	7 14 21 28	4 11 18 25	2 9 16 23 30	6 13 20 27
S	1 8 15 22 29	5 12 19 26	3 10 17 24 31	7 14 21 28
S	2 9 16 23 30	6 13 20 27	4 11 18 25	1 8 15 22 29

	September	October	November	December
M	6 13 20 27	4 11 18 25	1 8 15 22 29	6 13 20 2
T	7 14 21 28	5 12 19 26	2 9 16 23 30	7 14 21 2
W	1 8 15 22 29	6 13 20 27	3 10 17 24	1 8 15 22 2
T	2 9 16 23 30	7 14 21 28	4 11 18 25	2 9 16 23 3
F	3 10 17 24	1 8 15 22 29	5 12 19 26	3 10 17 24 3
S	4 11 18 25	2 9 16 23 30	6 13 20 27	4 11 18 25
S	5 12 19 26	3 10 17 24 31	7 14 21 28	5 12 19 26

13

	January	February	March	April
M	4 11 18 25	1 8 15 22 29	7 14 21 28	4 11 18 25
T	5 12 19 26	2 9 16 23	1 8 15 22 29	5 12 19 26
W	6 13 20 27	3 10 17 24	2 9 16 23 30	6 13 20 27
T	7 14 21 28	4 11 18 25	3 10 17 24 31	7 14 21 28
F	1 8 15 22 29	5 12 19 26	4 11 18 25	1 8 15 22 29
S	2 9 16 23 30	6 13 20 27	5 12 19 26	2 9 16 23 30
S	3 10 17 24 31	7 14 21 28	6 13 20 27	3 10 17 24

	May	June	July	August
M	2 9 16 23 30	6 13 20 27	4 11 18 25	1 8 15 22 29
T	3 10 17 24 31	7 14 21 28	5 12 19 26	2 9 16 23 30
W	4 11 18 25	1 8 15 22 29	6 13 20 27	3 10 17 24 31
T	5 12 19 26	2 9 16 23 30	7 14 21 28	4 11 18 25
F	6 13 20 27	3 10 17 24	1 8 15 22 29	5 12 19 26
S	7 14 21 28	4 11 18 25	2 9 16 23 30	6 13 20 27
S	1 8 15 22 29	5 12 19 26	3 10 17 24 31	7 14 21 28

	September	October	November	December
M	5 12 19 26	3 10 17 24 31	7 14 21 28	5 12 19 26
T	6 13 20 27	4 11 18 25	1 8 15 22 29	6 13 20 27
W	7 14 21 28	5 12 19 26	2 9 16 23 30	7 14 21 28
T	1 8 15 22 29	6 13 20 27	3 10 17 24	1 8 15 22 29
F	2 9 16 23 30	7 14 21 28	4 11 18 25	2 9 16 23 30
S	3 10 17 24	1 8 15 22 29	5 12 19 26	3 10 17 24 31
S	4 11 18 25	2 9 16 23 30	6 13 20 27	4 11 18 25

14

	January	February	March	April
M	3 10 17 24 31	7 14 21 28	6 13 20 27	3 10 17 2
T	4 11 18 25	1 8 15 22 29	7 14 21 28	4 11 18 2
W	5 12 19 26	2 9 16 23	1 8 15 22 29	5 12 19 2
T	6 13 20 27	3 10 17 24	2 9 16 23 30	6 13 20 2
F	7 14 21 28	4 11 18 25	3 10 17 24 31	7 14 21 2
S	1 8 15 22 29	5 12 19 26	4 11 18 25	1 8 15 22 2
S	2 9 16 23 30	6 13 20 27	5 12 19 26	2 9 16 23 3

	May	June	July	August
M	1 8 15 22 29	5 12 19 26	3 10 17 24 31	7 14 21 28
T	2 9 16 23 30	6 13 20 27	4 11 18 25	1 8 15 22 2
W	3 10 17 24 31	7 14 21 28	5 12 19 26	2 9 16 23 3
T	4 11 18 25	1 8 15 22 29	6 13 20 27	3 10 17 24 3
F	5 12 19 26	2 9 16 23 30	7 14 21 28	4 11 18 25
S	6 13 20 27	3 10 17 24	1 8 15 22 29	5 12 19 26
S	7 14 21 28	4 11 18 25	2 9 16 23 30	6 13 20 27

	September	October	November	December
M	4 11 18 25	2 9 16 23 30	6 13 20 27	4 11 18 2
T	5 12 19 26	3 10 17 24 31	7 14 21 28	5 12 19 2
W	6 13 20 27	4 11 18 25	1 8 15 22 29	6 13 20 2
T	7 14 21 28	5 12 19 26	2 9 16 23 30	7 14 21 2
F	1 8 15 22 29	6 13 20 27	3 10 17 24	1 8 15 22 2
S	2 9 16 23 30	7 14 21 28	4 11 18 25	2 9 16 23 3
S	3 10 17 24	1 8 15 22 29	5 12 19 26	3 10 17 24 3